HARVARD HISTORICAL MONOGRAPHS

LVIII

PUBLISHED UNDER THE DIRECTION

OF THE DEPARTMENT OF HISTORY

FROM THE INCOME OF

THE ROBERT LOUIS STROOCK FUND

THE FALL OF
STEIN

R. C. RAACK

HARVARD UNIVERSITY PRESS

CAMBRIDGE, MASSACHUSETTS

1965

FOR

C. F. R.
V. J. R.

PREFACE

The half-year beginning in June 1808, when Baron Stein returned to active leadership of the Prussian government, and ending in November 1808 with his withdrawal from service, was the most intensive period of activity in the short epoch of reform in Prussia. The movement to revive Prussia began after the battle of Jena in 1806 and the ensuing occupation had proved to King Frederick William III the need to find a new balance of forces in a society encrusted with bankrupt institutions. Stein, one of the strongest champions of reform, wanted to regenerate the state by enacting radical constitutional and administrative changes carrying the promise of thoroughgoing social transformations. In the fall of 1808, with the country poised between an old and a new order, the battle over the controversial innovations pre-empted Prussia's domestic political scene.

While deeply involved in this internal struggle, the Stein government was trying to preserve what was left of national independence in a Europe dominated by Napoleonic France. Recent events had fostered hopes that Bonaparte's hold on conquered Europe might be weakening. Some foresaw a shift in military alliances which could lead to the liberation of Europe. As diplomatic and domestic developments moved quickly together toward a climax in the fall of 1808, most of the chief figures of all the Prussian governments of the first four decades of the nineteenth century took part in the effort to resolve the dilemmas facing the languishing nation.

Ultimately at stake in these conflicts was the life of the Stein government itself, its tenure made precarious by the combination of men and forces opposed to its policies. The fall of Stein's ministry in November 1808 emerges in retrospect as a major turning point in German history, though most contemporaries believed that the men who followed Stein in office were of the same reformist stripe. It is argued here that this event foreshadows the outcome of the constitutional conflict in Prussia between 1815 and 1819, which Friedrich Meinecke and others have regarded as the decisive struggle for the reform movement.

Viewing these months as the crucible in which the mettle of Prussia's men of politics and their programs was tested, we perceive the historical significance of the fall of Stein. We are therefore led to ask not only why Stein fell, but also why it was that Stein's former colleagues did not carry out his mandate. For they not only succeeded him, but continued to occupy the leading chairs in the Prussian ministries for years after his resignation. The biographical evidence I have collected about Stein's friends and foes offers insights into the personalities of several erstwhile reformers which suggest how they came to fade unreluctantly into the featureless Restoration background, finishing their careers unsung as docile servants of the absolute monarchy. The evidence gathered about the strength and influence of the enemies of Stein, here more completely identified than ever before, gives us some measure of the opposition Stein and his friends faced. And though the picture of King Frederick William that I have sketched is not fundamentally new, we can see how important was his role, given the men gathered around him, in the events leading to the frustration of hopes for reform. From this information we may observe why the cause of reform and constitutional development, left in the hands of the men we shall be closely scrutinizing in action in the following pages, was unlikely to prosper.

Though many historians have recounted the dramatic events leading to the fall of the Stein government, I have taken as my special province for detailed investigation the personal intrigues and infighting among the small circle of men near the court just before Stein's resignation. The evidence I have found seems to show the need to explore the relation between what historians view as the larger historical movements—in this case the reform effort—and the constant harassments embodied in social and institutional life and the game of politics itself. Thus I have tried to put into perspec-

tive within a historical narrative the roles of chance and misunderstanding, clumsy bureaucratic machinery, patterns of action dictated
by irrelevant conventions, clashes of personality and petty aspects of
human relations, and the small vexations of the daily round. My
purpose has been to resuscitate, where possible, something more
than faceless shades and bloodless forces, and thus win the reader's
indulgence for retelling parts of a story of which the main outlines
are already known.

There is a wealth of archival sources available for the sort of
reconstruction of the events surrounding Stein's fall just outlined.
Where possible, I have deliberately used all the reportage that the
sources present to form a tableau having as many aspects as historical
onlookers left recorded. I believe that this arrangement—in which
facets are viewed singly by the participants before the total representation appears—helps to assert a sense of the uncertain movement
and incomplete revelation of developments as witnessed by contemporaries. From this method of storytelling I hope that the reader
will derive a sense of the making of history that will correlate with
his own experience, a dimension that can be obscured by the two-
dimensional, linear synthesis of the traditional narrative. May he
also gain an appreciation of the problems of the times as Stein and
his colleagues viewed them, and discern the complex interrelations
behind the superstructure of political influence at an autocratic court
like Prussia's. Perhaps this study of personal behavior within a
limited period will also serve to illuminate the acts of the same
political figures on other occasions in different circumstances where
sources may be less extensive.

My acknowledgments are more extensive than might be expected
in a study of this length. I have become especially cognizant, like
countless historians before me, of the debt we owe to the archivists
who catalogue and preserve the materials which are the stuff and
substance of our work. On many occasions, from their special knowledge of their holdings they have brought to my attention papers
which I should not myself have thought relevant to my study. I

would pay special respect to the archivists at the Deutsches Zentral-archiv, Abteilung II, in Merseburg, who readily assisted me with advice, materials, and microfilms. My debt is almost as great to other archivists in England, France, Germany, and Poland. The dispersal and loss of some of the chief German libraries in the course of the Second World War made it necessary to consult a number of different collections. A few volumes which appeared to be of importance for my study I have been unable to find. Fortunately, the great majority of printed sources were available to me in Widener Library at Harvard University, and it was there that the largest part of the research was done. To the Harvard librarians as well as to all the other librarians who assisted me I express my thanks.

At the beginning of my study in this period of German history Harvard University provided me with a fellowship for research abroad. A later grant from the Penrose Fund of the American Philosophical Association permitted me to continue the archival studies I had begun at that time. During this latter period of study I found the sources which led me to believe that a work of this scope might be completed successfully. An academic year spent as an exchange student at the University of Warsaw, under a grant from the Polish Ministry of Higher Education, allowed me to engage in research germane to this monograph, while at the same time I was able to work on another topic more relevant to my study there.

In the course of the writing I received most helpful editorial assistance and stylistic criticism from Professor Richard H. Wilde of California State College at Long Beach and from Professor Mack Walker of Harvard University. Professor W. M. Simon of Cornell University generously consented to read my manuscript, which benefited much from his special knowledge of the field. R. Arnold Ricks of Bennington College and Professor Eugene L. Asher of California State College at Long Beach also offered helpful advice about some sections of the text. I have tried to incorporate as many of their suggestions as possible into my work. Where this study approaches the standards of scholarship and literary style that I came to appreciate through my association as a graduate student with

Professor (now Dean) Franklin L. Ford of Harvard University, it owes much to the help of the friends and critics I have mentioned.

I am also obligated to Friedrich Laubisch of the Deutsche Akademie der Wissenschaften zu Berlin for a number of useful suggestions as well as for help in preparing transcriptions of difficult German texts. Professor Hans-Joachim Schoeps of the University of Erlangen-Nürnberg made available to me sections from the then unpublished manuscript of *Aus den Jahren Preussischer Not und Erneuerung: Tagebücher und Briefe der Gebrüder Gerlach und ihres Kreises, 1805–1820,* for which I am most grateful. Mrs. Martha Robinson of Quincy, Massachusetts, prepared a faultless copy of the penultimate text. Robert Jackson, of Berkeley, California, compiled the index. The extent of my obligation to my wife, who endured a number of small discomforts and a great deal of material deprivation, as well as the author at his labors, will be comprehended only by the wives of other scholars.

R. C. R.

San Francisco, California
February 1965

CONTENTS

THE FALL OF STEIN

ABBREVIATIONS

AAE Archives des affaires étrangères, Paris

AG Archives historiques du ministère de la guerre, Vincennes

APMW Archiwum państwowe miasta Wrocławia i województwa Wrocławskiego we Wrocławiu

CGA Correspondance de la grande Armée

CP Correspondance politique

DZA Deutsches Zentralarchiv, Abteilung II, Merseburg (formerly Preussisches Geheimes Staatsarchiv)

FO Foreign Office

F.W. Frederick William III

IB Immediatbericht

IS Immediatschreiben

KO Kabinettsorder

PRO Public Record Office, London

Rep. Repositorium

Stein Br. *Freiherr vom Stein: Briefe und amtliche Schriften*

Dates, unless otherwise noted, are New Style.

I

A CONSPIRACY
BORN OF DESPAIR

Disheartened, Baron Karl Friedrich vom Stein returned from Berlin to Königsberg through the chaste spring countryside. Nature's Maytide awakening could scarcely have been less appropriate to his mood. His mission to secure peace with France, the keystone of his foreign and domestic policy, had foundered. From Berlin as far as the Vistula crossing near Marienwerder, Stein, chief minister of the King of Prussia, was still obliged to carry French passports; to that distance eastward from Berlin the French army occupied the Prussian countryside as late as 1808.

It was to end this very occupation that he had gone to Berlin, headquarters of the French forces in Prussia. Stein's ministry, named in October 1807, had taken office just a year after Jena and Auerstädt, the battles which destroyed the army of Frederick the Great some twenty years after the death of that monarch. With the army, the main support of the Frederician edifice, the whole antiquated system of state had collapsed. Stein had quickly set in motion some of the political, administrative, and military reforms he thought Prussia had long needed. But his domestic program was really only begun when he realized that he must give first priority to securing a final treaty of peace with France. That treaty, and with it the fate of Prussia, lay wholly in Bonaparte's hands.

On an elaborately canopied floating pavilion moored in the Niemen River near Tilsit in July 1807, Napoleon and Alexander I of Russia had met to settle the peace of Europe. The Third Coalition against France had taken its place among its historical predecessors. Austria and Prussia lay vanquished; Russia exhausted; Ulm, Austerlitz, Jena, Auerstädt, and Friedland, the great French victories of these wars, had once more emblazoned eternal glory on the arms of France and struck renewed fear into the rulers of any remaining states which might oppose Napoleon. All Europe lay open to French aggression. Only the canny Alexander snatched profit from defeat at Tilsit. His immense territories stretched eastward far enough to daunt Bonaparte who, in 1808, still sensed the limits of his power. Unable to defeat the upstart, Alexander allowed himself to be wooed, then won. Glib and full of fancy, Napoleon secured the tsar as an ally against Britain and tendered his new friend a gratuity in the form of a part of the spoils of his Prussian campaign, the Bialystok area of New East Prussia.

The Treaty of Tilsit settled only a tentative pacification on central Europe. Prussia was shorn of almost half of its former territory, most of which fell to the Poles of the Grand Duchy of Warsaw in the east and to the French satellite Kingdom of Westphalia in the west. But the supplementary convention establishing the terms of the vast reparations to be paid by the defeated Prussians left open the exact mode and amount of payment as well as a final date for the evacuation. All Prussia up to the Vistula, excluding a few fortresses in Silesia and Pomerania, continued under French occupation. Even the delineation of the borders of the state, put into the hands of negotiating commissions, was opened up to chicanery.

The Prussian government, as Stein recognized, had been put on the rack of uncertainty. The state's economy could be rebuilt and credit re-established only when the whole amount of the nation's fiscal liabilities was known and the terms for repayment of the debt fixed. Until the territories the French had promised to restore to Prussia after the peace had been returned, the fundamental reforms he and his advisers contemplated could not be generally legislated. And while the fate of the state remained in doubt both domestically and diplomatically, the occupation continued as a moral and economic burden.

When only five months in office, Stein had yielded up his immediate control over the conduct of government affairs in Königsberg in order to go to Berlin to negotiate personally with Bonaparte's agent, Intendant-General Pierre Daru. He had hoped his physical presence there would betoken the earnest desire of the Prussian government to negotiate; moreover, he had calculated that the obsequious posture of waiting upon the emperor's lackeys, offensive though it might be to him personally as a Knight of the Empire, would appease the imperial vanity. But in the protracted negotiations nothing Stein had sought had been won. Daru and he had haggled through a succession of drafts; belatedly they had produced a treaty (March 9, 1808) fixing the terms of a settlement. The ultimate ratification, however, remained in Bonaparte's hands. Toward taking that final step, for reasons yet unknown to Stein, the French emperor would make no move. Napoleon, as Stein like all his adversaries had to learn, did not conduct diplomacy in accordance with established canons of statecraft.

Stein had reason to be bitterly disappointed by his failure in Berlin. He had taken many risks by leaving the seat of government in Königsberg with his ministry barely settled in office. His hope that he would succeed with the French where others had failed had proved false. Now, on his return from Berlin, most of the far-reaching reforms anticipated at the time of his nomination were still in committees. Nothing of significance for the administration of the state had been accomplished since the preceding fall. The state's financial plight had steadily worsened: the occupation had to be subsidized and the tax revenues from the vast majority of Prussian territory went into French hands or could not be collected.[1] His personal standing and prestige had surely declined as a consequence of his failure. No wonder that Stein's mood in June 1808 was despairing.

Stein took counsel with his friends and advisers and found them both downcast and alarmed. His report of French intransigence on

---

[1] The general background of Tilsit, Prussia's negotiations with France, and Stein's journey to Berlin can be found in Hans Haussherr, *Erfüllung und Befreiung: Der Kampf um die Durchführung des Tilsiter Friedens 1807/1808* (Hamburg, 1935), pts. 3 and 4, *passim;* and Gerhard Ritter, *Stein: Eine politische Biographie,* 3rd ed. (Stuttgart, 1958), ch. 10, *passim;* somewhat different in tone is Franz Mehring, *Zur preussischen Geschichte: Von Tilsit bis zur Reichsgründung* (Berlin, 1930), 53–55.

the question of ratification fitted into a general pattern of evidence they had amassed following Bonaparte's most recent actions in Spain. There the emperor had kidnapped and then forced the abdication of the Bourbon king and had replaced him with his brother, Joseph Bonaparte, King of Naples. Already imperial siblings occupied thrones in the Netherlands and Westphalia. The refusal of Bonaparte to grant final terms to the Prussians raised fears in Königsberg that the conqueror was playing a waiting game until his similar plans for the Prussian crown ripened, or until opportunities to carry out his other secret schemes were presented. The Prussians honestly feared at this time that the King of Prussia would fall victim to the fate of the King of Spain: that the remnant of the state would be annexed to Westphalia or Warsaw or become a satrapy governed directly from Paris.

In anticipation of the expected coup, Lt. Col. August Neithardt von Gneisenau and Col. Gerhard Johann von Scharnhorst, Stein's close military advisers, had devised a dangerous scheme to provoke an insurrection against the French in occupied Germany. Reports had come to them of the spontaneous uprising of the Spanish people against King Joseph and his French armies. They had heard that changes in the Vienna ministries portended a shift to an anti-French policy in Austria. In fact, in the spring and the early summer of 1808, intelligence reports constantly mentioned impending conflict or even hostile military confrontations between France and Austria. In such circumstances, it was difficult to separate rumor from fact; both were, in any case, sifted too often by desperate men through reason tempered by a will to believe. Every new story accelerated the impatience to turn plot into action and to prepare the armaments and network of insurrectionary organizations that such a scheme would require. For the leader of such a plan, Gneisenau and Scharnhorst needed the head of government, Stein.[2]

[2] On their fears for Prussia see Friedrich Thimme, "Zu den Erhebungsplänen der preussischen Patrioten im Sommer 1808: Ungedruckte Denkschriften Gneisenau's und Scharnhorst's," *Historische Zeitschrift*, LXXXVI (1901), 78–82, 89ff; Alfred Stern, "Gneisenaus Reise nach London im Jahre 1809 und ihre Vorgeschichte," *Historische Zeitschrift*, LXXXV (1900), 32; Gneisenau's memoir for Canning, 20

Strictly speaking, the idea of an uprising against the French that Gneisenau and Scharnhorst presented to Stein on his return was not original with them. Since Jena the more desperate Prussian patriots had sought to fend off conquest by France through the unleashing of some sort of popular insurrection. No doubt the examples of the French *levée* of 1793, as well as Gneisenau's impressions of the American Revolution, provided prototypes for the action they anticipated. At the height of the war between Prussia and France in 1807, many of those who, like Gneisenau, supported the insurrection scheme in its revived form in 1808 had sought to continue hostilities on a guerrilla basis. Even the sober Major Carl von Clausewitz had prepared such a plan at that time.[3] They had hoped for material and financial aid from England, aid which never arrived.[4] The negotiations which led to the preliminary peace at Tilsit then removed the immediate cause for action.

A few recent historians have argued that a plan of this sort could not have succeeded.[5] They have contended that the great majority

---

August 1809, PRO, FO, Prussia, 64/80 (part of which is included in Stern's article); Stein, IB, 14 August 1808, in Walter Hubatsch, ed., *Freiherr vom Stein: Briefe und amtliche Schriften,* II, pt. 2 (Stuttgart, 1960), 812–813; Ritter, *Stein,* 329–330; Paul Hassel, *Geschichte der preussischen Politik, 1807–1815* (Leipzig, 1881), pt. I, 174–175. Prussian ambassador Finckenstein in Vienna, beginning in May, reported the increasing war spirit and preparations in Austria (*ibid.,* 518–525).

[3] Hans Rothfels, "Eine Denkschrift Carls von Clausewitz aus den Jahren 1807–1808," *Preussische Jahrbücher,* CLXXVIII (1919), 223–245; Hassel, I, 217–218; Anton Ernstberger, *Eine deutsche Untergrundbewegung gegen Napoleon, 1806–1807* (Munich, 1955), 11, 12, 110, 112, 115; Albert Lionnet, *Die Erhebungspläne preussischer Patrioten Ende 1806 und Frühjahr 1807* (Berlin, 1914), 16, 35–40; Otto Karmin, *Sir Francis d'Ivernois, 1757–1842: Sa vie, son oeuvre, et son temps* (Geneva, 1920), 443.

[4] A. W. Ward and G. P. Gooch, eds., *The Cambridge History of British Foreign Policy,* I (Cambridge, Eng., 1922), 360; Lionnet, 114–124.

[5] Ritter, *Stein,* 336–340. Much of Ritter's argument against the plan seems to have been taken intact from Stein's old opponent, York von Wartenburg. See Johann G. Droysen, *Das Leben des Feldmarschalls Grafen York von Wartenburg,* 10th ed. (Leipzig, 1897), I, 160–161. Ritter refers on several occasions in his argument to the dissertation of his student Ulrich Meurer, "Die Rolle nationaler Leidenschaft der Massen in der Erhebung von 1813 gegen Napoleon," unpub. diss., University of Freiburg, 1953. Whatever the merit of Meurer's thesis (that the "masses" played little part in the patriotic war of 1813 because of their lack of national spirit), it would

of the Prussian people, the peasants, were parochial in their interests, ignorant and apathetic. As the argument runs, they would
have remained immobile and indifferent to a call to arms by the
king, in spite of the fact that the French occupation on the land
with its severe requisitions touched them directly. But Gneisenau
and Scharnhorst and the other advisers of the king, like Stein, who
later did take up the plan conditionally, heard few voices from
the peasantry. They knew that loyalty to the crown and state had
newly revived among the urban middle classes; they counted on
the nobility as a whole to follow unquestioningly the king's orders.
These voices they heard, for it was mostly men of insurrectionist
sympathy who surrounded the reform government. The hope of
the patriot military leaders, therefore, was to win over the king to
the idea of an organized insurrection under the Prussian aegis in
north Germany. The action, they imagined, would begin at the
outbreak of the coming Austro-French war and would depend, in
large part, on English military and financial support.[6] Not a small

---

not seem to be wholly relevant to the argument, for the patriots on this occasion were
thinking not only of a royal call to arms, but also of an intensive propaganda campaign to be conducted at every level to stir the people to action, a situation different
from 1813. Hence I must take note of the arguments of Heinz Heitzer, "Arbeiten
über die Geschichte der Befreiungskriege (1806–1813)," *Historische Forschungen in
der DDR* (Sonderheft of *Zeitschrift für Geschichtswissenschaft,* VIII Jg. (Berlin,
1960), 188–189, who, for all the wrong reasons, rightly questions the assumptions
of Ritter (and Meurer, 199n48). That others of far different political persuasion than
Stein's were excited by the prospect of a quick change in French fortunes is proved
by Friedrich von Gentz's remarks in a letter to Götzen, 19 October 1808, AG, CGA,
C2 80. Ritter, who has seen this letter, and identifies it from the handwriting as
Gentz's, uses it to prove that the Austrians (that is, Gentz) tried to temper the
violence of the Prussian patriots. I, on the other hand, use the same letter to show
the extent of Gentz's hopes for a rapid downfall of the French empire. Both ideas
are expressed in the letter, but Gentz's precautionary remarks to Götzen were made
in an effort to induce him to use a moderate approach to the Austrian court.
Some of the timid elements there were frightened by Stadion's notion of an uprising.
Hence Ritter's use of the letter, as it appears to me, could lead to the completely
false interpretation that Gentz was against the Prussian plans.

[6] Their plans were outlined in a Denkschrift of Scharnhorst dated "Mitte August
1808," *Stein Br.,* II (2), 821–824; Gneisenau to Frederick William, 10 August 1808,
PRO, FO, Prussia, 64/79—dated "August 1808" as printed in Rudolf Vaupel, ed.,
Die Reorganisation des preussischen Staates unter Stein und Hardenberg, II: Das

measure of the enthusiasm which they invested in the scheme was compounded of their desperate fear, a simple faith in the people of north Germany, as well as a conviction that a new war was in any case inevitable. Stein, as a responsible minister, had never before been confronted with such a proposal. Nor had the situation until now been such as to cause him to give serious consideration to such a plot. But on his return from Berlin, Stein was in just the mood to listen to such suggestions. A long-standing opponent of the excesses of the revolutionary system in France, he saw Prussia as the only state still capable of maintaining Germany and its culture intact. These political convictions, strong and unshakeable, were derived more from his heart than from his head. His colleagues had chosen him as the leader of their plan because, in the few short months of his ministry, they had already learned to rely on the vehemence of his feeling against Bonaparte and French tyranny in Europe. He and they lived in a generation of men that had known only revolutionary turmoil and the violence of war in adult life, and it was to arms that they quite naturally subscribed to restore the status which France's military prowess had taken from them.[7]

Stein's anti-French cast of mind had been reaffirmed ideologically during his stay in Berlin. A part of his visit had coincided in time

---

preussische Heer vom Tilsiter Frieden bis zur Befreiung, 1807–1814 (Leipzig, 1938), 549ff: "Man hat es in neuern Zeiten nicht genug beachtet, welche Streitmittel man aus grossen Städten ziehen kann" (550). Stein forwarded these plans to the king: Stein, Denkschrift, 11 August 1808, *Stein Br.*, II (2), 808–812; Stein, IB, 14 August 1808, *ibid.*, 812.

[7] Hans Haussherr, "Stein und Hardenberg," *Historische Zeitschrift*, CXC (1960), 271. Stein's colleague Schön wrote of him: "Stein lebte mit einem eminenden Geiste einer mit dem Herzen aufgefassten Idee, nämlich der des Vaterlandes und dieser mit ganzer Seele und mit vollem Gemüt und unbedingt mit gänzlicher Verleugnung seiner Person." Quoted by Hans Rothfels, *Theodor von Schön, Friedrich Wilhelm IV. und die Revolution von 1848* (Königsberg, 1937), 94. On Stein's concern with military virtues, which he wanted impressed on the crown prince, see Louise to Frau von Berg, 7 August 1808 in Karl Griewank, ed., *Königin Louise: Briefe und Aufzeichnungen* (Leipzig, n.d.), 362; and Georg Schuster, ed., *Die Jugend des Königs Friedrich Wilhelm IV und des Kaisers und Königs Wilhelm I: Tagebuchblätter ihres Erziehers Friedrich Delbrück* (Berlin, 1907), III, 181 (25 February 1809).

8 THE FALL OF STEIN

with the philosopher J. G. Fichte's series of lectures, the belatedly
famous "Addresses to the German Nation." Stein did not hear them
directly, but two of the Prussian agents with him in Berlin did—
J. A. Sack, head of the commission for direct negotiations with the
French, and Friedrich August von Stägemann, a member of Stein's
own party. At the very least Stein must have received from them
a general notion of the intensely nationalistic tone of the talks
even if he never read or heard them. Later he recommended the
written speeches for Clausewitz's perusal. Fichte's talks were not
an incitement to direct military action as so often portrayed.[8] They
were indeed a passionate rejection of it and a call for the triumph
of the intellectual virtues that Schiller had stressed in his poem
"Deutsche Grösse." But their general tone was assuredly a paean to
Deutschtum as well as to national resurrection through education.

While Stein was away in Berlin, Fichte's disciple, the Königsberg
professor J. W. Süvern, was delivering strikingly similar lectures
to audiences in the temporary capital. Not only were his lectures
inspired by nationalist feeling, he assigned to the statesman a role
as *Staatskünstler,* or architect of political affairs; his was the task
of leading the national group to greatness.[9] Some of the leading
men of Stein's administrative entourage and Queen Louise of
Prussia herself attended these talks. In fact, she took notes, either
on Stein's initiative or her own,[10] which were later submitted to
the minister for his study. It is significant that Süvern came (on
Stein's suggestion) into the government which succeeded Stein's
as a member of the Section for Instruction in the Ministry of the
Interior. As early as the summer of 1808, just after Stein's return

---

[8] See Rudolf Körner, "Die Wirkung der Reden Fichtes," *Forschungen zur brandenburgischen und preussischen Geschichte,* XL (1927), 65–87.

[9] See R. C. Raack, "The Course of Political Idealism in Prussia, 1806–1813," unpub.
diss., Harvard University, 1957, 132–135; J. H. Süvern, "Aus Süverns Vorlesungen
über Geschichte 1807–1808," *Mitteilungen aus dem Litteraturarchive in Berlin,* vol.
III (1901–1905). See the note of Altenstein to Stägemann, 17 May 1808, in Franz
Rühl, ed., *Aus der Franzosenzeit* (Leipzig, 1904), 99.

[10] On the queen's note taking see Louise to Frau von Berg, 27 May 1808,
Königin Luise: Briefe, 348; Louise to Scheffner, 20 June 1808, *ibid.,* 349; Stein to
Princess Marianne, 17 March 1811, *Stein Br.,* III (Stuttgart, 1961), 483.

from Berlin, Süvern was already being consulted—proof that Stein knew and esteemed his ideas.[11]

As a matter of fact, in the summer of 1808 the national awakening of the peoples of Europe was in the air, and Stein would have been hard put to avoid a general awareness of these ideas. The Prussian poet Heinrich von Kleist, in Dresden writing his gory "Hermannsschlacht," was animated by a suprarational patriotic wrath against the French. He had dedicated his pen wholly to the German nation, as his words of preface to the "Hermannsschlacht" reveal: "Wehe, mein Vaterland, dir! Die Leier, zum Ruhm dir, zu schlagen, / Ist, getreu dir im Schoss, mir, deinem Dichter, verwehrt." Ernst Moritz Arndt and *Turnvater* Jahn, the poets Theodor Körner and Max von Schenkendorf were, like Kleist, already sketching out their nationalist panegyrics for publication.

True, Stein was a responsible minister and they were poets and thinkers, but by temperament he was not the man to eschew rash action. With customary vigor, he had once cut through the indecision which held blocked all the reform plans awaiting enactment; by decisive acts he had made himself then the leader of the spirit and force of reform in Prussia. Now, in the early summer of 1808, swept along by the currents of the day and the promptings of his heart, what alternatives to the desperate plan of insurrection could he see?

We now know that the year 1808 and the Spanish insurrection mark the onset of the ebb tide of Napoleon's power. Contemporaries possessed no such hindsight. The first successes of the Spanish insurgents had been small when measured against the resources of France. In spite of the surprising French defeats, everyone still accounted to Bonaparte almost miraculous powers to turn disadvantage to his own favor. But Stein looked on from the same perspective as his advisers who made the plan; theirs was the desperate resolve of dying men who cannot refuse medicine not thoroughly tested. Stein could see the reforms needed to revive the state stymied, the state's finances ever weaker, its enemies stronger.

[11] On Süvern's influence see Raack, "Political Idealism in Prussia," 129–132.

In June, the rumor, seemingly well-founded, spread that Bonaparte would order French troops to take up stations in the few fortresses in Silesia left to the Prussians by the Treaty of Tilsit.[12] Would this be the first step toward a complete military occupation of Prussia? Better gamble all, the militants thought. With but one great campaign, perhaps a single victory, the enormous burdens of reparations and occupation would be lifted, the national territories restored and the state would vault to its prewar position of eminence.

The impending war between Austria and France seemed to offer the Prussians their great opportunity. To Stein and his advisers, the tragic example of Austria and Prussia divided against France as in 1805 and 1806 was a recent memory. What hope had their tiny kingdom in a French-organized Europe? A role in the French empire as part of Jerome Bonaparte's Kingdom of Westphalia after the King of Prussia had been levered off his throne by trickery? To play, at the very least, the humble part of tributary of France wedged between Bonaparte's loyal new allies, Alexander's Russia, the satellite Grand Duchy of Warsaw and Kingdom of Westphalia; to await penitently a treaty dictated by the conqueror whose foragers cruelly left nothing behind but the leaves to mask the naked countryside? Between a carefully planned uprising supported by England in conjunction with the anticipated Austrian attack on France and subservience to Napoleon, the Prussian patriots saw only one choice. They weighed the odds and chose the honorable risk over discretion.[13]

Seeing the question in this light, Stein too probably came to believe there was no choice but to adopt, in a contingent way at least, the insurrection plan of Gneisenau and Scharnhorst.[14] But if

---

[12] Ritter, *Stein,* 330; Hassel, I, 205.

[13] Max Lehmann, *Freiherr vom Stein,* II (Leipzig, 1903), 184.

[14] I cannot entirely agree with Gerhard Ritter's most recent assessment of the insurrection plan in *Staatskunst und Kriegshandwerk: Das Problem des "Militarismus" in Deutschland* (Munich, 1959), vol. I. In half a chapter on Gneisenau (ch. iv), he tries to show that Gneisenau's plans for an insurrection were fantastic. His theme is that the possible and the impossible must be considered in establishing the goal of any program. He argues that cool statesmanship (in contrast to Gneisenau's wild schemes) will ultimately prove the best guide for action, a point of view with which it would

he were to do this, he would have to lay the scheme before the king. All were agreed that nothing could be done without the king's consent.[15] Only his call to arms could summon up both the eager and the reluctant energies of the country to the battle *à outrance* which the circumstances would demand. Since arrangements for war would have to be carefully coordinated with the Austrians, the most careful and secret diplomatic preparations on the highest level would be necessary; such negotiations would reverse the tradition of years of hostility between the two German states.

Much was heard of the ascendency of the war party, led by Count Philip Stadion, in Vienna. Rumors of extensive Austrian military preparations, including a rearmament scheme which made use of popular levies, circulated in Königsberg as early as May.[16] Austria's nascent bellicose policy toward Bonaparte was born of the same desperation which affected Prussia: the notion that Bonaparte could not rest until every legitimate throne had toppled. The insurrection of the Spaniards for their king and tradition gave the needed example. Stadion, who in May and June still jockeyed for influence at the court amidst powerful counsels for peace, became convinced that Germans could do as Spaniards had done. He would join the peoples of Europe to liberate the Continent from tyranny.[17]

---

be difficult to disagree. But when he judges Gneisenau's plans as "too early" (104) he imposes upon the alternative plans Gneisenau and his friends had to judge the information he (Ritter) has gained from hindsight: that Napoleon would later overreach himself in Russia and hence a better situation for a war of liberation would develop. Gneisenau and the others, who did not know that Napoleon would come to greater grief in Moscow, believed that Napoleon already had overreached himself. They could hardly believe that a more favorable situation could develop. On Ritter, see Andreas Dorpalen, "Historiography as History: The Work of Gerhard Ritter," *Journal of Modern History*, XXXIV (1962), 1–18.

[15] Ritter's argument (*Stein*, 340) that the insurrection could not have succeeded without the king's consent quite obviously misses the point; none of the leaders planned initiating action without the king's consent. See above, note 6, and Alexander Gibson, memorandum, "The Misfortunes of Prussia," December 1808, PRO, FO, Prussia, 64/79.

[16] Finckenstein to F.W., 23 May, 18 June, and 9 July 1808, Hassel, I, 518–522; Ritter, *Stein*, 328–329.

[17] Major Lucey to Götzen, 30 August 1808, Hassel, I, 545; Finckenstein to F.W., 30 July and 6 August 1808, *ibid.*, 523–524; Helmut Rössler, *Oesterreichs Kampf um*

Probably the public mood in Prussia in 1808 was as close to that of Stein and the patriots as it would ever come. Two years of occupation by the French had turned the countryside as well as town against the invader.[18] The poor discipline of the French armies was one cause; that they were expected to live off the occupied land was another. Even the states allied to Bonaparte were not spared the requisitions and other miseries which became the lot of the conquered areas. The Poles of the Grand Duchy of Warsaw had to provide for the French armies stationed there and in neighboring Prussia. Warsaw and, to a certain extent, Posen were given the treatment of conquered cities, while the rural areas temporarily became a land of empty villages as the peasants hid themselves and their remaining stock. Marauding deserters were a continuing plague wherever the French armies had marched. After Tilsit, when the French retreated west of the Vistula, they took with them from all the areas they had occupied the movable foodstuffs and possessions of the peasants. By the spring of 1808 the *Danziger Zeitung,* French-controlled and censored, was reporting misery and hunger on the land from Stolp in Pomerania to Danzig.[19] In Berlin at the same time there was a serious dearth of bread, the dietary staple of the poor, which drove up prices.[20] It would seem probable, therefore, that a general call to fight for king and country would have

---

Deutschlands Befreiung: Die deutsche Politik der nationalen Führer Oesterreichs, 1805–1815 (Hamburg, 1940), I, 304–306, 322–323, 333–334; Adolf Beer, *Zehn Jahre österreichischer Politik, 1801–1810* (Leipzig, 1877), 317.

[18] Louis de Drusina to FO, 17 May and 5 July 1808, PRO, FO, Prussia, 64/78; G. Liebe, *Die französische Besatzung im Herzogtum Magdeburg, 1808–1811,* Neujahrsblätter hrsg. von der Historischen Kommission für die Provinz Sachsen und das Herzogtum Anhalt, vol. XXXV (Halle, 1911), 11–19.

[19] *Danziger Zeitung,* 16 June 1808; Rodgero Prümers, "Ein Posener Tagebuch aus der Franzosenzeit," *Zeitschrift der historischen Gesellschaft für die Provinz Posen,* XXI (1906), 258–259, 270–271; Stefan Kieniewicz and Witold Kula, eds., *Historia polski,* II, pt. 2 (Warsaw, 1958), 99, 102, 104.

[20] Magnus Friedrich von Bassewitz, *Die Kurmark Brandenburg im Zusammenhang mit den Schicksalen des Gesamtstaats Preussen während der Zeit vom 22. Oktober 1806 bis zum Ende des Jahres 1808,* II (Leipzig, 1852), 373, 391; Louis P. E. Bignon, *Histoire de France sous Napoléon,* VII (Paris, 1838), 383–389; Paul Schwartz, *Berlins Kriegsleiden in der Franzosenzeit* (Berlin, 1917), 20–21.

found a response among the peasantry and the lower economic groups of the towns almost as great as that anticipated in the plans of the patriots. If townsmen and peasants were to be summoned to fight, the king must play his role. But Frederick William III, of modest intellectual endowment, was, though honorable and righteous, hopelessly irresolute in matters of state policy. Like most weak men in power, he guarded jealously the technical exercise of his prerogatives. "I am a king," he once said, "and that which I command shall be done; nobody else has any voice in it."[21] Were he truly a king we may imagine that no one would have dared to raise a contradictory voice. But too often in past decisions he had revealed himself as a monarch unwilling to act except when forced by circumstance or by the necessity to defend what he judged to be inalienable.[22] Since Tilsit he had, in fact, become even more scrupulous in his effort to maintain royal privilege. But though Frederick William was most often unwilling to act until compelled to do so, he would usually hear out his advisers dutifully. His decision, if there were to be one, he would make alone.

The stiffening of his will against Napoleon was manifest in the

[21] Quoted and translated from Marwitz by Walter M. Simon, *The Failure of the Prussian Reform Movement, 1807–1819* (Ithaca, 1955), 10; see Gentz's opinion of Frederick William in 1815 in Prince Richard Metternich, ed., *Memoirs of Prince Metternich, 1773–1815,* trans. Mrs. Alexander Napier (New York, 1880), II, 557.

[22] Karl Griewank, "Hardenberg und die preussische Politik, 1804–1806," *Forschungen zur brandenburgischen und preussischen Geschichte,* XLVII (1935), 228, 272, 277–278; Metternich, *Memoirs,* I, 52–57; Reinhold Koser, "Die preussische Politik, 1796–1806," in *Zur preussischen und deutschen Geschichte* (Stuttgart, 1921), 264–265; Simon, *Failure of the Prussian Reform Movement,* 10; Friedrich Nippold, ed., *Erinnerungen aus dem Leben des General-Feldmarschalls Hermann von Boyen,* II (Leipzig, 1889), 18–19. There is a good summary of the changes in historical opinion on Frederick William in Alfred Herrmann, "Friedrich Wilhelm III. und sein Anteil an der Heeresreform bis 1813," *Historische Vierteljahrsschrift,* XI (1908), 485–489; and a rather painful effort at vindication of the king in Friedrich Thimme, "König Friedrich Wilhelm III.: Sein Anteil an der Konvention von Tauroggen und an der Reform von 1807–1812," *Forschungen zur brandenburgischen und preussischen Geschichte,* XVIII (1905), 1–59, *passim.* See also the very useful characterization by Eugene N. Anderson, *Nationalism and the Cultural Crisis in Prussia, 1806–1815* (New York, 1939), 257–295.

decision taken in Königsberg in late July to strengthen defenses in Silesia. The French, uneasy because of the rumors of war preparations in Austria and cognizant of their failure to provide a direct connection between Saxony and Warsaw, seem to have begun to regret not having taken the province long before.[23] Several of the major fortresses there had never fallen during the recent war and were still in Prussian hands. Now that France and Austria appeared to be moving toward a conflict, the leaders on both sides gave more thought to the Silesian forts and the strategic value of the province, which flanked Austria's Bohemian redoubt.[24] The rumors of preliminary French moves toward seizure of the forts persisted ominously.[25] An action of this type, an assault on his sovereign and documented rights, could compel even Frederick William, who clung stubbornly to the letter of an agreement, to take a risk. It was decided to rearm and victual the Silesian posts as a precaution.[26]

The mutual interest of Austria and Prussia in Silesia first directed Frederick William's attention to the problem of relations with the Habsburgs. As early as July 27, a letter for Queen Louise's signature was drafted which extended sincere greetings from Louise to the Austrian empress and proposed the closest cooperation between the two states in the future. Though the letter was probably not sent, it was obviously composed as a possible gambit to open the way for a rapprochement between Prussia and Austria.[27] Sending an agent to take charge of the rearmament in Silesia offered Stein and his ad-

[23] Gentz to Ompteda, 13 March 1808, in Ludwig von Ompteda, *Zur deutschen Geschichte in dem Jahrzehnt vor den Befreiungskriegen, II: Politischer Nachlass des hannoverischen Staats- und Cabinets-Ministers Ludwig von Ompteda aus den Jahren 1804 bis 1813* (Jena, 1869), Abt. 1, 379–380; Finckenstein to F.W., 14 May 1808, Hassel, I, 517–518; Max Lenz, "Napoleon I. und Preussen," *Cosmopolis*, IX (1898), 860.

[24] Max Lehmann, *Scharnhorst*, II (Leipzig, 1887), 184; Beer, 353; Rössler, I, 372.

[25] Ritter, *Stein*, 330; Hugo von Wiese, "Die patriotische Tätigkeit des Grafen Götzen in Schlesien in den Jahren 1808 und 1809," *Zeitschrift des Vereins für die Geschichte und Altertum Schlesiens*, XXVII (1893), 37.

[26] Ritter, *Stein*, 330, 332. On the king's stubbornness see Griewank, "Hardenberg und die preussische Politik," 272, 277; and Hassel, I, 201–203.

[27] Ritter, *Stein*, 332; Beer, 352–353; Louise to Empress Maria Ludovica, 25 July 1808, *Königin Luise: Briefe*, 362; Stein to F.W., 27 July 1808, *Stein Br.*, II (2), 797; Stein, Denkschrift, 11 August 1808, *ibid.*, 808–812.

visers an occasion to open up covert communication with the Austrians in Bohemia concerning mutual defense.

It is not completely certain that Frederick William was aware of the second of these assignments at the time of the departure of this agent, Count Friedrich von Götzen, for Silesia.[28] The plan, however, had been brought before him. Discussions with the Austrians would seem to have been a reasonable extension of Götzen's assignment, even if they related only to problems of the defense of Silesia. Hence Götzen's mission cannot be regarded as definite evidence that the king was actively considering a proposal for action against the French, except in the case that they initiated the hostilities by an assault on the forts. But surely he must have shared the disappointment of Stein at the failure to negotiate a final settlement with the French. Certainly he knew of the fate of the King of Spain and felt deeply the humiliation of his brother, Prince William of Prussia, who had sought since January to negotiate a treaty with Bonaparte. William's efforts had been to no more avail than Stein's; the brother of the Prussian king was, in effect, compelled to solicit attention in the imperial antechambers in Paris. Frederick William knew, as well, the dangerous situation of his country and of the depredations of the French, Polish, and Saxon troops in occupied Prussia and on the march from Saxony through Silesia. He was also aware that matters in the east were as unsettled as they were in the west: that the efforts to obtain a final demarcation of the borders with Danzig and Warsaw were a source of constant irritation to the

[28] Ritter, *Stein*, 332, 610–611n15; Stein, Denkschrift, 11 August 1808, *Stein Br.*, II (2), 808–812; Stein, IS, 21 August 1808, *ibid.*, 821; Stein to Goltz, 26 July 1808, *ibid.*, 794. It is Ritter who suggests that Götzen may not have had Frederick William's approval to open negotiations (*Stein*, 332). This follows Ritter's general line of argument that the patriots were working without the king's consent in their negotiations for war and insurrection. But in view of the fact that Frederick William approved of similar negotiations with the British government and opened up the topic of war with France with the tsar (see below, notes 33 and 34), there is no reason to believe Götzen could not have had a similar assignment. Ritter himself later concedes that the king knew of Götzen's negotiations with the Austrians, but did not terminate them, in spite of the fact that he was conducting a policy of peace through Foreign Minister Goltz at the same time (*Stein*, 611–612n15). If he knew of them later, why not earlier? And if he did not approve of them, why did he make no effort to call Götzen back?

Prussians.[29] Finally, he must have known that Prussia would have to keep up with the Austrians, and that an Austrian victory in Germany not shared by Prussia would bring in its train a serious alteration in the pre-Napoleonic balance of the forces inside central Europe.

Probably even Frederick William felt his timorous soul stirred by the thrill of hope which the uprising of the Spanish people had discharged across Europe. His ambassador in Paris reported not only the successes of the insurgents, but also the arrival of tangible English aid in the form of arms and material in the Spanish patriot camp. In early August there were reports that Napoleon would be forced to diminish the size of his garrisons in occupied Prussia and yet more intelligence about the increased strength of Austria's armaments. Finally, on the twelfth of August, Königsberg received official confirmation from Ambassador Brockhausen in Paris of the colossal defeat of the French by the Spanish irregulars at Bailén in late July.[30] This was followed within a few days by the equally stunning report of the uprising of the Spanish troops in Denmark and their subsequent escape to British ships operating off the coast. All this the French could not keep secret; moreover, the gravity of their situation was soon confirmed by the movement of large numbers of French troops from German garrisons to Spain.[31]

---

[29] The whole question of the relations between Prussia and the Grand Duchy of Warsaw has been considered extensively, if not without bias, by Juliusz Willaume: "Prusy a sprawa polska za Księstwa Warszawskiego," *Roczniki historyczne,* XVII (1948), 378–398; "Polsko-pruskie stosunki finansowo-gospodarcze (1807–1813)," *Roczniki historyczne,* XIX (1952), 99–132; "Rozgraniczenie Ks. Warszawskiego z Prusami," *Przegląd zachodni,* VII (1951), no. 1, 474–492; "Stosunki sąsiedzkie Księstwa Warszawskiego z Prusami," *Przegląd zachodni,* VII (1951), no. 3, 396–427. I have examined some of the archival sources Willaume has used. They do not seem to me to substantiate the black versus white interpretation Willaume gives them. See Archiwum główne akt dawnych, Warsaw, Akta rady stanu Xięstwa Warszawskiego (Korrespondencye z władzami pruskiemi), vol. 316.

[30] Brockhausen to F.W., 1, 11, and 24 July 1808, DZA, A.A.I., Rep. 1, No. 1234; Drusina to FO, 9, 12, 17, and 20 August 1808, PRO, FO, Prussia, 64/78; Hassel, I, 219, 225.

[31] Lehmann, *Scharnhorst,* II, 180; Bignon, VII, 363–364; Hermann Granier, ed., *Berichte aus der Berliner Franzosenzeit, 1807–1809* (Leipzig, 1913), 286–288.

By mid-August, therefore, the need for haste in any preparations to meet the new situation in external affairs must have been apparent to the king as well as to his advisers. Gneisenau, Scharnhorst, and Stein all outlined plans before the king for an insurrection in northern Germany. As a preliminary *démarche,* Stein proposed to clarify Prussia's situation by offering Bonaparte a direct alliance. If he refused, his fundamental hostility to Prussia could be considered proved and appropriate action taken; if he accepted, Prussia as France's ally could rearm openly while awaiting the moment to strike out against her with Austria. The king agreed to consider the suggestions.[32] Subsequently he approved initial steps toward organizing a Prussian-led insurrection in northern Germany which would coincide in time with the outbreak of the war between France and Austria. Acting under the influence of the news of continued French setbacks, Frederick William made the first important move toward implementation of the proposals. He wrote on the twenty-eighth of August to Alexander of Russia to ask what his attitude would be in the event of Austro-French conflict.[33] He followed up

[32] Ritter, *Stein*, 334. To show the English, with whom the Prussians were simultaneously opening negotiations for aid, that Prussia was not conducting a Janus-faced policy, the proposal for an alliance with France was secretly communicated to London. See the third document enclosed in the letter of Jacoby-Kloest to D'Ivernois, 14 August 1808, PRO, FO, Prussia, 64/79. It was apparently Scharnhorst who originally suggested the offer of alliance (Scharnhorst to Stein, 8 August 1808, *Stein Br.,* II (2), 806–808).

[33] The question of the king's approval of the plan of insurrection is given a completely self-contradictory treatment by Ritter. In the text Ritter notes: "Der König, ohne direkt zu widersprechen, machte seinen stillen Vorbehalt" (*Stein*, 337). This is based on Scharnhorst to Stein, 23 August 1808, *Stein Br.,* II (2), 825–826, where Scharnhorst notes that the king must be brought to say "yes" or "no." See Stein, Antwortkonzept, 24 August 1808, *ibid.,* 825. Ritter's original remark seems to imply that the king could not make up his mind or took no stand. But in view of the action he took to continue the negotiations with England (see Ritter, *Stein*, 608n12) and to sound out the tsar (see F.W. to Alexander, 28 August 1808, in Paul Bailleu, ed., *Briefwechsel König Friedrich Wilhelms III und der Königin Luise mit Kaiser Alexander I,* Leipzig, 1900, 174–177), it is obvious that he had given conditional approval to the preparation of the plan. At the top of the page (337) on which the above quotation appears, Ritter adds the caption "Erhebungspläne Gneisenaus. *Ablehnung* durch den König" (my italics). The remainder of remarks directed toward the question of the plot by Ritter then proceed from the wholly unfounded assumption

this inquiry by taking official cognizance for the first time of the secret negotiations for English aid.[34]

The attitudes of Russia and England were of vital significance for Prussia. As early as July, a request for English money and supplies had been delivered informally to London. Probably it did not at this time have the approval of the king.[35] But secret communication with London had always been kept open for just such a contingency, despite the formal state of war which had existed between Prussia and Great Britain since Tilsit. Under George Canning's

---

that Stein was carrying on a scheme to which the king had not consented (for instance, p. 353). In putting the rhetorical question, "Did Gneisenau, Scharnhorst and Stein . . . really believe they could persuade a Frederick William III?" (337), Ritter suggests that a negative response would be mandatory. But the fact was that the king agreed at this time to write to Alexander and negotiate for aid from the British. Even after Stein's resignation he was to send an emissary to the Austrians to discuss war plans (Rössler, I, 408), and was clearly ready to join the Austrians in war in the spring of 1809. See Udo Gaede, *Preussens Stellung zur Kriegsfrage im Jahre 1809* (Hannover, 1897), 100–102; Paul Bailleu, "Zur Geschichte des Jahres 1809," *Historische Zeitschrift*, LXXXIV (1900), 454–455; Lehmann, *Scharnhorst*, II, 273–279. Of course war is one thing, and war plus insurrection—the plan the patriots suggested in August—another. But we can be certain that the king was interested enough to permit preliminary soundings to be taken in the case of the former, and was aware of and had not completely closed his mind to the latter. See also Jacoby-Kloest to D'Ivernois, 4 September 1808 (the king has approved "tous les sinistres"), in Otto Karmin, "Documents relatifs à la correspondance secrète avec la cour de Berlin (1808–1809)," *Revue historique de la révolution et de l'empire*, IV (1913), 396; Alexander Gibson, memorandum, "The Misfortunes of Prussia," December 1808, PRO, FO, Prussia, 64/79; and Stein, Antwortkonzept, 24 August 1808, *Stein Br.*, II (2), 825–826. Scharnhorst, in a letter to the king of 13 December 1808, recalled to his majesty his acceptance of the plan (Vaupel, 783).

[34] The king may have decided to appeal indirectly for aid from England even earlier than the end of August: see Jacoby-Kloest to D'Ivernois, 14 August 1808, PRO, FO, Prussia, 64/79. This proposal would certainly seem to have the king's approval, since Jacoby transmitted simultaneously a copy of the official Prussian dispatch to Prince William of 12 August 1808, in which William is asked to put forward the suggestion of an alliance with France. It is doubtful that such an action would have been taken without his majesty's consent. See also Stein, Antwortkonzept, 24 August 1808, *Stein Br.*, II (2), 825–826.

[35] D'Ivernois to Canning, 10 July 1808, Karmin, "Documents relatifs," 391–393; Jacoby-Kloest to Canning, 12 July 1808, in Otto Karmin, "A propos des négotiations anglo-prussiennes de 1808," *Revue historique de l'histoire de la révolution et de l'empire*, VI (1915), 131.

foreign secretaryship, England reopened the policy of subsidizing anti-French diversions on the Continent.[36] Spain and Sweden in 1808 provided the first occasions to test the program. In fact, the news of the French losses in Spain seems to have hastened the formal announcement of the new policy in London.[37] To the secret Prussian feelers, Canning replied generally, though affirmatively, in a letter dated August 11, but his answer on the specific issue of direct aid to Prussia was not known in Königsberg until October 22.[38] The conditions he set out for British aid to a Prussian military effort indicated that he thought that only a combined effort of Russia and Prussia would have definite prospects for success.

Napoleon had assured Alexander at Tilsit that Prussia's continued existence was the result of his intercession.[39] Thereafter Frederick William felt himself to be wholly dependent on the tsar. The tsar's self-esteem was flattered by this role of protector insofar as it did not

[36] Raymond Carr, "Gustavus IV and the British Government, 1804–9," *English Historical Review*, LX (1945), 48; J. Holland Rose, "Canning and the Spanish Patriots in 1808," *American Historical Review*, XII (1906–07), 40; H. W. V. Temperley, *Life of Canning* (London, 1905), 84; Godfrey Davies, "English Foreign Policy," *Huntington Library Quarterly*, V (1942), 449, 452. Compare Paul Wittichen, "Friedrich von Gentz und die englische Politik, 1800–1814," *Preussische Jahrbücher*, CX (1902), 492; and the general judgment of British aid in Richard Glover, "Arms and the British Diplomat in the French Revolutionary Era," *Journal of Modern History*, XXIX (1957), 199–200.

[37] Baron Hardenberg, in Tilsit, had heard of the new English policy by the twelfth of August (Hardenberg Tagebuch, 12 August 1808, DZA, Rep. 92, Hardenberg, L29; see notes 34 and 38 above and below). See also Castlereagh's remarks, 4 July 1808, in T. C. Hansard, *The Parliamentary Debates*, ser. 1, XI (London, 1812), 1142–1143.

[38] Jacoby-Kloest reported to Königsberg on 10 August that England was supplying the Spanish patriots (Jacoby-Kloest to Goltz, 10 August 1808, DZA, A.A.I., Rep. 1, No. 1064). Canning's letter of 11 August 1808 to Jacoby-Kloest is in Karmin, "Documents relatifs," 589–594. For the king's consent to open negotiations with the English government, see enclosure no. 2 in Jacoby-Kloest to D'Ivernois, 14 August 1808, PRO, FO, Prussia, 64/79; Jacoby-Kloest to D'Ivernois, 22 October 1808, Karmin, "Documents relatifs," 583.

[39] O. P. Backus, "Stein and Russia's Prussian Policy from Tilsit to Vienna," unpub. diss., Yale University, 1949, 27–28; Bassewitz, *Die Kurmark, 1806–1808*, I (Leipzig, 1851), 409. Goltz was told the same thing; see Paul Bailleu, *Königin Luise: Ein Lebensbild* (Berlin, 1908), 247.

conflict, as it sometimes did, with his own interests.[40] The manner in which the King of Prussia had meanwhile recognized his debt, his constant supplications for Russian diplomatic aid to persuade Bonaparte to carry out the Treaty of Tilsit[41]—all of this appears to have gratified Alexander, whose protective attitude toward smaller nations appeared on occasion in other historical times and places. The consequence of his majesty's dependence on the tsar was that a final decision on the patriots' program lay in the tsar's hands. Even British aid, as has been seen, depended on Russo-Prussian cooperation. The king's letter to Alexander of August 28 was an effort to secure both. His willingness to agree to the opening of secret negotiations with the British, to which may be added his probable knowledge of the contacts with Austria through the Austrian chargé in Königsberg and Count Götzen in Silesia, are proofs that Frederick William was entertaining the idea of a Prussian-led insurrection in northern Germany in the event of an Austro-French war. The king's consent to a conditional plan was the first essential condition the patriots won. But none of the other contingencies upon which the conspirators based their plans developed as quickly as they had hoped.

The first great hopes for an uprising were to prove illusory, as the patriot leaders had found out long before Canning's letter arrived in Königsberg.[42] At Tilsit, Alexander had succumbed to the temptation of Napoleon's grandly imagined schemes; he had been temporarily immobilized by Bonaparte's aura of invincibility.[43] Through

---

[40] See, for example, the arguments Napoleon used with Alexander at Erfurt in Jean Hanoteau, ed., *Mémoires du général de Caulaincourt* (Paris, 1933), I, 272–273; Napoleon to Caulaincourt, 2 and 6 February 1808, in Léon Lecestre, ed., *Lettres inédites de Napoléon Ier*, 2nd ed. (Paris, 1897), I, 144, 146.

[41] F.W. to Alexander, 17 May 1808, *Briefwechsel F.W.–Alexander*, 173–174.

[42] Schladen to F.W., 19 August 1808, DZA, A.A.I., Rep. 1, No. 2409; Schöler to Altenstein, 31 August 1808, quoted by Ritter, *Stein*, 608n13; Alexander to F.W., 12 September 1808, Hassel, I, 374. Friedrich Schleiermacher, the patriotic pastor from Berlin, who was visiting at the time in Königsberg, reported the news of the tsar's stand (probably from Schladen's report) in a coded letter of 30 August 1808 to Georg Reimer. See R. C. Raack, "A New Schleiermacher Letter on the Conspiracy of 1808," *Zeitschrift für Religions- und Geistesgeschichte*, XVI (1964), 214, 221.

[43] Albert Vandal, *Napoléon et Alexandre Ier: L'Alliance russe sous le premier empire*, I (Paris, 1896), 56–57; Hassel, I, 184–185.

his alliance with the upstart, his greed and his vanity were promised satisfaction. Bonaparte conjured up vistas of great adventures in the Indies and the prospect of the partition of the Ottoman Empire.[44] Now engaged in a war with Sweden over Finland, Alexander had gotten a slice of Prussia's Polish conquest and occupied the Turkish provinces of Moldavia and Wallachia as the first fruits of his new alliance with France. These he hoped to add on a permanent basis to his empire; they were the lure Bonaparte had proffered in return for his continued freedom to arrange matters with Prussia at his own convenience.[45] To Alexander, who saw in the balance of forces of France, Austria, and Russia a guarantee of stability which would open the possibility of his arranging matters in his own sphere to suit himself, the continuation of peace in central Europe was a necessity. At this time, therefore, although for different reasons, both Alexander and Napoleon wanted it preserved.[46]

Worst of all for the plot and its consequences, the attempt to set up the mechanism was clumsy in almost all respects. The patriots felt the need to hasten the preparations under the press of events in August. Their notions of how and when the Austrians would act were based at that time more on rumor than on definite intelligence. Having a most imperfect knowledge of the timing and goals which would be set by Vienna's war party, having only the conditional agreement of their own leader to their plans, the unfolding of which obviously depended on so many decisions over which they had no control, they had quickly to arrange the mechanism for an insurrection in a country occupied for the most part by a hostile

[44] Napoleon to Alexander, 2 February 1808, *Correspondance de Napoléon Ier publiée par ordre de l'empereur Napoléon III,* XVI (Paris, 1864), 498; Napoleon to Alexander, 29 April 1808, *ibid.,* XVII (Paris, 1865), 47; Napoleon to Caulaincourt, 2 February 1808, *Lettres inédites de Napoléon,* I, 142–144.

[45] Napoleon to Alexander, 6 February 1808, *Lettres inédites de Napoléon,* I, 146.

[46] Vandal, I, 439. See Caulaincourt to Champagny, 28 August 1808, in Nicholas M. Romanoff, *Les Relations diplomatiques de la Russie et de la France d'après les rapports des ambassadeurs d'Alexandre et de Napoléon (1808–1812),* II (St. Petersburg, 1905), 324. On Russian representations for Prussia see Rumiantsev to Tolstoy, 25 March 1808 (O.S.), in N. K. Schilder, ed., *Posol'stvo grafa P. A. Tolstogo v Parizhe v 1807 i 1808 gg.* (St. Petersburg, 1893), 495; Tolstoy to Rumiantsev, 17 April 1808 (O.S.), *ibid.,* 503–504; Tolstoy to Champagny, 10 April 1808 (O.S.), *ibid.,* 507–508; Tolstoy to Rumiantsev, 6 August 1808 (O.S.), *ibid.,* 653–654.

army and filled with French spies. The imagined need for haste
forced them to collect arms almost openly. The same need meant
the recruiting of indiscreet, perhaps untrustworthy, subordinates—
zeal, after all, is the hallmark of the conspirator possessed by the
vision of quick redemption. Too much haste meant that the French
legion of spies was bound to uncover the plot in one form or another, and sooner rather than later.[47]

But the crisis, the result of inadvertent betrayal of the plan to the
French, came about sooner and in a more catastrophic way than
anyone, however skeptical, might have believed. On August 15, at
the height of the intense fervor generated by the news of Bailén and
of the arrival of English money and arms in Spain, a new spate of
seemingly authentic war rumors which had Napoleon departing
immediately for the Rhine frontier for a showdown battle with the
Austrians arrived in Königsberg. Word of the British landings in
Denmark to aid the Spanish troops there who had revolted against
their French commanders filtered in almost simultaneously. The
sudden dramatic reversal of Bonaparte's fortune was the topic of
conversation in every salon in Königsberg.[48]

Excited, Stein, under the impress of these startling events of the
past few days—which seemed to push rapidly forward the time for
decision—wrote out his fateful letter to Baron Sayn-Wittgenstein on Prussia's hopes for war. It contained the general outline of
the scheme of uprising he and his advisers were suggesting to the
king. Seized by the French from a Prussian courier near Berlin, the
letter proved to be the unlucky instrument which ultimately gave
Stein and his entire party over to his enemies, domestic and foreign.

For this ill-considered deed, Stein, not the circumstances alone,
was responsible. Not only was his letter addressed to an agent in

[47] For examples of the rashness of the conspirators see Gneisenau to Bärsch, 18
November 1808, Vaupel, 716; Heinrich Steffens, *Was ich erlebte*, VI (Breslau, 1842),
171–173, 176–180; Rudolf von Katte, "Der Streifzug des Karl Friedrichs von Katte
auf Magdeburg im April 1809," *Geschichts-Blätter für Stadt und Land Magdeburg*,
Jg. 70/71 (1935–36), 24.

[48] Alexander Gibson to FO, 21 August 1808, PRO, FO, Prussia, 64/79; Drusina to
FO, 9, 12, 17, and 20 August 1808, PRO, FO, Prussia, 64/78; Jacoby-Kloest to Goltz,
10 August 1808, DZA, A.A.I., Rep. 1, No. 1064.

whom he had no cause for confidence and who was to betray him personally on several later occasions, it was not even coded.[49] This simple precaution even his amateur coconspirators took.[50] His courier, moreover, was apprehended in the middle of the French-occupied Mark Brandenburg (where Stein surely knew in advance he would go) after having completed the first stage of his mission in Berlin.[51] The sending of the letter as well as the mode of transmission Stein chose were both acts of utter recklessness for a man in his position. That Stein was personally responsible for what later befell him as a consequence of the letter affair is undeniable.

Yet even time itself turned up among the untoward agents of fortune which arranged the circumstances of Stein's debacle. At the end of August a report of a new and more pacific attitude taken toward Prussia by Napoleon was received from Ambassador Brockhausen and Prince William in Paris. The emperor was now held ready to sign a final treaty of peace;[52] the very goal Stein and Prince William so long had sought now appeared miraculously within sight. The long months of uncertainty, which had precipitated Stein's patriotic rage, were over. The decision had been taken by Bonaparte in July,[53] though the embassy in Paris first learned of it on the eleventh of August. Even before the month passed, the

[49] See Ritter, *Stein,* 349, and below, Chapters V and VI. Stein's letter to a man of Wittgenstein's character astonished many: see Drusina to FO, 27 September 1808, PRO, FO, Prussia, 64/78; Gibson to FO, 23 September 1808, PRO, FO, Prussia, 64/79.

[50] See Schleiermacher to Reimer, 30 August 1808, in Raack, "A New Schleiermacher Letter," 211–212; and Wilhelm Dilthey, "Schleiermachers politische Gesinnung und Wirksamkeit," *Preussische Jahrbücher,* X (1862), 234–277, *passim.* There are many coded and otherwise concealed messages in the Schleiermacher correspondence for this period.

[51] See below, Chapter III.

[52] Stein had some earlier hint of Napoleon's change of attitude (Brockhausen to F.W., 11 July 1808, and F.W. to Brockhausen, 8 August 1808, DZA, A.A.I., Rep. 1, No. 1234) but he took it as encouragement to toughen Prussia's stand against Napoleon (Stein, Denkschrift, 11 August 1808, *Stein Br.,* II (2), 808–812). See also Brockhausen to F.W., 11 August 1808, DZA, A.A.I., Rep. 1, No. 1234; Prince William to F.W., 11 August 1808, Hassel, I, 418–419; F.W. to Alexander, 28 August 1808, *Briefwechsel F.W.–Alexander,* 174–177.

[53] Napoleon to Caulaincourt, 23 July 1808, *Lettres inédites de Napoléon,* I, 223–224.

emperor had ordered Daru in Berlin to take a more cooperative attitude toward the Prussians.[54] Identical news of Bonaparte's desire for a treaty came from Paris via St. Petersburg.[55] Napoleon's new willingness to seal up in legal form his German conquests was the first obvious result of what was to become known as his "Spanish ulcer." [56]

At the end of August, Stein and the king—neither yet knew of the capture of the royal courier—deliberately overlooked Napoleon's newest and brashest financial demands which had accompanied his most recent bid for peace. They sought to capitalize upon his military difficulties in Spain by urging a stiffer posture upon the emissaries in Paris.[57] It was clear, however, that the king saw this as a short-run tactic leading to a diplomatic denouement. Stein too must have realized that all he had sought during his long months in Berlin was now within reach. By this time he knew also that Alexander had prophesied disaster to the Austrians if they took up arms against Napoleon.[58] The tsar had announced that he would stand by his alliance with the French even if war with Austria ensued. Frederick William's perennial attitude of caution was once again confirmed. War with France would mean hostilities with Russia as well as no subsidies from England. For war on such terms the king had no stomach. Hence the conspiracy would have to be pushed into the background, whatever difficulties that might entail, while Stein and the king took the measure of the new stage

[54] Napoleon to Daru, 26 August 1808, in Léonce de Brotonne, ed., *Dernières lettres inédites de Napoléon Ier* (Paris, 1903), I, 349. A similar pacific posture taken toward Austria was reported by Metternich from Paris on 23 August (Rössler, I, 375).

[55] Schladen to F.W., 23 August 1808, DZA, A.A.I., Rep. 1, No. 2409; Alexander to F.W., 30 August 1808, *Briefwechsel F.W.–Alexander*, 177–178; Alexander to Napoleon, 25 August 1808, *Posol'stvo grafa P. A. Tolstogo v Parizhe*, 761.

[56] Napoleon to Caulaincourt, 21 July 1808, *Lettres inédites de Napoléon*, I, 224; Lenz, "Napoleon I. und Preussen," 861; Napoleon to Alexander, 8 August 1808, *Correspondance de Napoléon*, XVII, 360; Vandal, I, 435; Edouard Driault, *Napoléon et l'Europe*, III (Paris, 1917), 346.

[57] Stein, Note (Votum) to IB of Prince William, 11 August 1808 (see Hassel, I, 418–419), 24 August 1808, *Stein Br.*, II (2), 826; Stein, Denkschrift, 30 August 1808, *ibid.*, 844–846.

[58] Alexander to F.W., 12 September 1808, *Briefwechsel F.W.–Alexander*, 178–179.

of the negotiations. But by this time, Stein's letter, a product of his war fever of early August, seized on the twenty-sixth of the month, was already in Napoleon's hands.[59]

[59] For Stein's explanation of the circumstances surrounding the writing of the letter, see Stein to Alexander, 21 September 1808, *Stein Br.,* II (2), 866–867; and Stein to Wittgenstein, 3 October 1808, *ibid.,* 883–884.

II

ON THE EVE OF CRISIS:
STEIN'S FRIENDS AND FOES

We have seen how the unwillingness of the French to make terms with Prussia and Stein's prolonged though vain hopes that they could be encouraged to do so had drawn out his stay in Berlin through the spring of 1808. In his long absence from Königsberg, the spirit of success and confidence engendered by the quick, successful reform legislation of the preceding fall had gradually dissipated. A slowing down of action would surely have occurred in any case, once the eternal wrangle of commission work began. But Stein's absence deprived the government of the force and decisiveness which it required.

The broad outlines of the reformers' platform with its bold proposals had been developed because of their commitment to the Prussian state. Stein and some of his closest collaborators held, as we have noted, a fundamental conviction that the continued existence of Prussia was vital to the future of Germany. Hence they had become convinced that the political breakdown after the military defeats of 1806 made necessary a rebuilding of the civil and military administration as well as the establishment of a basis for popular participation in government. The latter, in fact, some considered to be philosophically self-evident and morally necessary. The fact that Prussia's neighbors to the east and west, under the impetus of the notions of rationalization and improvement of society which Bonaparte's France carried over from the eighteenth century, were taking giant steps away from the feudal past made the same work in Prussia all the more urgent. Stein's legislative proposals, as we shall see, were similar in nature to the measures being enacted all over Europe to meet the challenge of the new age which had begun with the French Revolution. But as there was no general agreement among politically active Prussians on the type and extent of the reforms needed by the defeated state, Stein's program met determined opposition from powerful groups inside the nation. With Stein away in Berlin, the hopes of his domestic enemies, ideological and temperamental conservatives and partisans of the old system, began to revive. Insofar as these adversaries supplied a rationale for their politics, beyond a simple attachment to the bygone order, they argued, in general, that defeat in battle did not compel a thoroughgoing "revolution"; this term, with its obvious pejorative overtone of Jacobinism, they applied recklessly to any innovation. Their chief canon of reference, as might be expected, was the state of Frederick the Great, which they held to be the epitome of political art. All deviations from that model they viewed as unnecessary or even dangerous.[1] With the main author of their discontent removed, they had begun to recover confidence, take stock of their resources, and rediscover their influence at court. In the absence of direct evidence, this would seem to be the most plausible explanation of the origin of the powerful coalition which, by midsummer of 1808, was preparing to attack Stein and his party openly.

The fact was that Stein and the reformers, in their short tenure of office, had failed to clear out the Augean stables at the Prussian court. Indeed, fundamentally moderate men, like Stein and his

[1] On Stein's loss of time in Berlin, see Ritter, *Stein,* 325–327; Mehring, *Zur preussischen Geschichte,* 53–55. Outside pressures to reform Prussia are discussed by Erwin Hölzle, "Das Napoleonische Staatssystem in Deutschland," *Historische Zeitschrift,* CXLVIII (1933), 285–287; and Ritter, *Stein,* 317; Mehring, *Zur preussischen Geschichte,* 139. Hölzle (290) illustrates the power of example with a most interesting quotation from Hardenberg's Riga *Denkschrift* of 1807: "Die Gewalt dieser Grundsätze ist so gross, sie sind so allgemein anerkannt und verbreitet, dass der Staat, der sie nicht annimmt, entweder seinem Untergang oder der erzwungenen Annahme entgegensehen muss." On the king's attitude toward reform see Otto Hintze, "Die preussische Reformbestrebungen vor 1806," *Historische Zeitschrift,* LXXVI (1896), 415–416. Good characterizations of the opposition to Stein are given by Mehring, *Zur preussischen Geschichte,* 60–61; and Simon, *Failure of the Prussian Reform Movement,* 12–13.

reform-minded predecessor, Baron Karl August von Hardenberg, could not have conceived the sort of cleansing, even carried out in the name of revolution, which would have been necessary to remove their adversaries from the king's hearing. Frederick William, in any case, would never have permitted it. Though he knew that the pre-Jena system of state was inadequate and that its leaders had been personally besmirched by the defeat which had brought it down, he still kept a coterie of the old party about him. Whether out of loyalty, charity, or preference—we do not know which—Frederick William preferred the opponents of Stein for his courtiers.

Stein's enemies had been taken completely aback by the speed of the first reform legislation and by the quick establishment of commissions to plan other important changes. Stein had moved swiftly and directly, capitalizing on the preliminary labors of Hardenberg and other innovators of the foregoing administration. The enactments which eliminated serfdom and certain class barriers to professional and social mobility envisaged an end to the feudal organization of society. The abolition of patrimonial justice in order to terminate the last hold of landlord over tenant was contemplated. The opening of the army and bureaucracy to men of talent irrespective of class background, the establishment of a cabinet system of responsible ministers bearing fixed portfolios, and the creation of popularly chosen, representative governments in the cities—these reforms, in the planning stage, were next on the agenda to be decreed. With them, old Prussia would be overturned domestically. The position of the nobility, founded on property and privilege, would be undermined. Many of Stein's enemies viewed all this as subverting the Prussia of tradition. Crass egalitarians would create a new state which a man of dignity and honor, as many partisans of the older society understood these two concepts, could not accept. Seen through conservative eyes, domestic forces, not the French, were destroying the nation, and this in the name of saving it.

In addition to the enemies of Stein by ideological conviction (inso far as such a pure type existed), the antireform camp included disgruntled officials and courtiers, ex-ministers still longing for

office and restoration of their influence, and undoubtedly some unabashed opportunists as well. Some had found themselves displaced
in the circle of royal influence by the interposition of the reform
party. Some were struck from the rolls of the civil service for reasons
of economy; some were dismissed for failing to follow the court to
Königsberg. Others had readjusted to the new Napoleonic order in
Europe and hailed its stability as a bulwark against Jacobinism;
they saw personal or national salvation only in cooperation with the
French. Each of Stein's foes held his own political conviction and
purpose; in general they shared only their hostility to the ministry
and to the reforms, a compliant or favorable attitude toward the
French, and an insistence on resurrecting the "system" of Frederick
the Great, whatever that might have become by the year of its
demise, 1806.

Stein, of course, knew of the danger from these elements. But
he could not deal effectively with them and simultaneously bring
about a treaty with the French. He saw his paramount interest
served first by the trip to Berlin; those enemies who were immediately a menace remained behind, concentrated around the court in
Königsberg. Yet these had, or were to have, significant aid from
allies in Berlin. In fact their cabal against the reform government,
for such it became, was only to succeed because of intrigue against
Stein carried on in both cities.

In Berlin, the main opposition was concentrated in the hands
of the ex-ministers and former advisers whom Stein and Hardenberg had displaced, aristocrats like Friedrich Wilhelm von Zastrow
and Otto Friedrich von Voss and, later, the commoner Karl
Friedrich Beyme. Little biographical information about any of
these men is available; insofar as archival sources once existed, they
appear to have perished in the catastrophe of 1945. Of Zastrow, who
had preceded Baron Hardenberg as Minister of Foreign Affairs,
we know least of all. Friedrich von Gentz, later Metternich's secretary, whose acidulous biographical vignettes inevitably color any
account of his times, knew Zastrow and the others from the years
of his service to Prussia. Gentz described him as having his sole

competence in military organization. Beyond that talent he had no other. He lacked an expanded purview of affairs and was wealthy, "passionate, vain, revengeful, partisan, envious, intolerant." [2] Clausewitz described him more simply as "cautious and devious" (*umsichtig und gewandt*).[3] In the spring of 1807 Zastrow had left the king's service to return to Berlin. The reasons for his change of milieu are not wholly clear, but chief among them was a bitter conflict with Hardenberg which nearly came to an exchange with pistols at dawn.[4] His family biographer, a later Zastrow, attributed his resignation to his vain opposition to the continuation of the war at that time (just a few months before the Treaty of Tilsit), opposition allegedly stemming from his mistrust of Prussia's Russian ally. As a matter of fact, even some unimpeachable reformers like Friedrich von Schroetter had opposed continuing the war though for different reasons; that is, considering the looting and devastation wrought in the East Prussian countryside by the Russian troops, to be Russia's ally was as bad as being France's enemy.[5] But Zastrow's enemies charged that his desire for a reconciliation with France was really based upon his desire to retain his vast estates in formerly Prussian Poland, which the Warsaw government would confiscate from an enemy leader. Toward this end he was alleged to have been in secret communication with the French from the beginning of the war.[6] The latter story, though unproven, is neither implausible nor impossible, since Zastrow, almost immediately after the defeat at Jena, had been assigned by the king to meet Bonaparte in Berlin. The purpose of his mission, to which he ardently subscribed, was

[2] Paul Wittichen, "Das preussische Kabinett und Friedrich von Gentz: Eine Denkschrift aus dem Jahre 1800," *Historische Zeitschrift*, LXXXIX (1902), 256.

[3] Carl von Clausewitz, *Nachrichten über Preussen in seiner grossen Katastrophe* (Berlin, 1888), 436.

[4] On Zastrow and Hardenberg, see Bassewitz, *Die Kurmark, 1806–1808*, I, 371–372, 380–382.

[5] Gottlieb Krause, *Der preussische Provinzialminister Freiherr von Schroetter und sein Anteil an der Steinschen Reformgesetzgebung*, pt. 1 (Königsberg, 1898), 63–66, 69. See Bassewitz, *Die Kurmark, 1806–1808*, I, 406, on the behavior of Russian troops near Memel. Schroetter, accused of victualing the Russian troops insufficiently, argued that supplies were not available (*ibid.*, 390).

[6] Gibson to FO, 10 October 1808, PRO, FO, Prussia, 64/79. Ritter, *Stein*, 610n9, speculates that Zastrow later tried to betray Stein to get the lands back.

to find a common ground, if any existed, for an armistice. In any case, the family chronicler does nothing in his account based upon the Zastrow archive to mitigate the charges made against his ancestor. In fact, Zastrow's biography seems almost deliberately muddied at this point.[7]

Like Zastrow, Otto von Voss was an ex-minister of the King of Prussia. He had been forced out of the government when Hardenberg came in in April 1807. He then returned to French-occupied Berlin, where he took up the unofficial leadership of the Junkers, or aristocratic party, in the Mark. Originally a proponent of the war (which would, of course, have put him in opposition to Zastrow earlier), he was friendly with Stein as late as 1807.[8] In May 1808 he was named by Stein to the post of head of the Prussian delegation in Berlin for negotiations with the occupying authorities.[9] The first occupant of that place, the patriot J. A. Sack, had fought with Daru and been declared persona non grata by the French. Stein obviously had cause to hope that Voss's relations with the French authorities would be better than Sack's, for Voss, after Tilsit, apparently had decided that cooperation with France was Prussia's sole hope. Voss's appointment must be viewed as a part of Stein's "policy of fulfillment" through which, in May, he still hoped to bring an end to the occupation and a final treaty of peace with France.[10] Voss was a violent opponent of the "revolutionizing" of the country by the re-

---

[7] Otto von Zastrow, *Die Zastrowen: Zusammengestellt in den Jahren 1862 bis 1869 aus dem ausgefundenen Materialen . . .* , I (Berlin, 1872), 81–82; see also *Allgemeine deutsche Biographie,* XLIV (Leipzig, 1898), 721–723. Leopold von Gerlach, in his "Familiengeschichte," also put Zastrow in the peace party. See Hans Joachim Schoeps, ed., *Aus den Jahren preussischer Not und Erneuerung: Tagebücher und Briefe der Gebrüder Gerlach und ihres Kreises, 1805–1820* (Berlin, 1963), 72.

[8] On Voss and Hardenberg see the Theodor von Schön Nachlass, in the former Königsberg State Archive, now in Göttingen, No. 61, p. 32. On Voss, see Bassewitz, *Die Kurmark, 1806–1808,* I, 416; and *Allgemeine deutsche Biographie,* XL (Leipzig, 1895), 352–360. Two letters of Voss with important indications of his political views for this time are those to Prince Hatzfeldt of 10 and 21 February 1809, in APMW, Archiwum Hatzfeldt'ów, No. 673.

[9] Stein, IB, 8 May 1808, *Stein Br.,* II (2), 726; F.W. to Stein, 15 May 1808, *ibid.,* 734. See also, on the disagreement between Sack and Daru, Leopold von Gerlach's "Familiengeschichte," in Schoeps, *Aus den Jahren preussischer Not,* 73.

[10] Hassel, I, 173; Ritter, *Stein,* 325–326. Ritter's phrase alludes to Stresemann.

formers and, like Zastrow, he was both personally and politically Hardenberg's enemy. Probably he considered Stein to be little more than Hardenberg's creature as well as his own rival for the coveted post of chief minister. His nomination by Stein to the important place in Berlin is as incomprehensible today as it was to Hardenberg then,[11] for Voss immediately pretended to power and title equal to Stein's.[12] From the first day of his appointment, he used his official position to intrigue against the man who had put him in office.

Stein's antagonists in Berlin were crafty and capable; his Königsberg opponents compensated for their manifest incapacity by their proximity to the seat of authority. Indecisive Frederick William loved to surround himself with courtiers who were his equivalent in talent and vision. Many of the court offices were merely symbolic, yet served as a haven for the stalwarts of the old order, those who owed their posts to birth and influence. Most important, such office holding guaranteed a convenient entree for antireform opinions into the royal society.

In this latter entourage was the antique military governor of Königsberg, Field Marshal Friedrich Adolf von Kalckreuth, the king's adjutant, on whom young Major Clausewitz blamed a good part of the debacle at Jena.[13] Later Kalckreuth had, not without honor, defended Danzig. The king then assigned him to negotiate with the French the Königsberg Convention (July 12, 1807) to implement the Treaty of Tilsit. It was the unastute Kalckreuth who had failed in that document to close the reparations loophole, leaving the adjudication of that critical matter to the future—the very issue which drew Stein away to his long absence in Berlin in the spring. By the summer of 1808, Kalckreuth had transformed himself into the leader of the party of reconciliation with France. For this, and for allegedly telling the French consul all he knew, Gneisenau called him the chief French agent in Königsberg.[14]

[11] Hardenberg Tagebuch, 20 May 1808, DZA, Rep. 92, Hardenberg, L29; Hardenberg to Altenstein, 21 May 1808, 14 September 1808, DZA, Rep. 92, Altenstein, B14.
[12] He objected to holding a "herabsetzende Abstufung" vis-à-vis Stein (Voss, IB, 2 June 1808, *Stein Br.*, II (2), 742–743).
[13] Clausewitz, *Nachrichten*, 517, 530–531.
[14] On Kalckreuth, see *Allgemeine deutsche Biographie*, XVI (Leipzig, 1882), 34–

Also high up among the king's confidants was the court general Karl Leopold von Köckritz, a friend of Count Christian von Haugwitz, one of the authors of the discredited pro-French policy pursued by Prussia before Jena. His enemies mocked him as "a well-powdered nullity." [15] Of Köckritz the brilliant, sourish Gentz wrote: "He is a man who has neither brains, nor education, nor knowledge, nor talent for any affair, nor any sociable qualities; an officer of the narrowest, vulgarest class, a cipher in the real meaning of the word." For this royal lap dog Gentz had but one bit of praise: he refused to participate in any cabal.[16] But even this quality, as we shall see, had vanished since Gentz had gathered the material for his Prussian cameos.

Perhaps more important at court than either Kalckreuth or Köckritz, because of her position as lady in waiting to the queen, was the octogenarian Countess Sophie von Voss (no relation to Otto). [17] Although her political understanding was probably rudimentary, through her influence factionaries could gain access to the beautiful and capricious Louise, whose feminine whims the king never learned to discount.

Outside the *Hofpartei*—called by some of its opponents, punning on the leaders' names, the "Kakodämonen" [18] (from the Greek *kakodaimones,* or "evil spirits")—Stein had another powerful enemy: Karl Friedrich Beyme, the king's bourgeois favorite. As in the case of so many of Stein's influential contemporaries in Prussia,

---

38. Gneisenau's comment on him is in a memoir for Canning, summer 1809, in PRO, FO, Prussia, 64/80. Gneisenau's opinion appears confirmed by a letter of Altenstein to Stägemann, 1 May 1808, Rühl, *Aus der Franzosenzeit,* 92. See also Gneisenau, Denkschrift, 24 August 1808, Vaupel, 566.

[15] On Haugwitz and Köckritz, see *Allgemeine deutsche Biographie,* XV (Leipzig, 1882), 116–117; Gneisenau's memoir for Canning, summer 1809, in PRO, FO, Prussia, 64/80; Clausewitz, *Nachrichten,* 449.

[16] The quotation from Gentz is printed by Wittichen, "Das preussische Kabinett und Gentz," 255–256. See Stein's similar view of Köckritz in Ritter, *Stein,* 152.

[17] On Countess Voss, see *Allgemeine deutsche Biographie,* XL (Leipzig, 1896), 361–366. Sophie Marie von Pannewitz, Countess von Voss, *Sixty-nine Years at the Court of Prussia,* trans. Emilie and Agnes Stephenson, 2 vols. (London, 1876), is her diary, reputedly expurgated.

[18] The term "Kakodämonen" is used by Sack in a letter to Stein of 23 November 1808, *Stein Br.,* II (2), 986.

regrettably little biographical research has been expended on Beyme. Unlike Stein's titled adversaries, he had long been associated with the idea of reform of the Prussian state.[19] In that respect, he was at one with the king's own vague interests. A few of his contemporaries respected his driving energy; most others denounced him as a parvenu striving toward the top, an unprincipled conniver, ruthless in his quest for influence.[20] Though a commoner, he enjoyed the confidence of a monarch who apparently made few distinctions on account of birth among his aides; but he was judged less generously among those of higher station as a ridiculous though dangerous upstart. To high-born Metternich, who had served as the Habsburgs' ambassador in Berlin before Jena, Beyme was nothing more than a "Prussian Jacobin." [21]

Gentz had served Prussia when Beyme's influence with the king was greatest. Around 1800, according to him, Beyme was the most important man in civil affairs in the state. He held great power over each of the ministries. Gentz conceded that Beyme was capable and astute, but there praise stopped: "He is one of the philosophizing half-educated . . . Everything which calls itself enlightenment or which will reform the state or which masks itself in the guise of philosophy he protects . . . insatiably ambitious . . . arrogant and illiberal." [22]

[19] On Beyme see Karl Disch, "Der Kabinettsrath Beyme und die auswärtige Politik Preussens in den Jahren 1805–1806," *Forschungen zur brandenburgischen und preussischen Geschichte,* XLI (1928), 331–366, and XLII (1929), 93–134; Ludwig Dehio, "Eine Reform-Denkschrift Beymes aus dem Sommer 1806," *ibid.,* XXXVIII (1926), 321–338; *Allgemeine deutsche Biographie,* II (Leipzig, 1875), 601–605; and Hintze, "Die preussische Reformbestrebungen vor 1806," 416.

[20] Gneisenau to Stein, 15 February 1809, *Stein Br.,* III, 45; Erich von Bodelschwingh, *Das Leben des Ober-Praesidenten Freiherrn von Vincke,* pt. 1 (Berlin, 1853), 371; Disch, 333 and n. 6. See also Clausewitz, *Nachrichten,* 452–453. Clausewitz asserted that Beyme's greatest talent was his ability to gain the king's confidence.

[21] Quoted by Kurt von Raumer, *Deutschland um 1800: Krise und Neugestaltung, 1789–1815, Handbuch der deutschen Geschichte,* ed. by Leo Just, III, pt. 1, (Constance, 1961), 181; and by Disch, 335.

[22] Quoted by Wittichen, "Das preussische Kabinett und Gentz," 257–258. Beyme's letters are full of expressions of his interest in self-improvement and "self-completion." See Beyme to Karl von Schroetter in "Briefe des Grafen von Beyme aus den Jahren

By the cast of his mind as well as the judgments of his faculties, Beyme revealed himself as a disciple of the philosopher Fichte. Beyme had heard Fichte's lectures on the progress of man through the stages of history to a higher development, "The Characteristics of the Present Age," in Berlin in 1804 and 1805. While giving those lectures, Fichte was still in his "French period"; that is, he esteemed France as the nation destined to lead Europe to a higher historical stage. Then both he and Beyme, each in his own way, switched cockades when the French and Prussian systems clashed in 1806. But neither philosopher nor statesman ever abandoned faith in man's progress through expanding the realm where reason held sway.[23] The goal did not change; history instead chose another vehicle for man's ascent to Utopia.

Long before Jena, Hardenberg regarded Beyme as a danger to his own position of influence with the king.[24] Though Hardenberg broke with pre-Jena Prussia's policy of pacifying Bonaparte, Beyme remained loyal to it up to the eve of Jena. But as soon as the war began, he became just as ardent a patriot as he had been pacifer before. Thereby he became the enemy of Zastrow, who, as we have seen, had urged the king just after Jena to meet Napoleon's terms for peace. In the winter of 1806 and 1807, Beyme became once again, as in 1800, though still without the requisite title, the real prime minister, the commoner who directed Prussia. He had escaped the obloquy which befell the author of the pro-French policy, Haugwitz.[25] And whatever the nature of the rivalry which had existed

---

1797, 1807 und 1808," *Allgemeine Conservative Monatsschrift*, II (1886), 937–949, *passim*.

[23] Johann Gottlieb Fichte, *The Popular Works of Fichte, II: The Characteristics of the Present Age*, trans. William Smith (London, 1847). See Beyme to Schön, 25 December (falsely dated October) 1808, in Theodor von Schön, *Aus den Papieren des Ministers und Burggrafen von Marienburg Theodor von Schön*, I (Halle, 1875), 83–84.

[24] Bassewitz, *Die Kurmark, 1806–1808*, I, 350; Raumer, 219; Koser, "Die preussische Politik," 260.

[25] Bassewitz, *Die Kurmark, 1806–1808*, I, 353, 380, 407; Fritz Valjavec, *Die Entstehung der politischen Strömungen in Deutschland, 1770–1815* (Munich, 1951), 377–378. On Haugwitz see Clausewitz, *Nachrichten*, 449–451; and Metternich, *Memoirs*, II, 24–25.

between him and Hardenberg before the catastrophe, he made Hardenberg his own candidate to replace Zastrow as foreign minister in the spring of 1807. At that time, Beyme stayed on as adviser to the king.

When Napoleon ordered that Hardenberg, whom he wrongly gauged on wholly inadequate evidence as an irreconcilable enemy of France, be exiled after Tilsit, both Beyme and Hardenberg advised the king to entrust the conduct of affairs to Stein. But Stein immediately demanded that Beyme be put away from his place of influence near the king.[26] After considerable discussion it was agreed that Beyme would remain in Königsberg until the dissolution of the old advisory council (*Kabinett*) in late spring; he would then take up a judicial post in Berlin. The queen undertook to salve his hurt by urging that he accept a temporary withdrawal with good grace.[27] He followed the advice and at first made sporadic efforts to cooperate with Stein, though never terminating his persistent caviling against the minister and his reformer colleagues, Baron Karl vom Stein zum Altenstein and Theodor von Schön. The impression given by the scanty evidence is that Beyme could not resist meddling, though officially out of office, whenever the opportunity was presented.[28]

Stein had been only five months in office when he departed for Berlin in the spring of 1808. Beyme, ostensibly returned to private life, remained behind in Königsberg. Apparently he had believed that his exile from the royal circle was truly to be only temporary and that Stein would turn over the direction of affairs to him during his absence in Berlin. When Stein did not do this,[29] Beyme began, it appears, to work actively against him.

[26] Ritter, *Stein*, 206–210; Bassewitz, *Die Kurmark, 1806–1808*, I, 340–372. Even before the outbreak of the war in 1806 Napoleon had come to regard Hardenberg as an enemy of France (see Ritter, *Stein*, 150). Stein and Hardenberg had already tried and failed to push Beyme out in December 1806 (*ibid.*, 168–169, 173–175).

[27] Ritter, *Stein*, 208–209; Bassewitz, *Die Kurmark, 1806–1808*, I, 454–461.

[28] Bassewitz, *Die Kurmark, 1806–1808*, I, 340–382, *passim;* Beyme to Schroetter, 14 October and 29 November 1807, "Briefe des Grafen von Beyme," 941, 944. Altenstein and Beyme were old foes (see Ritter, *Stein*, 204–210).

[29] Ritter, *Stein*, 245.

Though beset by many enemies, Stein was not without influential support in Königsberg. The king, while he may not have found in Stein his perfect counterpart for the ministry, respected him and was willing to underwrite his general program. More important perhaps for the strength of Stein's position was the support of the queen. By many she was considered the stronger of the royal pair. In the spring of 1808, she was emotionally as violent a partisan of Stein and his cause as she was his enemy a bare six months later. Fickle in heart and an easy victim to intrigue,[30] she had been Beyme's supporter in the fall of 1807; only half a year later she was his foe. Similarly, the worshipful admiration she showered on Stein that spring and summer was to be forgotten by December, when she took credit before the French consul for his fall from power.[31]

In the spring of 1808, the queen had learned of the opposition to Stein. She had reported it to him immediately—proof of her support for him at this time. A cabal, she said, had been formed and was "boring" from within.[32] Two weeks later, she informed him through a mutual friend that "Chaisenbau"—surely a deliberate attempt to obfuscate "Gneisenau"—wanted him to return immediately to Königsberg.[33] Beyme was charging Stein behind his back with being too yielding toward the French in the negotiations. In her indictment of the efforts to turn the king against the first minister, the queen grouped some of Stein's closest coworkers in Königsberg: Privy Councilor Wilhelm Anton Klewitz and the passionate reformist liberals Theodor von Schön and one of the two

---

[30] Louise de Prusse, Princesse Antoine Radziwill, *Quarante-cinq années de ma vie, 1770 à 1815*, 2nd ed. (Paris, 1911), 299.

[31] Clérembault to Davout, 25 November 1808, AG, CGA, C2 81; confirmed by Godefroy Cavaignac, "La Saisie de la lettre de Stein en 1808," *Revue historique*, LX (1896), 77.

[32] On Queen Louise's support for Stein see Louise to Stein, 31 March 1808, *Königin Luise: Briefe*, 334; Louise to Frau von Berg, 4 May 1808, *ibid.*, 345. For her warnings to Stein see Louise to Stein, 1 May 1808, *ibid.*, 343; Louise to Frau von Berg, 17 May 1808, *ibid.*, 345–346.

[33] Gneisenau in his memoir of the summer of 1808 (PRO, FO, Prussia, 64/80) said his call was an effort to bring Stein back because of the important implications of the Spanish insurrection.

barons Schroetter.[34] With these she lumped together Zastrow, who was in Berlin, and Borstell, the conservative military adviser and opponent of Scharnhorst.[35]

What is to be made of the diffuse charges contained in the queen's bill of indictment against Stein's "enemies"? Not only did she name Zastrow and Beyme, each enemy to the other in the previous year, but also several well-known colleagues of Stein against whom only the flimsiest chain of evidence of disloyalty can be fashioned. Hence, on the surface of things, one might well discredit the queen's information. She had collected all the rumors and evidences of disloyalty and dissatisfaction she knew of, juxtaposed them helter-skelter, and had sent them off to Berlin. More than anything, it would seem, the queen's letters reflect her concern for the kingdom, the fate of which she associated with Stein's mission and reform ministry, as well as her own unwritten, perhaps unthought, wish that he return quickly to command matters in Königsberg.

It may well be that Schön, Schroetter, and Klewitz actually were unhappy at the time because of Stein's long absence and his consequent failure to direct the reform group. Among the reformers there must have been much bickering over many details. The dogmatic, utopian Schön would have been the last person to stifle his opinion in the name of tact. There are several later indications of discontent among Stein's aides in which the names Schön and Schroetter appear, but no solid proof that they were ever willing to conspire against the king's first minister.[36] Yet the cabal the queen mentioned

---

[34] Queen Louise apparently referred to Friedrich von Schroetter.

[35] Louise to Frau von Berg, 17 May 1808, *Königin Luise: Briefe,* 345–346. See Ritter, *Stein,* 245. On Scharnhorst and Borstell, see Rudolf Stadelmann, "Das Duell zwischen Scharnhorst und Borstell im Dezember 1807," *Historische Zeitschrift,* CLXI (1940), 263–276.

[36] Rothfels, *Schön,* ch. 1, has a good discussion of Schön. Schön was also opposed to Stein's plan for the reorganization of the cabinet and ministries; see Dohna to Merckel, 1 April 1809, in Otto Linke, "Der Geschäftsbericht des Ministers Grafen zu Dohna," *Jahresbericht der schlesischen Gesellschaft für vaterländische Kultur,* LXXX (1902), Abt. 3, p. 3. On Schroetter, see Drusina to FO, 20 October 1808, PRO, FO, Prussia, 64/78; and Mehring, *Zur preussischen Geschichte,* 60, on the nature of Schroetter's opposition to Stein's plan for the end of patrimonial justice. Karl von Schroetter, the justice minister, was said to be displeased with the new articles of war

and the naming of Beyme, about whom Stein received information from another source, cannot be ignored.[37] True, in April Beyme had made through Stein's trusted coworker F. A. von Stägemann a protest of complete loyalty to the minister. He wrote that he wished Stein would hurry back to Königsberg to put affairs there in order once more.[38] But irrespective of this protestation, evidences of Beyme's duplicity and conniving are too abundant to permit ignoring the queen's charge, which is confirmed elsewhere. It was the first sign of a direct effort to work on the king behind the minister's back. At almost the same time as his letter to Stägemann, Beyme was complaining to the king of Stein's conduct of affairs.[39] He implied that Stein, not as clever as he should be, was being used by the French against the interest of Prussia. The date of his letter, which was written just before the queen's revelations to Stein, shows that it was one source of the queen's information about Beyme. By publicly worrying Beyme must have intended to impeach Stein's conduct of foreign affairs at the same time as he proved his concern for Prussia. There is no more reason to accept as sincere his hopes that Stein return to Königsberg to take over the conduct of government than there is to credit as genuine the feelings expressed in his subsequent letter to Stein: that he would gladly leave Königsberg if only he were certain he possessed the minister's confidence.[40] Beyme obviously knew that Stein was behind this exclu-

(Delbrück, *Tagebuchblätter*, 1 September 1808, III, 48). See also Raack, "A New Schleiermacher Letter," 219n29.   ,

[37] Stein recognized the problem: see Stein to Altenstein, 29 April 1808, *Stein Br.*, II (2), 722; see also Stägemann to Frau von Stägemann, 15 May 1808, Rühl, *Aus der Franzosenzeit*, 96; Altenstein to Stägemann, 17 May 1808, *ibid.*, 98.

[38] Beyme to Stägemann, 21 April 1808, Rühl, *Aus der Franzosenzeit*, 85–86.

[39] Beyme: "Ich will ihm [Stein] damit keinen Vorwurf machen, weil die bisherige Erfahrung gezeigt hat, dass auch der Klügste den französischen Fallstricken nicht hat entgehen können." And: "Euere Königliche Majestät haben dort keinen Minister, sondern nur einen Bevollmächtigten, der sich aber von den Franzosen als Euerer Majestät Minister gegen Ihr Interesse brauchen lässt" (Beyme to F.W., 12 May 1808, Hassel, I, 561–562. Nevertheless, on the very same day the king expressed his complete confidence in Beyme. See Hermann Hüffer, *Die Kabinettsregierung in Preussen und Johann Wilhelm Lombard* . . . (Leipzig, 1891), 408).

[40] Beyme to Stein, 2 June 1808, *Stein Br.*, II (2), 742.

sion from his position of influence; their reconciliation of the previous October had been no more than superficial. Shortly after Stein's return to Königsberg in early June, Beyme, as had been agreed upon six months before, left the provisional capital for his estate at Steglitz, just outside Berlin.[41] No one within the reform party lamented his going. Stein thereafter served alone, without benefit of Beyme's unofficial advice to the king.

The return of Stein from Berlin and the political exile of Beyme marked the beginning of the second phase of the great freshet of reforms associated with Stein's name. Two general plans of reorganization, one for the military forces and one for the civil government, were in preparation in the summer of 1808.

As a first step which served as an earnest of intent, Stein let out on half pay many members of the government service. Pressed for money and in quest of financial and organizational reform, he considered them superfluous.[42] Their exclusion would benefit the work, long under way, on the reform of the central cabinet organization. On this, Stein's own ideas ran parallel to those of Altenstein. Altenstein, who was a close confidant of Hardenberg, had been one of Stein's closest collaborators at the beginning of his ministry. He and his brother-in-law Karl Friedrich Nagler were in constant communication with Hardenberg and supplied the ex-minister with his whole stock of inside information about court and government affairs. In the summer of 1808, Stein adopted Altenstein's idea for a state council. There was to be one chief minister responsible for the work of a number of subalterns. The united cabinet, led by the prime minister, would advise the king in place of the plethora of equal departmental ministries, each individually answerable to the king, which had been the organization before. The acceptance of Altenstein's system, originally put forth in his Riga Program (*Rigaer Denkschrift*) of September 1807, showed the influence Altenstein had in the Stein administration.[43]

---

[41] Beyme to Stein, 2 June 1808, *Stein Br.*, II (2), 741–742 and 741n12; Ritter, *Stein*, 209–210.   [42] Ritter, *Stein*, 245.   [43] Ritter, *Stein*, 240–242.

A revision at the level of local administration in the cities and counties was also worked out in the summer of 1808. Leadership in this sphere was given to the East Prussian Kantian liberal, Baron Friedrich Leopold von Schroetter. His proposals, put forward at the end of August, envisaged the introduction of a modicum of self-government.[44] The cities and rural counties of Prussia were to be granted a measure of popular control over their own elected administrations. If this program were enacted as Schroetter proposed, it would be at the expense of the power of the nobles; as the chief component of the royal civil service, this class had governed the nation in the name of the king until this time.

Another committee responsible for judicial and legal reforms had made a specific proposal for the termination of patrimonial justice; this was the estate owners' last real legal hold over the peasants who had been released from bondage to the land by the edicts of the preceding October.[45] All these changes, which would alter drastically the future social and political structure of Prussia, were in moot at the same time that Scharnhorst and Stein in the summer of 1808 pushed through a basic overhauling of the military.[46]

Reorganization of the army as planned by Scharnhorst met with great opposition not only within the military reform commission itself but from many among the old leadership as well, those attached to existing organization and procedure, and from ideological and temperamental conservatives in general. This latter group, to which must be added a number of ancient soldiers like Kalckreuth and Köckritz, had easy access to the king. As in the case of the civil reforms, the military reorganization portended a completely new casting of army and society. The East Elbian nobility of service, the Junkers, had had almost exclusive control of the military under the king's general direction. Now class, the existing gauge of merit for officer candidates, was to be replaced by ability and education. The author of this proposal, as well as of so many of the new

[44] Ritter, *Stein*, 251.
[45] Ritter, *Stein*, 230–231.
[46] William O. Shanahan, *Prussian Military Reforms, 1786–1813* (New York, 1945), 129.

ordinances like the civil obligation to universal service, was Major Carl von Grolman. Of bourgeois origin, he was a zealous proponent of the idea of insurrection. At one time, even Gneisenau was led to call him a "crass Jacobin," a judgment which coincided by and large with that of his conservative in-laws, the Gerlachs.[47]

The enactment of these innovations Stein now geared to his own energetic pace, setting off a flurry of activity after the long spring of quiescent study. Rumor already suggested that he had added to his specific program the quick development of a representative, constitutional assembly. Such an idea had appeared in several forms on many occasions in Stein's and Gneisenau's proposals for military action. Most frequently a meeting of the estates was mentioned.[48] The patriots saw the estates as a means of rallying popular support and gaining public sympathy for the crown. But any meeting, even on a class basis, would give a voice to the representatives of groups never before heard from in Prussia. The portent of the meeting of the estates, to the conservative opponents of Stein, was the same one they could see in all his legislation: a radical unbalancing of the body politic.

Thus the tempo and nature of reform activity in the summer of 1808 augured a quick and decisive change in the contours of power and influence in the country. In this we may find the cause of the sudden crystallization of the opposition to Stein. Some elements of the antireform groups were now desperately willing to use any means to destroy the regiment of domestic "Jacobins," whose extreme notions would undermine the state to an extent far greater than they could expect from the French tyrant himself.

But at the same time, as opposition to his program grew, Stein held the trust of the king and the complete confidence of the queen.

---

[47] Shanahan, 131–132, 137; Georg H. Pertz, *Das Leben des Ministers Freiherrn vom Stein,* 2nd ed., II (Berlin, 1851), 187–188. For Gneisenau on Grolman see Lehmann, *Scharnhorst,* II, 17; for the Gerlachs' opinion as expressed in Leopold von Gerlach's "Familiengeschichte," see Schoeps, *Aus den Jahren preussischer Not,* 61.

[48] Stern, "Gneisenaus Reise," 33; Gneisenau's memoir of 10 August 1808, PRO, FO, Prussia, 64/79 (in Vaupel, 549ff); Gneisenau, Denkschrift, ca. 27 September 1808, PRO, FO, Prussia, 64/79 (see Vaupel, 597); Boyen to F.W., 29 September 1808, DZA, Rep. 89a, XVIII, 1.

He seems then to have reached the height of his influence at court. Even the educational plans he prepared for the little crown prince and his brother were submitted by the queen to the king.[49] Stein thought that the type of education the princes were receiving was insufficiently manly to form a stalwart, decisive king. The minister's striking faith in the therapeutic possibilities of pedagogy shows him to be ensconced, with Fichte and Süvern, in the ideological milieu of his time;[50] more important, the queen's acceptance of Stein's notions not only demonstrates her faith in him, but also her sensitivity to the weaknesses of her husband, which she had no desire to see recapitulated in her sons.

Probably the direct, upright baron supplied at this point in the queen's life the element of strength which her husband lacked. He was the embodiment of a program which held out hope for the future in her exile's environment of despair. Stein, as an idealized savior, had become an important part of Louise's mental underpinning; the nimbus which he bore in her eyes must have extended to his colleagues and to the reforms themselves. It was probably he, and the sense of purpose which his ministry gave, that inspired her to hear the lectures of Professor Süvern on the art of the statesman. She had pledged to submit the notes she took for Stein's perusal, though she feared ostentatiously that he would find them (and her?) muddleheaded. Her letters to him and about him dating from this time are strongly permeated with that saccharine note of helplessness before masculinity affected by a coquette who intends to flatter.[51] This role she had once played to Napoleon, and she would later play to Alexander; with both monarchs she attempted to use

[49] Louise to Stein, 31 March 1808, *Königin Luise: Briefe*, 334–335; Louise to Frau von Berg, summer 1808, *ibid.*, 358: "For my sons there will be an Ancillon [Stein's choice], not a La Harpe." See also Louise to Frau von Berg, 7 and 20 August 1808, *ibid.*, 362–363, 366.

[50] Note the Pestalozzian vogue reflected in the lectures of Fichte and Süvern, and the establishment of the University of Berlin in 1810 under the direction of Wilhelm von Humboldt, who was nominated by Stein; see Raack, "Political Idealism in Prussia," 129–135.

[51] Louise to Stein, 31 March and 1 May 1808, *Königin Luise: Briefe*, 334, 343; Louise to Scheffner, 20 June 1808, *ibid.*, 349; Louise to Frau von Berg, 20 August 1808, *ibid.*, 366.

her feminine wiles to aid her beleaguered husband.[52] Louise intuitively recognized the importance of Stein's strength of character to her weak consort and the position of her sons, and this must have carried her attachment to him temporarily beyond simple gratitude for services successfully performed. She had reported to him the intrigues, both real and fancied, she heard of; her emotional attachment to Stein then led her to mix on his behalf in the politics of state, of which she knew really very little. Her opinion of him, based as it was on her very human need for his strength and confidence, was reinforced by those about her whom she trusted. Her sister-in-law Princess Louise and her husband, Prince Anton Radziwill, as well as the king's sister-in-law Princess Marianne, the wife of the absent negotiator Prince William of Prussia, formed a powerful coterie of support for Stein at court.[53] How important the attachment of the queen's support to Stein's cause was at this time in establishing a favorable attitude toward him on the part of the king cannot be directly measured. Certainly, however, it abetted him and his cause in the moments when the fainthearted monarch was racked by doubt about the far-reaching consequences of the reformers' extravagant proposals.

Hence unless some major blow from outside were struck against him—and this no one anticipated though some surely lived in hope—Stein's position was as secure as ministries could be in the summer of 1808. Unbeknown to him, some of his own helpers were personally disaffected already. Yet his prestige was too great at this

---

[52] On Louise and Napoleon in Tilsit see Bassewitz, *Die Kurmark, 1806–1808,* I, 410; Bailleu, *Königin Luise,* 242–249; less flattering to Louise is M. A. Thiers, *Histoire du consulat et de l'empire,* VII (Paris, 1874), 664–665, 669. Boyen believed that the queen tried to use people. Since the king was opposed to her interference in state affairs, she had to act unobtrusively (see Boyen, *Erinnerungen,* II, 18–19, 24). My general characterization of Louise is supported by Mehring, *Zur preussischen Geschichte,* 62–63.

[53] Prince Anton Radziwill to Princess Louise, 18 June 1808, 26 June 1808, Archiwum główne akt dawnych, Warsaw, Archiwum Radziwiłłowie, Oddział XIII, Listy w książach 13; Leonie Wuppermann, *Prinzessin Marianne von Preussen geborene Prinzessin von Hessen-Homburg in den Jahren 1804–1808* (Bonn, 1942), 166–168; Princess Wilhelm to Stein, 5 September and 26 November 1808, *Stein Br.,* II (2), 848, 994.

time for this antagonism to be manifested; it was necessarily confined to private expressions of discontent.

But as the summer advanced, Stein occupied himself more and more with the conspiracy against Napoleonic rule in Germany and correspondingly less with the course of reform. This turning from the main path was doubtlessly much regretted by some of his coworkers. The evidence is weak, but it appears that the Kantian liberals among them—Schön and Schroetter on the basis of their past opinions—would have opposed the course of military action as a fruitless, utopian distraction. Some of the others, as we shall see, opposed it for entirely different reasons.[54] But whatever the nature of the discontents within the reform camp, there were certain to be a great many among a party which spanned such a spectrum of personalities and ideologies. The ministers and counselors did not always stand together on every issue; nevertheless, at this time their disagreements seem to have been confined for the most part within the normal channels of political exchange. Stein's really dangerous enemies were still outside the ministry, at court and in Berlin.

[54] Schleiermacher's coded letter to Reimer of 30 August 1808 refers to a conspiracy to replace Stein, but I have been unable to identify definitely all of the cover names in the letter with specific individuals (see Raack, "A New Schleiermacher Letter," 209–223). On Schön's and Schroetter's opposition see above, note 36, and Haussherr, *Erfüllung und Befreiung*, 246. For Schön on the conspiracy, see Schön, *Papiere*, II (Berlin, 1875), 51, and IV (Berlin, 1876), 573–582. See also Schön on Scharnhorst in the Schön Nachlass, No. 61, pp. 14–15, 17, 26–27. The Nachlass copy of Schön on Scharnhorst varies at times from the printed text (*Papiere*, IV, 537ff). Schön and Schroetter were apparently friendly: see Schön to Schroetter, 10 and 13 December 1808, Schön Nachlass, No. 27.

III

THE CONSEQUENCES
OF CONTUMELY

Since May, with the outbreak of the Spanish uprising and the first rumors of the rearmament of the Austrians, the commanders of French forces all over Europe had taken fright at the prospect of insurrection in their own areas of authority. By the middle of the summer, Napoleon himself was anxious enough about what he heard from his agents to turn his attention to the matter of Austrian rearmament and the prospect of a new German war. The conference with the tsar he arranged for Erfurt in October was a product of his anxiety; he sought to use the Russian alliance to France's advantage in the pacification of the Austrians.[1]

To be sure, Spain was only the most dramatic scene. But there the shaky foundation of the Bonapartist house of cards was first revealed. In the summer of 1808, the dislocation in Napoleon's crude and hurriedly constructed empire intensified daily. Madrid fell to the insurgents. Warsaw and Italy emptied as French troops were hastened to Spain. Dissatisfaction with French control was spread by an influential pro-Prussian party inside the Polish grand duchy itself.[2] The pope made an open attack on the civil code, a sign of the widening breach between himself and the tyrant. In the ports of northern Europe within Napoleon's Continental System hatred festered against the French-imposed blockade of British trade which slowly strangled the trade of Europe. In the Netherlands, Bona-

---

[1] Vandal, I, 431; J. Vidal de la Blanche, *La Régénération de la Prusse après Iéna* (Paris, 1910), 385.
[2] Davout to Napoleon, 26 June and 29 October 1808, in Charles de Mazade, ed., *Correspondance du Maréchal Davout . . . 1801–1815* (Paris, 1885), II, 248, 315; Brockhausen to F.W., 21 February 1808, Hassel, I, 496.

parte's personal arrogance had made his more moderate brother Louis, the formerly unloved King of Holland, almost popular. Nor was the discontent with the French in Germany confined to the east; in the south and west evidence mounted that a nationalist call to arms would not go unheeded. Indeed, so serious had the situation become in the emperor's eyes that he began at long last to regard seriously the anti-Bonapartist ranting of Madame de Staël.[3] Europe, which but a few short months before had lain prostrate at the conqueror's feet, stirred perceptibly once again.

Evidence of the increasingly unsubmissive attitude in Germany alarmed the French authorities there. They were supplied by spies and paid agents with an abundance of information and misinformation. Most of the reports they got were garbled even when a kernel of truth did exist. In addition to the honest failures of observation and reporting, the agents invented and exaggerated—so it appears—in order to enhance the ostensible value of their service to their employers. The fact was that in the French headquarters in Berlin the mass of accumulated evidence soon gave a wholly erroneous picture of the plot.

The French knew that the Prussians were recruiting among unemployed former soldiers for adherents to the conspiracy. Letters seeking volunteers were constantly recovered from the post.[4] The archives of the Ministry of War in Vincennes dating from this period are crammed with the correspondence of obviously innocent parties sent on to Paris for examination by the inordinately suspicious censors.[5] As it appears, the French believed that the central

[3] Napoleon to Fouché, 28 June 1808, *Lettres inédites de Napoléon,* I, 210; Vandal, I, 435; Albert Sorel, *L'Europe et la révolution française,* 5th ed., VII (Paris, 1904), 281–287.

[4] Report of the Grand Army to the Minister of War, 5 June and 23 July 1808, AG, CGA, C2 77 (part included by Granier, *Aus der Berliner Franzosenzeit,* 278); Report of the Grand Army to the Minister of War, 4 August 1808, *ibid.,* C2 78; Soult to Napoleon, 31 August 1808, *ibid.,* C2 79; Soult to Napoleon, 3 and 13 September 1808, in Godefroy Cavaignac, *La Formation de la Prusse contemporaine,* I (Paris, 1897), 496–497.

[5] AG, CGA, C2 78 and C2 79, *passim.* Note also the contents of the records of the Ministry of Foreign Affairs (esp. AAE, CP, Prusse 1808, 243), which indicate that

commander of the web of conspiracy was the notorious English agent Friedrich von Gentz, who worked out of Töplitz in Bohemia. All enemies of France, they were convinced, would find succor there from the Austrian authorities.[6]

In Pomerania, so it was said, the famous Major Ferdinand von Schill, who had so effectively maneuvered against the French during the recent Prussian war, was raising a corps to fight with the Austrians in the coming conflict. Schill and his father-in-law, General Ernst von Rüchel, were alleged to be heart and soul of the insurrection forces in the north.[7] The French were also told that a close connection between the Austrians and Prussians had been achieved.[8] In Silesia, where Prussian, Austrian, and French troops were in closest proximity, the situation was, as we have seen, already tense. Marshal Louis Nicholas Davout, described as the "ne plus ultra of suspicion," in command at the time in Breslau, reported that all the Prussian officers had already received orders to prepare to march.[9]

In these circumstances, when fact and fancy became increasingly harder to separate even by those who had a will to do so, the French officials began scrutinizing every letter and crediting every whisper of suspicion. On the twenty-second of August, the com-

---

much of the official Prussian correspondence fell into French hands and that the Prussian code had been partially broken by the French.

[6] Paul R. Sweet, *Friedrich von Gentz: Defender of the Old Order* (Madison, 1941), 147; Soult to Napoleon, 31 August 1808, AG, CGA, C2 79 (part quoted in Cavaignac, *La Formation de la Prusse,* I, 495); Hassel, I, 169.

[7] L. (?) to Soult, 2 September 1808, AG, CGA, C2 79; Soult to Napoleon, 31 August 1808, *ibid.*

[8] Soult to Napoleon, 13 September 1808, Cavaignac, *La Formation de la Prusse,* I, 495.

[9] Davout was equally suspicious in his dealings with the Warsaw Poles; see H. A. L. Fisher, *Studies in Napoleonic Statesmanship: Germany* (Oxford, 1903), 154. The phrase was applied to Davout by Sack: see Sack to Stein, 23 November 1808, *Stein Br.,* II (2), 986; also Davout to Napoleon, 13 September 1808, Davout, *Correspondance,* II, 283. Soult reported the news of a plot afoot to massacre all the French in Prussia under cover of darkness at the first word of Austrian victory. But Soult also took pains to observe (which appears to set him apart from Davout) that he was aware that his devotion to the emperor's cause might cause him to overstress the danger from the Prussians; see Soult to Napoleon, 31 August 1808, AG, CGA, C2 79.

mander of the French forces in Berlin got word that an *Assessor* Koppe, reputedly an important Prussian agent, en route from London to Königsberg via Hamburg, would be passing through the city. Koppe, it was said, had lately been in London in secret negotiations. While he had indeed been in London a year before, the fact was that he had long since been in Paris as courier to Prince William. Furthermore, he had just left Königsberg for Berlin and Hamburg bearing private letters and official dispatches.[10] Some letters he had already delivered to members of the royal family still in Berlin. Acting on the basis of the mistaken report, the French gave orders to seize Koppe. He was apprehended on the twenty-fifth of August just outside Berlin at the beginning of the second leg of his journey to Hamburg.[11] He still had with him, among other notes and dispatches official and unofficial, letters from Stein to an Altona (Hamburg) banker and to Baron Wilhelm Ludwig zu Sayn-Wittgenstein. In them Stein expressed his confidence in the ability of Prussia to pay the contributions and reparations so far levied against her, at least through the winter. This private opinion belied the statement the Prussian emissaries in Paris had made of their financial capabilities. Even more indiscreet was the impulsively candid letter to Wittgenstein. Stein encouraged him to spread the spirit of insurrection in western Germany. War, Stein wrote, impended between France and Austria. The animus against the French was spreading daily. Europe's future would be staked on the outcome of the impending conflict.[12]

[10] Soult to Napoleon, 22 August 1808, AG, CGA, C2 78; Nagler to Koppe (?), 14 August 1808, Cavaignac, *La Formation de la Prusse*, I, 490. Koppe apparently did not leave Königsberg until the sixteenth, for he carried a message of that date from Goltz to Voss (DZA, A.A.I., Rep. 1, No. 1064).

[11] Soult to Napoleon, 26 August 1808, Cavaignac, *La Formation de la Prusse*, I, 492–493; Report of General Lauer, 28 August 1808, *ibid.*, 493–494; Soult to Napoleon, 31 August 1808, AG, CGA, C2 79. Koppe had delivered some official correspondence to Voss: Goltz to Voss, 16 August 1808, DZA, A.A.I., Rep. 1, No. 1064.

[12] Stein to Wittgenstein, 15 August 1808, *Stein Br.*, II (2), 813–818; Ritter, *Stein*, 346. There is a French translation of the letter in AG, CGA, C2 78 (folder of 15 August 1808). Copies of Stein's letter of 15 August 1808 to J. Dehn (the Altona banker) as well as his letters to Wittgenstein are in AAE, CP, Prusse, 1808, 242.

The arrest of Koppe was an unlucky turn of fortune's wheel illustrating how small things, even based on false information, influence the fate of nations. The information given the French against Koppe must have been pure invention deliberately contrived from a vague rumor by an agent desperately trying to establish his usefulness. But the prizes won fortuitously by the French were Stein's letters (about which no one had advance information) and an innocent note from old Countess Voss to Wittgenstein, both to be full of consequences for Stein and the government of Prussia during the next few months.[13]

The French marshals were elated by this accidental success. The letters were sent immediately to Paris for the emperor's perusal. They arrived just as he was pressing home the negotiations with Prince William and the extraordinary delegation of Prussians which had awaited his pleasure for over half a year.

The first result of the capture of the letters came with their introduction into these negotiations between the French Foreign Minister Jean Baptiste Champagny and the Prussian delegation at Paris. The chief minister of the King of Prussia had been caught flagrantly spinning out a dangerous intrigue against the Emperor Napoleon. The honorable Prince William was seriously embarrassed by Stein's indiscretions; furthermore, the arguments of the Prussians against the allegedly onerous financial clauses were undermined. Bonaparte, who lacked the scruples Prince William held, cleverly used the letters to increase the pressure on the Prussian negotiators. Champagny now presented a twenty-four-hour ultimatum for signing the latest terms.[14]

[13] Soult to Napoleon, 26 August 1808, Cavaignac, *La Formation de la Prusse,* I, 492–493. On the letter of Countess Voss, see below, Chapter V.

[14] Ritter, *Stein,* 342–347. But Ritter's account does not take account of the inclinations of Ambassador Brockhausen and Prince William to accept the French conditions if some improvement of the financial clauses could be worked out. Brockhausen, in fact, seems to have been ready to sign and hope for better financial arrangements at some later date. See Brockhausen to F.W., 2 September 1808, DZA, A.A.I., Rep. 1, No. 1234; and Prince William to F.W., Hassel, I, 482–484. Ritter goes to some effort to vindicate Prince William (as does Hassel, I, 245–246). But it would appear that

In point of fact, Bonaparte's terms were not changed significantly over those first presented in August. But even the latter conditions considerably exceeded the preliminary agreements made at Tilsit as well as those made in Berlin in the spring. The sums termed "reparations" had been greatly inflated and other new conditions imposed. Most important among the latter, the Prussian army henceforth was to be limited to 42,000 men. The clause on military strength obviously reflected Napoleon's recognition of the developing danger to France's position in central Europe since the beginning of the Spanish crisis.[15]

Hence the misadventure of Stein's letter to Wittgenstein did not force upon the Prussian emissaries a new set of outrageous terms. Rather, Brockhausen, the ambassador in Paris who joined Prince William in the negotiations, had quite made up his mind to sign the same agreement without much more higgling on the day before they learned from Champagny of Stein's blunder. Brockhausen reported to the king his conviction that the vagueness of the terms would still permit a tolerable range of independent action. Most important, the evacuation would finally be effected. The period of seemingly endless uncertainty which in Hardenberg's and Stein's eyes as well as his own was the root of most of the state's problems would be terminated.[16] Brockhausen was certain that Prussia could pay the higher reparations the French now asked. Prince William himself, while opposing the financial clauses, nevertheless argued

---

Napoleon, not wanting the whole issue to be discussed at Erfurt in Alexander's presence, was more eager than the Prussians to make peace at this time. Hence it would seem that the Prussians had everything to gain by drawing out the negotiations and pressing either for better terms or for an appeal to the tsar. It is unjustifiable to suggest, as Ritter does, that the Prussians, defenseless, had to sign or Napoleon would march. Napoleon, as everyone knew, was soon to meet Alexander. A French march on Prussia, with the Erfurt meeting impending, was obviously out of the question. Thus it can be argued that the Prussians had everything to gain, in spite of the Stein letter affair, by refusing to sign and that Prince William and his colleagues had crumpled too soon. We may suspect that Brockhausen's relative satisfaction with the terms before he knew of the Stein letter inclined him to advise the prince to sign.

[15] Ritter, *Stein*, 347.
[16] On Hardenberg's view of the negotiations with the French, see below, Chapter V.

that the remainder of the terms were as good as the Prussians could expect in the circumstances. The Russian ambassador supported this view. Brockhausen thought that the French might be persuaded to lengthen the period of payment; and the end of the occupation would so lighten the burden on the state's finances that it could make up its obligations. In short, much of his argument paralleled the rationale for Stein's negotiating trip to Berlin in the spring.

Yet the Prussian negotiators were under instructions from Königsberg to break off the talks if Napoleon remained intransigent and the August terms could not be improved. These instructions had been sent long before, however, when Stein and the king, under the impress of the news of French reverses of mid-August, had believed that Napoleon would be forced to soften his terms.[17] Brockhausen and his fellow negotiators, as of the second of September, had no confidence in the notion on which these guidelines for discussion were based. They argued, to the contrary, that Austria and France would come to some sort of agreement and that Austria would disarm; Russia, they predicted, would never sustain the hopes for an uprising. Now, as before, Brockhausen put no stock in the Spaniards' ability to maintain their war against Bonaparte's military sorcery. Withal, they argued that, since Prussia could pay the sums demanded (as Stein's seized letters tended to confirm), peace should be made and the evacuation secured. The military reductions might be avoided in many ways; Brockhausen suggested, among other things, the establishment of a militia.[18]

The king was probably not unhappy when he received these latest French demands in the middle of September.[19] To him they represented definite prospects of peace, though the conditions were

---

[17] Hassel, I, 241–242. See above, note 14, and Brockhausen to F.W., 9 September 1808, Hassel, I, 508–509. See, on the attitude of Count Tolstoy (the Russian ambassador), René Bittard des Portes, "Les Préliminaires de l'entrevue d'Erfurt (1808)," *Revue d'histoire diplomatique,* IV (1890), 107. Tolstoy, however, noted that he could give no other advice, for he had received no instructions to back up the Prussians, and the French knew it. See Tolstoy to Rumiantsev, 8 September 1808, *Posol'stvo grafa P. A. Tolstogo v Parizhe,* 677–678.

[18] Brockhausen to F.W., 2 September 1808, DZA, A.A.I., Rep. 1, No. 1234.

[19] Delbrück, *Tagebuchblätter,* 13 September 1808, III, 54.

hard. It must have been Stein, therefore, who convinced him not to come to immediate terms with the tyrant's new and higher blackmail. Stein insisted in opposition to Brockhausen's arguments that Napoleon's weaker position should force him to yield on some points instead of increasing his demands. He contended that the new impositions were proof that lasting reconciliation with Bonaparte was impossible: imperial agreements, like Tilsit, were made solely to be broken, and Prussian concessions only elicited more demands. His conviction that the final solution of Franco-Prussian problems must inevitably be military was therefore reaffirmed.[20]

But by this time Alexander's dislike for Austrian war preparations was probably known in Königsberg. One important argument for the policy of insurrection was thus undermined. The tsar, en route to Erfurt, would pass through Königsberg within a few days; thus there would be some opportunity to change his views on the matter.[21] Could Stein persuade him to reconsider his commitment to France?

At least a decision on an answer to the new French terms for Prussia could be staved off until the tsar had been consulted. He was, after all, a guarantor of the Peace of Tilsit and had accepted a certain moral responsibility for Prussia at that time. And if the king was going to rely on Alexander,[22] some actual indication of the extent of his support would have to be gained. Conversations would force Alexander to reveal what he intended to do for Prussia now that Napoleon's inflated demands had been advanced. In the

[20] Stein, Denkschrift, 30 August, 8 and 14 September 1808, Stein Br., II (2), 844–846, 850–852, 857–860. See F.W. to Prince William, 16 September 1808, Hassel, I, 492–493; F.W. to Brockhausen, 16 September 1808, DZA, A.A.I., Rep. 1, No. 1234; Ritter, Stein, 342–343. Note how Napoleon, when the fancy took him, simply changed the terms of the agreements with the Prussians: as after the Königsberg agreement of July 1807 (Bassewitz, Die Kurmark, 1806–1808, I, 430–436); twice in August 1808 (Hassel, I, 237–241); and even after Erfurt (ibid., 286).

[21] Ritter, Stein, 608n13, and compare 343–345. Louise to Alexander, 6 September 1808, Königin Luise: Briefe, 368, suggests that it was already known at this time that Alexander would abide by his alliance with Bonaparte. See above, Chapter I. Stein's Denkschrift of 18 September 1808, Stein Br., II (2), 861–865, was apparently written with a view to influencing Alexander as well as Frederick William.

[22] F.W. to Prince William, 16 September 1808, Hassel, I, 492–493.

meantime it was quite conceivable that events themselves would bring about a reconsideration of Russia's and, consequently, of Prussia's position. If Austria continued to arm and the Spanish continued victorious, the European balance of power would quickly be shifted. But Stein realized that, whether these expectations were fulfilled or not, the feverish preparations for an insurrection which occupied all in the month of August would have to be suspended. He would await the result of another try at diplomacy. Let Alexander fulfill his role as protector of the Prussians at Erfurt if he had a mind to; so Stein calculated. Coming thus to a policy of watchful waiting, Stein at last found himself in complete harmony with the views of Frederick William.

Even while awaiting Alexander, having made these mental adjustments and altered his policy, Stein stood under the premonitory shadow of a diplomatic debacle. Although French authorities had tried to keep the news of Koppe's arrest a secret, that had proved to be impossible. The patriots had as many spies in Berlin as the French. Once the story was out, the organization of clandestine patriots sent off a messenger to the innocent Wittgenstein—by implication they assumed him to be one of their own—to advise him to flee to avoid certain arrest.[23] Wittgenstein, who was at the baths at Doberan in Mecklenburg, had no idea of the content of Stein's letter. Nonplused, the messenger reported back the ungrateful baron's treatment of him, that given Mortimer by Leicester in

---

[23] Koppe may have carried some messages from the leaders of the insurrection in Königsberg as far as Berlin. His arrival in Berlin coincides with the hasty departure for Königsberg of the patriotic pastor Schleiermacher, whose trip had as its purpose obtaining clarification of the role of the Berliners in the conspiracy. See Schleiermacher Tagebuch, 20 August 1808, Schleiermacher Nachlass; and Raack, "A New Schleiermacher Letter," 210–223. On the advice to Wittgenstein to flee see M.Q., ed., *Denkwürdigkeiten aus dem Leben des Generals der Infanterie von Hüser* (Berlin, 1877), 74–75. This source was given to me by Professor Richard Samuel of the University of Melbourne. Wittgenstein wrote to a Berlin acquaintance that he had learned by mail on 2 September of the capture of Koppe on 30 August (Wittgenstein to Faudel, 2 September 1808, AG, CGA, C2 79). But see Chapter V, note 110, below.

Schiller's *Maria Stuart*: "Fort! Ich kenn Euch nicht, / Ich habe nichts gemein mit Meuchelmördern." [24]

The same news of the apprehension of Koppe was quickly carried to Königsberg, arriving there about the first of September. Stein seems first to have doubted that the compromising letter was found on Koppe, but he told the king what had happened and what dangerous implications the dispatches could have. The king, vexed, reputedly told Stein: "Sie haben gewiss einen dumm [*sic*] Streich gemacht!" [25] Yet his first reaction was not to jettison his first minister; instead he decided to play the aggrieved party and protest to the French the arrest of a royal courier. He hoped to force the French to return Koppe's pouches and keep silent on the contents. Count August Wilhelm von der Goltz, the titular foreign minister, was charged with making a strong, straight-faced diplomatic representation to the French authorities in Berlin. He alleged that Koppe, a diplomatic courier, carried official letters affecting financial matters which, being closed with the royal seal, must remain inviolate. Koppe was also said to be carrying some personal valuables belonging to Wittgenstein. Goltz asked for their return.[26] Voss, the Prussian representative in Berlin, was instructed to take parallel steps. On the ninth of September, he handed Daru a protest containing a statement of the king's unhappiness over the detaining of his courier (poor Koppe long since having been sent off to France for further interrogation and confinement). For additional effect,

[24] Act 4, Scene 4. English translation: "Hence! I know you not, / I have nothing in common with assassins."

[25] Breese to Stein, 26 August 1808, *Stein Br.*, II (2), 839–840. The king's remark ("You certainly pulled a dumb stunt") in Report of French spy to Soult, 23 August 1808, AG, CGA, C2 78 (and in Cavaignac, *La Formation de la Prusse*, I, 498), is evidently somewhat embellished, but the sentiment appears to be authentic. Schleiermacher, who was commenting in his letters to Reimer on the situation in Königsberg, wrote on 6 September 1808 of some worry about the consequences of Stein's "conte courante." This may relate to the uncertainty over the fate of the letter which prevailed at the time. See Dilthey, "Schleiermachers politische Gesinnung und Wirksamkeit," 260.

[26] Goltz to Daru, 1 September 1808, AAE, CP, Prusse, 1808, 243, pp. 242–243.

Voss reminded Daru that Koppe had the complete confidence of Minister Stein.[27] This hapless ploy he advanced because he knew that a year before Bonaparte had fancied Stein friendly to the French system and supported him for high office.[28] All of this shows, of course, how successfully the French kept secret the contents of Stein's letter. Voss did not even know two weeks after the arrest what Koppe's pouch had contained. Considering Voss's subsequent behavior, this protest on Stein's behalf shows that he still conscientiously fulfilled his responsibilities. At this time he had no reason to doubt that Stein, who had the support of the French as well as of the king, held an impregnable ministerial position.

By chance—they knew nothing as yet of Stein's errant letter—Stein's aristocratic enemies in Königsberg had chosen this infelicitous moment to connive at his downfall. The flood of reform proposals and, in particular, the enactment at this time of the military reforms abruptly faced them, as we have seen, with the outline of the new Prussia. Stein was only indirectly concerned with the military legislation, but it had the same portent as his own legislative works: the end of the privileged position of the nobility. Thus Stein had to take a stand with the king in favor of the work of the Military Reorganization Commission. Some thought he had enough enemies and should therefore avoid the additional burden.[29] Stein's party was, in addition, not wholly united on the issue.[30] And the king himself, though he recognized the logical consequences of the battle of Jena, had as usual to be pushed by Scharnhorst and his aides into supporting the reforms.[31] But once he had made up his mind, he gave the military innovators his favor. The promotion of Gneisenau to colonel, which took place on the fourteenth of September, was a public sign of the king's commitment.[32] It illus-

---

[27] Voss to Daru, 9 September 1808, *ibid.*, p. 245.

[28] Ritter, *Stein,* 204–205.

[29] Major Röder to Count Götzen, 13 September 1808, Vaupel, 582.

[30] See the remarks of Karl von Schroetter in Delbrück, *Tagebuchblätter,* 1 September 1808, III, 48.

[31] Herrmann, "Friedrich Wilhelm III. und sein Anteil an der Heeresreform bis 1813," 503n3.

[32] KO to Gneisenau, 14 September 1808, Vaupel, 583–584. Breese to Stein, 26

trates in addition that Frederick William, who knew Gneisenau
to be an ardent supporter of the insurrection, had not yet completely
turned his back on that plan in spite of the seizure of Koppe.
This modest gesture of support for the patriot party must have
been important at the very instant when Stein was under increasing
attack from his enemies at court. It may very well have been planned
by the king in part for its timely effect. The agrarian reform proc-
lamations of the foregoing October had contributed indirectly to
temporary social dislocations in Silesia. The misery of the population
in that occupied province and the false hopes raised by garbled
versions of the edicts had led to a small-scale peasants' revolt in the
summer of 1808.[33] The French forces in occupation had to be called
upon to put down the unrest. Marshal Kalckreuth in Königsberg,
the soul of the opposition to Stein,[34] was a Silesian landowner. So
were many others among Stein's foes. No doubt they read into this
short-lived affair the dangers of the Great Fear of 1789; the events
of the revolutionary epoch scarred the memory of every landholding
aristocrat of the day. Now French troops led by former lieutenants
of the armies of the revolution put down the unrest the "Jacobins"
in Königsberg had fomented.

Kalckreuth had opened a bold campaign against Stein on the first
of September, the date of the publication of the new articles of
war. At his estate in Spandienen, not far from the temporary capital,
Kalckreuth gathered a picked society including the king and queen.
Stein, because of his high position, had been sent a perfunctory in-
vitation. But Kalckreuth counted on the minister's usual busy sched-
ule—Stein's excuse for passing up most social affairs—to prevent
his attendance. The purpose of the gathering, as it appeared to all
including Stein, was to surround the king with Stein's enemies and

---

August 1808, *Stein Br.*, II (2), 839–840, which announces Koppe's arrest, would have
been in Königsberg by the thirty-first of August or the first of September.

[33] Stein to Bismarck, 7 September 1808, *Stein Br.*, II (2), 848–849; KO to Karl von
Schroetter, 7 September 1808, *ibid.*, 849; Simon, *Failure of the Prussian Reform
Movement*, 24–25; Ritter, *Stein*, 338.

[34] Stein called "der listige, geschwätzige, hämische Kalckreuth" the chief opponent
of the military reform (Stein, Autobiographische Aufzeichnungen, 12 July 1811,
Stein Br., III, 546).

to overwhelm him with complaints against the ministry. But when the chief of government arrived, to Kalckreuth's great surprise, the usually wooden king, who must have sensed the intrigue lurking, pointedly demonstrated great friendliness to him. This occurred in spite of the fact that the king may have heard that very day from Stein of the possible capture of the incriminating letters.[35]

The king's mild rebuff to Kalckreuth and his conniving friends at the salon in Spandienen was a small exception to his general attitude of toleration toward almost any act that did not directly impinge on his own prerogatives. He liked the society of men of all political views. But since the reformers had tasks at hand, they were seldom near him, whereas daily meals at the royal table, court and military ceremonies, and social events put the king into more frequent contact with the very people whose idle hands maneuvered the opposition to Stein and the new program for Prussia.

Nor did this indirect chastisement of Stein's enemies prove enduring. Unabashed, the claque of opposition grew steadily. On the fourteenth of September Stein's friend, Princess Marianne, wife of Prince William, complained to her absent husband of the swelling party spirit.[36] Stein, conscious of the danger, tried to move against Kalckreuth indirectly through a prosecution for violation of the laws restricting trade with the enemy. The charge related to the marshal's estates in Silesia.[37] But for some reason, most probably the king's intervention, nothing ever came of it. The nagging op-

[35] Delbrück, *Tagebuchblätter*, 1 September 1808, III, 48; Boyen, *Erinnerungen*, I (Leipzig, 1889), 332–333. Stein got another warning of the intrigues against him from Princess Wilhelm at about the same time (Princess Wilhelm to Stein, 5 September 1808, *Stein Br.*, II (2), 848). Stein apparently associated her warning with the scene with Kalckreuth: "Die Geschichte mit dem M[arshall?] hart und die Vorbereitung zur Szene in Spandienen" (Stein's marginal note, *ibid.*). Ritter erroneously suggests that the tip came before the salon episode (*Stein*, 334, 612n23). See Raack, "A New Schleiermacher Letter," 219–220.

[36] See Delbrück, *Tagebuchblätter*, *passim*, which regularly lists the guests at the king's table. Princess Wilhelm wrote to Prince Wilhelm on 14 September 1808: "Der Parteigeist ist eingerissen und man hofft stark auf Dich zur Stütze der wahren und schönen Partei" (Wuppermann, 164).

[37] Pertz, *Stein*, II, 143.

position to Stein continued to win by default an almost daily hearing in the royal circle.

We have already seen that Stein and his programs had outspoken friends as well as enemies—many shadings of opinion are comprised in the mosaic we have attempted to delineate of the court of Frederick William. Princess Marianne had been apprised of the insurrection scheme by Stein, Scharnhorst, Gneisenau, and Legation Counselor Nagler shortly after it had been proposed to the king.[38] She wrote an intimation of what the patriots intended to her husband, Prince William, and also apparently gave them the hope (false, as it turned out) that he would lead the armies of the insurrection.[39] Nagler, a friend of Hardenberg as well as the brother-in-law of Altenstein, was a trusted partisan of the scheme at this time.[40] Princess Marianne appears to have volunteered to try to bring the queen around to support of the plan. But in spite of her trust in Stein, the queen remained aloof.[41]

I hope the reader will by now be convinced that the range of action open to Stein in domestic as well as in foreign affairs was really very limited. He could articulate policies but he could not determine them. Arguments from all sides could be presented to the king, but there is no evidence that he ever participated in the give

[38] Princess Wilhelm to Prince Wilhelm, 25 August 1808, Wuppermann, 146.

[39] Princess Wilhelm to Prince Wilhelm, 14 September 1808, Wuppermann, 164–165.

[40] Stein had proposed Nagler for the post of agent to Vienna to coordinate plans with the Austrians (Stein, Denkschrift, 1 August 1808, *Stein Br.,* II (2), 811). See also Radziwill, 298, on the friendship between Nagler and Stein. Nagler helped explain the plans of insurrection to Princess Wilhelm (Princess Wilhelm to Prince Wilhelm, 25 August 1808, Wuppermann, 146). Nagler was also present at an assembly of prominent patriots just before Schleiermacher's departure from Königsberg (Schleiermacher Tagebuch, 23 September 1808, Schleiermacher Nachlass).

[41] Ritter, *Stein,* 358, gives no evidence for his assertion that the queen supported the conspiracy at one time. Tessa Klatt, *Das politische Wirken der Königin Luise von Preussen* (Berlin, 1937), argues on the basis of evidence drawn from the year 1809 that she was against it. The best indication that the queen had not been won over is the letter of Princess Wilhelm to Stein of 5 September 1808, *Stein Br.,* II (2), 848. But compare the report of a French spy to Bignon, 29 August 1808, AG, CGA, C2 79, which is undoubtedly a fabrication.

and take of discussion; rather, he listened, then decided for himself. He must have been impassive, even unreachable. In such conditions of policy making, it must at all times have been difficult for Stein to estimate his position. It would be even more difficult to know where the king stood on an issue until he had, in the course of weeks or even months following the presentation of a program by the minister, made his decision. Until that time, a new step in any direction toward a resolution of the question under consideration would have been impossible.

How can one account for the strange conduct of Frederick William III? Only by hazarding a guess, based on the scanty evidence of his outward behavior preserved in the historical record. From this I would suggest that he was a sovereign who esteemed himself too little. This twist of personality, so unusual in a reigning monarch, would explain his unwillingness to defend his decisions in the forum of argument. Such behavior could also have been prompted by his vision of himself as a divinely appointed, absolute king, a vision which contrasted awkwardly with his known propensity toward accepting the destruction of special status of the nobility and of other privileged echelons of Prussian society. Their position in the state, after all, like his own, was sanctified by tradition and what they also imagined to be a God-given right.[42] Would it be fair, then, to characterize Frederick William as an enlightened despot *manqué?* The image of himself as absolute, his conviction that his was the duty to better the lot of all his subjects, was joined to a consistent reluctance, founded on some feeling of personal inadequacy, to face a difficult choice and debate alternative courses as well as a stubborn refusal to reconsider those decisions he had already taken.

If this sketch of the personality of Frederick William is approximate, then we can perhaps gain a better understanding of his relation to Stein and the others who surrounded him. Whereas he

---

[42] York von Wartenburg once made the same sort of argument—that the basis of the special privilege of the crown and the nobility was identical—to Prince Wilhelm (see Droysen, *York*, I, 157).

might respect the chief minister for his clarity of thought, he would not necessarily cherish his company. Stein was too rigorous in his logic, too direct and outspoken, too impatient. He would pay too little attention to the formalities of the relations in the court and even with the king himself. Could he conceal from the king that he privately judged him "hollow, dull and trivial"? [43] In his deep honesty and utter sincerity, his disdain of hypocrisy and inability to affect unearned respect, he would too often brusquely push aside the fabric of illusion with which Frederick William defended himself from the harshness of a world which disobeyed absolute monarchs. That Stein's outspoken loyalty to Germany was a "higher cause" beyond his love for the sovereign and regal house he served must have been only too apparent to the king on many occasions. Would it be fair to say, then, that much of the time the king felt ill at ease with Stein? Put in absolute terms (which neither would have defined), they employed each other because their temporary ends happened to coincide. It is true that the king did trust some men. But it would seem that the basis for his trust in these cases was far different from the basis of his respect for Stein. All his favorites of this period—Hardenberg, Beyme, Alexander (and even old Kalckreuth)—had in common suaveness, grace, and a sentimental and superficial loyalty and honesty. All of them, with the exception of the tsar, who had no need to do so, effectively masked any loyalty they might have had beyond that to Frederick William. And all of them, unlike Stein, who saved his tears for his pillow, seem to have been able to satisfy the emotional requirements of the king, apparently a critical need and a prerequisite for gaining his confidence, at the same time as they hid from him the jarring force of their independent intellects. [44]

---

[43] Stein had been forced out of an earlier cabinet in January 1807 after a direct conflict with the king that culminated in an exchange of bitter words (see Ritter, *Stein*, 177–178). For Stein's opinion of the king, see *ibid.*, 359.

[44] "Ich habe ihn nie geliebt" (F.W. on Stein, quoted by Bailleu, *Königin Luise*, 297). See also the account of the spontaneous weeping of Frederick William and Hardenberg at their meeting near Königsberg on 10 November (*ibid.*, 298, and see below, Chapter V).

Given this view of the relation between the king and his minister, the extent to which the Prussian king trusted the fate of his nation to Alexander must have been especially perplexing to Stein. Frederick William, even if only for lack of any other hope, trusted Alexander to maintain Prussia's interests. It may be that the king's lack of self-confidence, reinforced as it was by his awareness of the extent of his own responsibility for what had occurred in 1806, left him no other option. He may have known that Bonaparte had told Alexander at Tilsit that only the intercession of the tsar had kept him from ending the independent existence of Prussia and driving the House of Hohenzollern out of Germany. He was aware of the fact that Alexander had been urging Napoleon over the past year to conclude his peace with Prussia. What he did not know was that Russian intercession, at most lukewarm, was conditioned by the tsar's own interests. Napoleon had given Alexander clearly to understand that he would continue to maintain his silence on the issue of Russia's occupation of the Turkish provinces of Moldavia and Wallachia just as long as Alexander did not press the issue of a treaty with Prussia. There is no evidence that Alexander did not understand this rather direct line of argument and temper his complaints on behalf of Frederick William accordingly.[45]

Stein, even if not in full possession of the facts of the case, thought that Alexander was fundamentally a poor champion for Prussia. He was much more realistic than the king in assessing the tsar's promises and his performance.[46] But the joyful news of Napoleon's decision to seal up the treaty with Prussia was delivered in a roundabout way from St. Petersburg as well as directly from Ambassador

---

[45] Napoleon to Caulaincourt, 2 February and 21 July 1808, *Lettres inédites de Napoléon*, I, 144, 223; F.W. to Schladen, 30 July and 10 and 13 August 1808, and Schladen to F.W., 19 August 1808, DZA, A.A.I., Rep. 1, No. 2409. On the strange way Russian foreign policy was conducted—Count Tolstoy, the ambassador in Paris, had had no instructions from St. Petersburg since June—see above, note 17, and Brockhausen to F.W., 2 September 1809, *ibid.*, No. 1234.

[46] Stein, Antwortkonzept, 24 August 1808, *Stein Br.*, II (2), 825–826; Stein, Denkschrift, 8 September 1808, *ibid.*, 850–852.

Brockhausen in Paris.[47] With this, Frederick William's preconceptions seemed to have been confirmed, Stein's doubts proven groundless; the yielding of Bonaparte at long last appeared to be a direct response to Russian cajolery and pressure. In the king's eyes, Alexander's stature had increased enormously, reinforced fortuitously by the vagaries of Napoleonic diplomacy.

The facts of the situation were quite different. Napoleon had long before decided to arrange the Prussian settlement to meet his own particular requirements. As early as February 1808 he had told Prince William that he might make the convention in the summer and that, if he did, it would be in response to his political rather than his financial needs.[48] The rationale that underlay Bonaparte's volunteering that date is obscure. Certainly, however, the Spanish affair and its ramifications were the circumstances which forced him to fulfill his prophecy. But in any case, the date of the final convention with Prussia was set by Napoleon alone, whatever his purpose at the time.

Hence, when Alexander arrived in Königsberg on the eighteenth of September he already held Prussia's destiny in his hands, a condition Stein was inevitably, if reluctantly, compelled to recognize. At least with Alexander present a decision on the limits of Prussia's appeal for a better treaty could finally be taken. Then, at the conference on the common affairs of the two states held by king and tsar, Stein attended and gave such a good accounting of himself and Prussia's case that he won the confidence of the tsar to an extent which was to stand him well in the future. From all that was said, it appears that Alexander volunteered to take a far stronger stand on Prussia's behalf than Stein had previously thought or hoped he would.

The conference was followed by an eighty-course dinner, which

[47] Schladen to F.W., 23 August 1808, and F.W. to Schladen, 5 September 1808, DZA, A.A.I., Rep. 1, No. 2409; Hassel, I, 252; Alexander to Napoleon, 25 August 1808, *Posol'stvo grafa P. A. Tolstogo v Parizhe*, 761.

[48] Enclosure no. 1 in Jacoby-Kloest to D'Ivernois, 14 August 1808, PRO, FO, Prussia, 64/79; Lenz, "Napoleon I. und Preussen," 861.

exceeded by far the diminished resources of the Prussian court. A fête at Kalckreuth's country estate in Spandienen followed on the twentieth. Each social event was graced by the beautiful Queen Louise; we may be sure that gallant Alexander was not as unappreciative of that decorative lady as Bonaparte had once been. Then, after the bourgeois court in its straitened circumstances bedded down for the night, Countess von Truchsess, one of the queen's ladies in waiting, joined Alexander in rites to Priapus. A dour English agent unsentimentally implied that she had been put up to the work for *raisons d'état*.[49] But we can scarcely imagine either Stein or the king giving her the assignment, and we must remain in the dark as to who did if the countess was really not following the yearnings of her heart. Alexander, in any case, was both pleased and impressed by his visit to the court and left behind many promises of what he would accomplish for Prussia at Erfurt.[50] The English agent thought he could be relied upon to forget everything he had promised as soon as he found some other "Fair-one"; but to accept this point of view would be to denigrate the important role Stein had played in winning Alexander over to a strong representation of the Prussian cause.

Up to this point Stein had gained some small part of what he wanted and he had done so by diplomatic means. He had forestalled the king's original desire to go along with the recent French terms reported by Brockhausen. Instead, Alexander was pledged to seek to lower the amount reported as Napoleon's most recent financial demand and shorten the term of the occupation once the convention had been signed.[51] Stein could hope that something like

[49] Kalckreuth had been high in Alexander's esteem since his defense of Danzig: see F.W. to Louise, 10 June 1807, in Karl Griewank, ed., *Briefwechsel der Königin Luise mit ihrem Gemahl Friedrich Wilhelm III, 1793–1810* (Leipzig, 1929), 329 and n. 2. See also Gibson to FO, 21 September 1808, PRO, FO, Prussia, 64/79.

[50] F.W. to Goltz, 28 September (sent 29 September) 1808, DZA, A.A.I., Rep. 1, No. 1234; Ritter, *Stein,* 344–345.

[51] Jacoby-Kloest to D'Ivernois, 21 September 1808, PRO, FO, Prussia, 64/79 (dated 20 September 1808 in Karmin, "Documents relatifs," 578–580); Hassel, I, 260; Ritter, *Stein,* 346–348.

the draft of conditions arranged by him and Daru in the spring might finally be negotiated. For the interim, the preparations for the rearmament of Prussia and for the uprising were still under way. Prussia, Stein could hope, might win both a tolerable treaty and an opportunity to save itself by arms at some later, more favorable moment.

To make certain that Alexander kept to his agreement, Stein decided to go along, ostensibly to visit in Leipzig, but really to await the effect of Alexander's talks with Bonaparte in Erfurt. He would be close by the tsar to render advice and support or to seal the terms of the convention when the occasion arose. In fact, the last word would be his. The tsar had shown himself amenable to Stein's arguments in Königsberg. The king, the weakest of the three, would be left behind to ratify the product of their diplomatic art. With a favorable result, Stein could end the occupation of the country and its financial difficulties on the best available terms. Thereafter, he could continue his rearmament while biding his time to see just what the Austrians would do.

For the creation of this seemingly favorable cluster of choices credit is due to Stein for the force of his personality and his logic, and to Bonaparte for proving Stein's point. By raising his terms so far beyond those granted at Tilsit and those negotiated in good faith by Kalckreuth in Königsberg and Stein in Berlin, Bonaparte appeared at last to have overreached himself. Alexander, who like the rest of Europe no longer saw Bonaparte as the utterly invincible conqueror and who was less under the spell of the great man's personality than he had been in defeat at Tilsit, was committed to engage his personal honor in a firm representation of Prussia's cause. And Stein would be nearby to see that he did so. Stein had cause to be pleased with the turn of events which Alexander's visit had begun. Yet it should be noted that he had come over from outright rejection of Brockhausen's proposals for accepting Napoleon's terms to support of Alexander's decision to win relatively slight modifications in those same terms. Within the three days of the tsar's visit he had abandoned his warlike posture in favor of a peaceful one, however temporary he intended it to be.

Then calamity struck. A few hours after Alexander's departure for Erfurt, a courier arrived in his camp bearing the news of the Paris convention signed on the eighth of September by Prince William. With him came the account of the seizure of Stein's letter; it had been published in the *Journal de l'Empire* with an appropriately derisive commentary. The same news was quickly forwarded to Königsberg. With it the king learned for the first time of the effect of the captured letter on the negotiations in Paris.[52]

The royal household in Königsberg stirred with excitement, though at first no one outside the ministry knew the cause. "Tout est perdu," Foreign Minister Goltz muttered, chalk-faced, to those courtiers awaiting information before the king's chamber. Stein's protected status—if it had ever been more than an illusion—had vanished forthwith. It was immediately decided to send Goltz in Stein's place to Erfurt. Though signed by Prince William, the Paris agreement still needed the king's ratification and therefore might yet be altered. Alexander agreed to continue his mission under the conditions determined before,[53] but the strength Stein would have added to the cause would be deprived him. Goltz, we shall see, was not Stein. The Prussian cause suffered yet another disadvantage: the moral burden imposed by Stein's letter. On top of all this, Goltz and Alexander were given an additional charge, that of winning, presumably at the expense of some additional concessions to Bona-

---

[52] F.W. to Brockhausen, 28 September (sent 29 September) 1808, DZA, A.A.I., Rep. 1, No. 1234; Stein to Wittgenstein, 3 October 1808, *Stein Br.,* II (2), 883–884; Report of French spy to Soult, 29 September 1808 (information identified as coming from Baron von Bielefeld—see Chapter IV, below—and Köckritz), AG, CGA, C2 79.

[53] Report of French spy, 30 September 1808, AG, CGA, C2 79; Soult to Napoleon, 28 September 1808, Cavaignac, *La Formation de la Prusse,* I, 499–501; F.W. to Brockhausen, 28 September (sent 29 September) 1808, DZA, A.A.I., Rep. 1, No. 1234; Hassel, I, 261–263; Ritter, *Stein,* 349; Delbrück, *Tagebuchblätter,* 22 September 1808, III, 62–63. On Stein as one of Napoleon's choices at Tilsit (with Count Friedrich von Schulenberg and Zastrow!), see Serge Tatischeff, *Alexandre Ier et Napoléon d'après leur correspondance inédite, 1801–1812* (Paris, 1891), 155.

parte, a pardon for Stein on the ground that the king could not dispense with his services.[54]

At long last Stein's domestic opponents had found the weapon they had been seeking: by his own error, he had compromised himself, the monarch, and the state. By his ineptitude he had made himself the public enemy of Bonaparte. The question was, what use could Stein's enemies make of his grand *faux pas*?

[54] Prince Hatzfeldt, Tagebuch, 28 September (falsely dated August) 1808, APMW, Archiwum Hatzfeldt'ów, No. 743; F.W. to Alexander, 21 September 1808, *Briefwechsel F.W.–Alexander,* 179–180; Louise to Alexander, 29 September 1808, *Königin Luise: Briefe,* 373–374; Drusina to FO, 27 September 1808, PRO, FO, Prussia, 64/78; Jacoby-Kloest to D'Ivernois, 21 September 1808, *ibid.,* 64/79.

IV

STEIN REPRIEVED

Stein's first reaction to the immediate crisis brought about by the publication and denunciation of his letter was to submit his resignation to the king. Such appeared to be the path of honor. He suggested that the king place him under arrest in the fortress of Pillau, a gesture which he believed would exonerate the Prussian government itself from Bonaparte's charges.[1] No one, including Stein, seems to have doubted that Frederick William would dismiss his first minister.[2] Hence Stein's decision to demit voluntarily must be viewed in this light. But, as in so much else, the king was slow in coming to a decision, perhaps reluctant to make one. The queen still supported the minister;[3] the king himself had only recently heard the most extravagant praise for him from Alexander himself. He knew that the policy of conspiracy in whose service Stein had been ensnared had his own cautious approval.[4] Most important, Stein at the time had no serious rivals; his very pre-eminence left the king without a prospective replace-

[1] Radziwill, 294; confirmed by Drusina to FO, 27 September 1808, PRO, FO, Prussia, 64/78. The king gave Princess Wilhelm the idea that it was his notion to put Stein in the fortress (Wuppermann, 170). Chasot to F.W., 12 October 1808, DZA, Rep. 92, F.W. III, B VIIa, 7c, confirms only that Stein offered his resignation.

[2] Countess Voss, *Sixty-nine Years at the Court of Prussia*, 21 September 1808, I, 150; Gibson to FO, 24 and 27 September 1808, PRO, FO, Prussia, 64/79. Princess Wilhelm wrote in her diary: "Stein kann nicht bleiben, wir verlieren alles mit ihm sogar den Kredit" (Wuppermann, 170). Even the king at first thought Stein was lost to Prussia: see F.W. to Alexander, 21 September 1808, *Briefwechsel F.W.–Alexander*, 179–180.

[3] Louise to Alexander, 28 September 1808, *Königin Luise: Briefe*, 373–374. See also Marie von Brühl to Clausewitz, 4 October 1808, in Karl Linnebach, ed., *Karl und Marie von Clausewitz: Ein Lebensbild in Briefen und Tagebuchblättern* (Berlin, 1916), 472.

[4] See Chapter I, above.

ment. The reform legislation, which the king did not wish to see stymied, was not yet wholly prepared; some ordinances which had been completed had not yet been issued. If at all possible, Stein would have to be saved. The king did remove him from any further role in the conduct of foreign affairs— a demonstration that the minister would no longer be a menace to the French system. To this mild rebuke was joined an order which excluded the minister from the king's society. With Stein thus censured, Goltz was sent off to enlist the tsar's aid in winning a pardon for the minister.[5] This charge Alexander, who got a special plea on Stein's behalf from Queen Louise, could not fail to heed.

The agreement made by Prince William in Paris still needed ratification by the king. Frederick William was at first inclined not to complete the submission of Prussia to Bonaparte's terms; he apparently continued to hope for an improvement in the financial covenant to be worked out by Alexander.[6] But on the twenty-seventh of September, six days after Alexander left Königsberg for Erfurt, word arrived that the Swedish army was only seventeen miles from St. Petersburg.[7] If true, the tsar's bargaining position, on which the king relied, would be seriously weakened. Just a day later a new dispatch from Ambassador Brockhausen was received. Napoleon was reported to have shown a willingness to soften the financial conditions of the settlement.[8] On the twenty-ninth, Prince William's report of his parting interview with the emperor came in. Bonaparte had been all joviality, exuding wishes for peace between France and Prussia.[9]

[5] Stein to Alexander, 21 September 1808, *Stein Br.*, II (2), 866–867; F.W. to Alexander, 21 September 1808, *Briefwechsel F.W.–Alexander,* 179–180. See Chapter III, note 54, above.

[6] Louise to Alexander, 29 September 1808, *Königin Luise: Briefe,* 373–374. Stein at first advised the king to ratify the convention if no alternative existed: Stein, Votum (without date, marked by Goltz "received evening of 21 September"), *Stein Br.*, II (2), 867.

[7] Delbrück, *Tagebuchblätter,* 27 September 1808, III, 67.

[8] Brockhausen to F.W., 16 September 1808 (marked "decoded 28 September 1808"), DZA, A.A.I., Rep. 1, No. 1234.

[9] Brockhausen to F.W., 16 September 1808, DZA, A.A.I., Rep. 1, No. 1234; F.W. to

The king's initial inclination against ratification was quickly forgotten; he now had some meager sustenance for his hopes for peace. Only a quick ratification, he knew, could lead to re-entry into his capital before winter made travel difficult. A courier conveying full powers to Goltz to ratify the terms of the treaty therefore departed that day. As if to obviate a conflict with his chief minister, the king did not inform Stein that the power to ratify had been sent to Goltz.[10] To what we may attribute this strange line of behavior aside from a quirk of Frederick William's personality is uncertain —he had made a decision and he held the power to act, but in his secret self he probably knew that Stein could easily overturn the flimsy, emotion-charged rationale which led him to his choice. Whatever else might be said, however, it was not a policy which contributed in any way to establishing a salutary clarity of purpose and direction to guide the conduct of the state.

If we review briefly Stein's conduct of foreign affairs since the first news of the new French willingness to come to terms had arrived in Königsberg, we can see how strikingly Stein's and the king's conceptions of Prussia's future status had begun to diverge. The turn in relations with France which the definite prospect of a peaceful settlement introduced should have been reflected by a corresponding change in Prussia's policy. Frederick William, in keeping with the logic of the new situation as well as his own predisposition, had staked all on the prospect of turning over Prussia's future to Alexander's care. We can only imagine his secret gasp of

---

Brockhausen, 28 September (sent 29 September) 1808, *ibid.*; Stein to Wittgenstein, 3 October 1808, *Stein Br.*, II (2), 883; Ritter, *Stein,* 350.

[10] F.W. to Brockhausen, 28 September (sent 29 September) 1808, DZA, A.A.I., Rep. 1, No. 1234; F.W. to Goltz, 29 September 1808, Hassel, I, 575–576; Louise to Alexander, 29 September 1808, *Königin Luise: Briefe,* 373–374; Ritter, *Stein,* 350. Hardenberg, in Tilsit, apparently learned that the ratification had been sent before Stein did (Hardenberg Tagebuch, 7 October 1808, DZA, Rep. 92, Hardenberg, L29). See Stein to Götzen, 4 or 5 October 1808, *Stein Br.,* II (2), 885; and Stein, Denkschrift, 12 October 1808, *ibid.,* 889–891. The king later put the blame for forcing him to sign the convention on Stein's letter and the threat of 170,000 French troops (F.W. to Alexander [letter drafted by Nagler], 12 May 1809, *Briefwechsel F.W.–Alexander,* 188–189).

relief as the tsar took over the responsibility for the final decision. The same policy had been accepted by Stein at the time of Alexander's visit. We have seen how, in deciding to accompany the tsar to Erfurt, he had made the most of the limited alternatives available once Russia's good offices had been proffered. But Stein was skeptical of any long-term commitment to Prussia by Alexander. It also seems evident that, by this time, he was so caught up in the grand scheme of insurrection that he was quite unable to accept the finality of Prussia's new situation as a dependent of the Franco-Russian system in Europe. For whether or not Stein realized it, satellite status for the indefinite future was the actual import of the king's decision. Yet Stein continued to anticipate a military solution as the only final one for Prussia's problems; the tsar might save a half-dead Prussia, but Stein wanted to rebuild it physically as it had been. He thought in terms of full salvation; the insurrection, which had been originally proposed as a contingent program, was becoming his chief article of faith.[11] Then, suddenly, the word of the contretemps and of the harsh terms of the convention had arrived, linked to the revelation of his own indiscretion. The sarcastic commentaries which mocked him publicly in the French-controlled press fed his rancorous feeling against Napoleon. By this time, if not before, we may be sure that he had taken up the insurrection plan with single-minded dedication, whatever temporary sidesteps the exigencies of the moment might dictate.

In spite of the fact that the king had made his own decision in the case of the ratification, Stein was still in charge of the programs, such as the preparation of the insurrection, which he had introduced. He had received no new line of direction from the king, who continued to keep his own counsel and apparently shunned discussion

[11] Stein had never put the insurrection scheme completely out of his mind: see Stein, Denkschrift, 30 August 1808, *Stein Br.*, II (2), 844–846; Stein Denkschrift, 18 September 1808, *ibid.*, 863–864; Stein to Götzen, 23 September 1808, *ibid.*, 867–868. Gneisenau, for example, had argued since the first indications that Bonaparte's hold might be weakening that the idea of the war and insurrection could never be dropped because Napoleon would have to be crushed completely (see Gneisenau, Denkschrift, 10 August 1808, PRO, FO, Prussia, 64/79, in Vaupel, 547–552).

with the chief of administration. Stein knew nothing of the directive sent to Goltz and had no instructions from the king to stop preparations for the uprising. Thus he furthered the dangerous policy which had originally been approved, including the conversations Count Götzen was conducting with the Austrians. He did not apprise the king of each new step pursuant to the development of his plans. But his independent mode of action was not just a timely innovation in the relation between monarch and servant. Stein simply could not hamstring the conduct of affairs by facing the king with the minute decisions on day-to-day implementation of policies. Yet it is apparent that Stein, in this matter, was acting well beyond the king's intent, even if not beyond his expressed will. The fact was that the king and Stein were pursuing foreign policies with utterly different goals.[12]

One consequence of the news of the signature of the treaty and of Stein's blunder was to force the whole controversy over the uprising into the open. The patriots, who did not learn of the ratification for a fortnight, began to argue desperately against it. The elaborate net of insurrection had been spread throughout Germany. As zealots flocked to the clandestine cells to hear the leaders divulge their plans, all sense of caution was soon swept away. In the mutual expressions of patriotic hopes the sense of commitment to a single

[12] Stein to Götzen, 23 September and 4 or 5 October 1808, *Stein Br.*, II (2), 867–868, 885; Stein, Denkschrift, 12 October 1808, *ibid.*, 889–891. Ritter puts a better interpretation on the king's conduct of affairs, and does not point out that the king's failure to notify his chief minister of the ratification was an indication of a curious method of conducting governmental affairs (*Stein*, 350). He accuses Stein of conducting a "Doppelpolitik" in order to inveigle Prussia without the knowledge of the king in the war he hoped the Austrians were about to begin (353; at top of page: "Gewagtes Doppelspiel Steins.") But the argument he conducts in a footnote (610–611n15) leads him to the conclusion: "Richtig ist daran aber doch so viel, dass der König über die 'geheimen Relationen' Götzens in Österreich im *allgemeinen* orientiert war, ebenso über die schlesischen Rüstungen, und beides einstweilen weiter geschehen liess, trotz der von Goltz gleichzeitig betriebenen Versöhnungspolitik." Hence it would appear that the difference between the king and Stein on this was a matter of degree and, of course, ultimate intent. But the king was not so far removed from the "Doppelspiel" Stein conducted behind his back as at first appears from Ritter's arguments.

cause waxed. Their feeling of solidarity was heightened by the prospect of comradeship in feats of strength and daring. In the eyes of the committed, the organizations of the conspiracy, rather than the long-term policies they had been created to fulfill, became self-justifying. The members came to see the societies as offering the sole prospect of success for the resurrection of Prussia and Germany.[13] It would be difficult to believe that those who conceived it originally—Gneisenau, Scharnhorst, and Stein—could have escaped a paternal dedication to their brainchild. To some extent, and I think we gather from Stein's case how easily it could occur, the contingent policy tended to become the only policy.

Gneisenau had always been the most impassioned champion of insurrection and hence stood with Stein against the ratification. He argued in a bold memoir to the king that the onerous financial conditions of the treaty could not be fulfilled. He proposed that the king should summon the Prussian estates to a meeting to consider the terms. This would not only postpone any decision, it would allow the king to use the meeting as a sounding board which would help rally the support of the whole nation against ratification.[14]

Gneisenau combined this argument for popularizing the opposition to France with one in favor of the expansion of the organs of self-government. A meeting of any sort of representative body was almost unknown in Prussia, though the idea, as we have seen, was already under study by Stein and his party. The examples of the American Revolution and the rally of the French people to the revolutionary state which inspired Gneisenau were radical indeed for Prussia, but they found the support of Stein.[15] The mass insurrection had become bound up closely in the minds of these patriots

[13] There is no satisfactory account of the conspiracy of 1808. See Chapter I, above, and my article "A New Schleiermacher Letter," *passim*.

[14] Gneisenau, Denkschrift (called "Reflections on the Situation in Prussia in September 1808" in the English translation by Alexander Gibson, PRO, FO, Prussia, 64/79), September 1808, Vaupel, 593–597; Boyen to F.W., DZA, Rep. 89a, XLVIII, 1. According to Gibson to FO, 27 September 1808, PRO, FO, Prussia, 64/79, Gneisenau, Grolman, and Scharnhorst had that day sent a letter to the king saying that they could no longer serve unless "energetic measures" were taken.

[15] Stein, Denkschrift, 12 October 1808, *Stein Br.*, II (2), 889–891; Ritter, *Stein*, 351.

with the political reform they thought would win the people's support for state and monarchy. The cause of war had been joined to the cause of popular government.

Stein's domestic opposition also sensed the connection between political innovation and insurrection. For them, his now public letter confirmed the charge of dangerous incitements made against him. The formation of the Tugendbund, which originally had had national pedagogical and charitable ends, but which soon was infiltrated by the insurrectionaries, cast a new pall of fear. The prospect of peasants with pikes and pitchforks led by committees of public virtue scouring the countryside for French soldiers redoubled the intensity of the visions of revolution the aristocrats dreamed.[16] Their fears, coupled with their new hope which derived from Stein's embarrassment, amplified their already strident voices; in Königsberg the composition of the government to replace Stein's was now openly discussed.[17] From Berlin the minister heard that his foes were rallying boldly behind Voss.[18]

Against these enemies of Stein Gneisenau had argued, in defense of the insurrection, that the proponents of ratification were mostly those persons whose advanced age or longing for the pleasures of domesticity in the capital inclined them to peaceful pursuits. Others he flatly identified as cowards.[19] But in truth, the most cogently reasoned attacks came from genuine conservatives, who were as critical of the insurrection as they were of the whole idea of liberalization joined to it. Not all were tremulously or treasonably pro-French, as Gneisenau implied. Rough-hewn York von Wartenburg, the archetypical Junker cavalier, whose famous deed during the Wars of Liberation was later to be crucial in turning Prussia against

[16] The discontent of the aristocracy is excellently summarized by Max Lehmann, *Freiherr vom Stein,* II (Leipzig, 1903), 593–594. On the Tugendbund, see Ritter, *Stein,* 338–339.

[17] Gneisenau, Denkschrift, September 1808, PRO, FO, Prussia, 64/79 (in Vaupel, 595); Gibson to FO, 22 September 1808, PRO, FO, Prussia, 64/79; Drusina to FO, *ibid.,* 64/78.

[18] Stein, IB, 26 September 1808, *Stein Br.,* II (2), 875–876.

[19] Gneisenau, Denkschrift, September 1808, PRO, FO, Prussia, 64/79 (in Vaupel, 593–597).

France, now accused Stein of seeking to "lead the peasants to El-
dorado" with his uprising. To him Stein was wrong not because he
raised secret societies to drive out the French, but because he had
jeopardized the crown by doing so.

We may take York's unsophisticated arguments against Stein's
reforms as representative enough, even if they were partially a dis-
tillation of the ideas and slogans of his cronies in the conservative
Königsberg Perponcher Klub. The truth is that these opponents of
Stein and their friends in the *Hofpartei* nowhere left recorded a
political philosophy as such, and we must be content with the un-
systematic notions they here and there advanced against the reforms.
Most in the Perponcher group complained that while Berlin had
been occupied in "old Fritz's" time after similar military defeats, no
one then had thought that a domestic revolution was necessary.
Ideas such as Stein's they denounced as "philosophical blather"
(*Geschwätz*) dreamed up by businessmen and professors who had
"poorly digested Adam Smith." To them, ending the "so-called en-
slavement" of the peasants, as Stein proposed, was an attack on the
fundament of the social order. Stein's "Plusmachersystem" was as
alien to the Prussian soul as Smith; it too had been imported from
England.[20]

Far more sophisticated than York's formulation of the argument
against reform and insurrection was the persuasive memoir written
by Chief Assistant Equerry (*Vice-Ober-Stallmeister*) Ludwig von
Jagow in October. Like York, he did not directly denounce the idea
of insurrection, but maintained that it was impractical in the circumstances. Those who shared his stand, he alleged, were not lacking in
patriotism—the charge the activists like Gneisenau had obviously

---

[20] Droysen, *York*, I, 152–154. York was hardly an original political thinker. The
ideas undoubtedly reflect those current in his circle. The very same appeal to Frederick
the Great, for example, appeared in a French-approved denunciation of the Stein
reforms which appeared in Berlin's *Vossische Zeitung* on 26 November 1808. The
Perponcher Club was probably named after a Baron Perponcher. Schön later recalled
it as the center of the opposition to Stein in Königsberg and as having had a connection with Voss; see Franz Rühl, ed., *Briefwechsel des Ministers und Burggrafen von
Marienburg Theodor von Schön mit G. F. Pertz and J. G. Droysen* (Leipzig, 1896),
42–43, 217.

raised with more than a little success—nor were they pro-French. Jagow, a friend of Zastrow, added what he intended as a warning to the king: actions taken in foreign affairs without royal consent could embarrass the monarchy and menace the conduct of government.[21]

Jagow's complaints were echoed by other respectable conservatives. A later letter to the king from Otto von Gerlach, who, though an opponent of the "liberal" tone of Stein's government, was a personal enemy of Voss, admonished the king that an anti-French insurrection involving peasants might have revolutionary implications. There was no question of Gerlach's patriotism or of his hostility toward the French.[22] Arch-Junker Friedrich von der Marwitz made a similar complaint.[23]

As in the case of York and Jagow, no charge of direct personal involvement could be made against Gerlach and Marwitz. They did not connive against Stein's ministry as did the most vociferous enemies from the conservative faction, Voss and the *Hofpartei*. Nor could any complaint of personal office seeking be laid at their doors. So even if the king discounted the opinions of the court fools who surrounded him because he recognized that their passions or ambition had distracted their reason, he could not ignore these views.

We have but one indication of what stand Frederick William actually took between the two camps, one instance in which he showed unusual annoyance with the harrassment of the partisan struggle over treaty ratification. On the twenty-seventh of September the patriot author of the military reforms, Major Grolman, had strewn the parade ground in Königsberg with leaflets attacking the Paris convention. The same day, the king, who on almost every other occasion had managed to preserve an almost other-worldly detachment from the hurly-burly political struggle, ordered Grolman jail-

---

[21] DZA, Rep. 92, F.W. III, B VI, 22. Jagow's memoir may have been written to counter Grolman's circular. See below, note 25. On Jagow, see Hassel, I, 206.

[22] Gerlach to F.W., 6 December 1808, DZA, Rep. 89a, L5, printed in Schoeps, *Aus den Jahren preussischer Not*, 363–364. See Leonie Keyserling, *Studien zu den Entwicklungsjahren der Brüder Gerlach* (Heidelberg, 1913), 14.

[23] Friedrich Meusel, *Friedrich August Ludwig von der Marwitz: Ein märkischer Edelmann im Zeitalter der Befreiungskriege*, I (Berlin, 1908), 500.

ed. More significant, he told Kalckreuth, the military governor of Königsberg, to impose a harsh censorship on the public expression of opinion in the city. Was this because Grolman's action brought to his attention for the first time what the ultimate consequences of the line of political evolution that he had benignly encouraged might be? May we speculate that the later advisers he found who promised him reform without popular involvement—"Demokratische Grundsätze in einer monarchischen Regierung," in Hardenberg's splendidly elusive phrase[24]—had hit upon a line of argument which was especially appealing to the king?

We do not know whether Kalckreuth or the king was responsible for initially suggesting the ban on political action in the capital. But the results, a narrowing of the range of political action (which, in any case, had never been very broad) was not a hopeful sign for the reform party. Kalckreuth, of course, delectated in the measure of influence and power he won from the Grolman affair. He issued the prohibition on expression to the armed forces, then told Schroetter, Minister for the Province of East Prussia, to issue an identical regulation for the civil and academic governments. Schroetter protested that no cause for such action had been given by the civil population, but the king backed Kalckreuth. Stein, not consulted by the king on his decision, thought the antique marshal was going out of his way to humiliate Schroetter. Schroetter's openly liberal position—he was one of the East Prussian Kantians—would have been especially obnoxious to the courtier group. Stein, in the circumstances, had to content himself with a sarcastic but private marginal note for Schroetter to the effect that Kalckreuth had the necessary authority to issue all the orders himself.[25]

---

[24] Georg Winter, ed., *Die Reorganisation des preussischen Staates unter Stein und Hardenberg*, pt. 1: *Vom Beginn des Kampfes gegen die Kabinettsregierung bis zum Wiedereintritt des Ministers vom Stein* (Leipzig, 1931), 306.

[25] Delbrück, *Tagebücher,* 28 and 29 September 1808, III, 67–68; Clausewitz to Marie von Brühl, 13 October 1808, Clausewitz, *Briefe,* 174; Gibson to FO, 10 October 1808, PRO, FO, Prussia, 64/79; Schroetter to F.W., 3 October 1808, and F.W. to Schroetter, 7 October 1808 (Stein's marginal note on Schroetter's letter to the king), DZA, Rep. 89a, LII. See also Scharnhorst to Götzen, 29 September 1808, in Karl Linnebach, ed., *Scharnhorsts Briefe,* I (Munich, 1914), 348.

The Grolman affair showed just how much less effective Stein had become within a week after his public incrimination. The very fact that the king and the first minister no longer met made him less persuasive in presenting his point of view. At this very time his enemies had boldly opened their struggle for succession. He was forced to complain now that "les pitoyables"—he meant his enemies at court—were able to frustrate all positive action.[26]

In contrast to the weakness of Stein and his friends, the conservative opposition had easily the best of two possible lines of argument; they could reason on the one hand that Stein's mistakes had forced a disastrous peace treaty on the nation, or they could maintain on the other hand that Stein was pushing the nation toward an unwanted, calamitous war with France. The question was whether these courtiers and their friends in Berlin, his enemies long before the exposure of his unlucky letter, would be able to thrust him aside and succeed to his mantle.

To contemporaries it appeared that the consequences of Stein's diplomatic blunder would ultimately be decided by Napoleon. At the outset the French emperor appears to have been determined to punish Stein personally. Intolerant and willful, Bonaparte was not the man to forgive and forget. When the occasion demanded he could be tactful and moderate; but his normal stance toward those who crossed his path was arrogant and brutal. The murder of the Duke of Enghien is a case in point. In this case as in any other there was only one certainty: his whim would be incalculable.[27]

There is no reason to believe that Napoleon had any deep understanding of Stein or his character, or of affairs in general at the Königsberg court. His empire spread too widely for a single mind, even Napoleon's, to compass it. His bureaucracy was too hastily as-

---

[26] Scharnhorst to Götzen, 4 October 1808, Scharnhorst, *Briefe,* I, 349; Stein to Götzen, 4 or 5 October 1808, *Stein Br.,* II (2), 885.

[27] A good characterization of Napoleon is in Metternich to Stadion, 24 September 1808, Metternich, *Memoirs,* II, 283. In 1804, the Bourbon Duke of Enghien was kidnapped from neutral territory and summarily executed for his alleged involvement in a plot on Napoleon's life.

sembled to be competent, too much aware of the necessity to serve his fancy to question his orders. We may presume that he glanced hurriedly through the reports submitted by his marshals from Germany. Some of the information, gossip, and rumor they reported as intelligence must have stuck in the corner of his mind. Recall that only a year before in far different, if somewhat baffling, circumstances he had named Stein with others of far different political persuasion as possible replacements for Hardenberg. As with the nomination, Napoleon in this second case involving Stein presumably drew a hasty inference on the basis of the inadequate evidence he had. The captured letter simply confirmed the general impression of recruitment, rearmament, and the organization of an insurrection against the French which the reports of his generals and spies had produced.[28] Marshal Nicolas Soult had reported from Berlin on the thirty-first of August that all Königsberg, with the sole exception of Marshal Kalckreuth, supported a war policy.[29] The condemnation and punishment of Stein was one way Napoleon could quickly set a timely example for those Prussians who might try to emulate the annoying Spaniards.

"Ces prussiens sont de pauvres et misérables gens"; so had Bonaparte expressed his customary contempt for his most recent enemies. Stein's letter he had called "extraordinary," by which he meant extraordinarily foolish even for a Prussian.[30] In the momentum of his first fury he had ordered his brother Jerome, whom he wrongly assumed to be Stein's royal master, to call the errant knight to the bar of royal Westphalian justice. If he did not appear, his family lands should be sequestered.[31] In the final draft of the convention which Champagny presented to the Prussian emissaries for signature on the eighth of September Napoleon had also inserted a new clause requiring dismissal of all of the servants of the king of Prussia who

[28] See above, Chapter III. Constantin de Grunwald, *Stein: L'Ennemi de Napoléon* (Paris, 1936), 167, also agrees that Napoleon knew little of Stein.
[29] Cavaignac, *La Formation de la Prusse*, I, 495.
[30] Napoleon to Soult, 4 September 1808, *Lettres inédites de Napoléon*, I, 238.
[31] Napoleon to Jerome Napoleon, 6 September 1808, *Lettres inédites de Napoléon*, I, 239.

came originally from lands no longer Prussian.[32] These blows were
aimed (rather inaccurately, since neither of the sweeping categories
Bonaparte had so far specified included Stein) at Stein and others
whom Napoleon suspected of making up the militant party. Hardenberg and Nagler as well as Stein had been denounced as "Hano-
verians" of English sympathy in one of the free-swinging reports of
a French spy in Berlin.[33] Soult regularly forwarded such reports,
embellished by his own summary of intelligence, to Paris. Napoleon's
confusion may have stemmed from this.

Then, two days after the convention had been signed by Prince
William, Bonaparte arbitrarily ordered a completely new condition
to be imposed. Perhaps he felt his spleen insufficiently vented; more
probably the later report by Soult, cited above, of the hostility toward
him in Königsberg renewed his anger. It may also be that he had
suddenly learned that Stein would not be among those whom the
terms of the convention would exclude from Prussian service. As on
so many occasions before, Napoleon, for whatever reason, simply
chose to amend the terms unilaterally in his own favor in order to
rectify omissions in the treaty. Curiously, however, he sent his new
condition—which was that Stein would be put out by the King of
Prussia or the king would not return to his capital[34]—to Soult in
Berlin. But he made no direct communication of this requirement to
the Prussian king or to Prince William, though William had remained in Paris and met the emperor once again before his departure.[35] Was it that, for tactical reasons, he preferred to reserve
the new demand for the discussions in Erfurt when the ratifications
were to be exchanged? Whatever his reasons, the question came up
first at Erfurt, where Goltz, with Alexander's support, was seeking a
pardon for Stein.

[32] Ritter, *Stein,* 353.
[33] Report of French spy, 8 August 1808, AG, CGA, C2 79.
[34] Napoleon to Soult, 10 September 1808, *Correspondance de Napoléon,* XVII, 503.
[35] D'Aubier to Goltz, 4 December 1808, DZA, Rep. 63, 88, No. 598; Sack to Stein,
26 November 1808, *Stein Br.,* II (2), 995–996. Note that Napoleon made no demand
for Stein's removal in his conversation with Prince William and Brockhausen of 15
September 1808: Prince William to F.W., 15 September 1808, Hassel, I, 489–492;
Brockhausen to F.W., 16 September 1808, DZA, A.A.I., Rep. 1, No. 1234.

In the succeeding weeks the reports of French agents transmitted to Paris continued to confirm the intelligence that an uprising was in preparation in Germany. Marshal Davout in Silesia, who reported patriotic formations even more sinister than those in Berlin, observed that the recently exposed letter of Stein confirmed his previous reports.[36] The rumors they heard of the newly founded Tugendbund, or "Frères de vertu," ascribed to that society both cabalistic and rebellious purposes. The French, steeped as they were in the lore of revolution, found in the very name of the society a challenge to their system.

Yet it should be noted that Bonaparte rarely permitted himself the luxury of giving credence to the erroneous intelligence he was given. On occasion, when his own short patience was strained, he would issue a violent, blanket proscription, lashing out against his tormenters. For example, the first great animus against Stein had as an irrational by-product an imperial anathema pronounced against a Prussian of lesser consequence, General Rüchel.[37] But Bonaparte, with his peculiar combination of arrogance and skepticism, still discounted most of the information he received. Perhaps he did so because he was able to see only the highlights of any diplomatic situation and did not lose himself in trivia; perhaps he understood that his lackeys overelaborated the dangers in their bailiwicks. They had, after all, a stake in keeping things stirred up in order to demonstrate their own capacity to keep control in difficult times; they shared, it may be presumed, a natural wish to enhance the importance of their sectors of command. In these conditions, their own self-interest weighted their judgments. It is also quite true that the business of France had become the business of war, and Napoleon's generals the captains of industry. Mirabeau's remark about the eighteenth-century Prussian garrison state could be applied to Napoleonic France. Metternich, the Habsburg ambassador to Paris in 1808, observed to Count Stadion that fall: "One might say that

---

[36] Davout to Napoleon, 22 September 1808, Davout, *Correspondance*, II, 293–294.
[37] Napoleon to Soult, 4 September 1808, *Lettres inédites de Napoléon*, I, 238; Soult to Napoleon, 13 September 1808, AG, CGA, C2 79.

France is peopled entirely by soldiers and by citizens created to work for them by the sweat of their brows." [38] Fortunately for Bonaparte, in this case he was so unable to overcome his personal contempt for the Germans that he ignored most of what his agents, the honest, the self-deceived, and the schemers alike, told him. He would have done so even if all he heard had been perfectly true. He simply ascribed the persistent, to him puny and ridiculous, effort to raise a force against him in Germany to Prussian "military mania." [39]

Meanwhile, in Berlin, news of Stein's indiscretion had brought a quick fall in his reputation and a headlong scramble for safe places among the members of the court party there. Baroness Stein, who resided in the city, had at first taken some pains to deny the authenticity of the letter.[40] But once all doubts vanished, Stein's still circumspect antagonists quickly sensed the importance of the event and recognized from the tone of the published commentary accompanying the letter that Napoleon's attack was meant to render the minister prostrate. Their response to the crisis which threatened their government revealed the degree to which some Prussians would use the French for their own purposes, or grovel before them.

For a few days, the motto of those Berliners who desired to preserve their status with the French authorities was "sauve-qui-peut." Not more than a moment after the cock had thrice crowed, Voss, Prince Ferdinand of Prussia (the king's nephew), and Prince Ludwig Ferdinand von Hatzfeldt appeared voluntarily before Soult to proclaim themselves as utterly deceived by the head of their government. Hatzfeldt, of the Silesian aristocracy, was diplomatic repre-

[38] Letter of 24 September 1808, Metternich, *Memoirs*, II, 284.

[39] Napoleon was quoted as saying (no doubt in French) that the Germans, "*Schlafmützen* . . . are happy when the cabbage is picked and stored in the cellar." The story comes from Friedrich Carl Freiherr von Müffling, *Aus meinem Leben*, 2nd ed. (Berlin, 1855), 23. Napoleon to Soult, 10 September 1808, *Correspondance de Napoléon*, XVII, 503.

[40] Report of French spy to Soult, 29 September 1808, AG, CGA, C2 79. Stein's letter was in general much condemned in Berlin. See Agnes von Gerlach to Marie von Raumer, 19 September and 1 October 1808, in Schoeps, *Aus den Jahren preussischer Not*, 359–360, 361.

sentative in Berlin and Dresden of the Catholic prince primate and archchancellor (the former Electoral Prince of Mainz) and had actively served the Prussian government previously.[41] Voss, the official Prussian chief of delegation in Berlin, joined the others in lamenting that Stein had made them appear ridiculous. Their friendships with the French authorities, they said, had been misused by Stein to mask a sordid intrigue completely alien to their elegant characters.[42]

[41] Hatzfeldt had been left behind at the time of the evacuation of Berlin in 1806 and was charged with saving a cache of rifles stored in the Zeughaus for the Prussians. He had failed to accomplish this before the French arrived and was captured and almost shot as a Prussian spy according to Hans Haussherr, *Die Stunde Hardenbergs* (Hamburg, 1943), 14; and Schwartz, *Berlins Kriegsleiden,* 10. He was saved by a plea from his wife, a Schulenberg by birth, to Napoleon. By September 1808 he was assisting the French generals in Berlin in their efforts to discover suspicious persons. He gave tips on travelers and even helped the French in their interrogations; see Ernst Salzer, ed., *Denkwürdigkeiten des Generals Friedrich von Eisenhart, 1769–1839* (Berlin, 1910), 174–179; and Report of French spy, 3 September 1808, AG, CGA, C2 79. This work he probably thought a part of his function as diplomatic representative of the prince primate, one of the most important of Napoleon's German princelings. Though Hatzfeldt's estates were mainly in Silesia, he appears to have decided about the time of the end of the French evacuation to leave Prussia. He recommended to the prince primate that he close his Berlin office (Hatzfeldt also served the prince primate in Dresden). See his Tagebuch, 25 November 1808, APMW, Archiwum Hatzfeldt'ów, No. 743. Davout, who commended his good service to Napoleon, also reported to Napoleon on 17 December 1808 (Davout, *Correspondance,* II, 324) that Hatzfeldt would leave Berlin. An article in the Frankfurt (where the prince primate had his seat of government) newspaper, quoted a Berlin report of 27 November that Hatzfeldt would leave Prussia permanently. But this was corrected officially in a story in Berlin's *Vossische Zeitung* on 24 December 1808. This report, obviously fabricated, was laced with extravagant praise for Hatzfeldt and contained testimonials to the esteem in which he was held by his fellow citizens. Stein always regarded him as one of his Francophile enemies in Berlin: see Stein, Autobiographische Aufzeichnungen, 12 July 1811, *Stein Br.,* III, 546; and Stein, Autobiographie, January 1823, in Erich Botzenhart, ed., *Freiherr vom Stein: Briefwechsel, Denkschriften, Aufzeichnungen,* VI (Berlin, n.d.,), 171. In 1812, Hatzfeldt supplied Hardenberg with a list of anti-French suspects whom he suggested removing from the government; see Alfred Stern, *Abhandlungen und Aktenstücke zur Geschichte der preussischen Reformzeit, 1807–1815* (Leipzig, 1885), 376–377. On the prince primate, see Hubert Becher, *Der deutsche Primas: Eine Untersuchung zur deutschen Kirchengeschichte in der ersten Hälfte des neunzehnten Jahrhunderts* (Colmar, 1944), ch. iv, *passim.*

[42] Soult to Napoleon, 19 September 1808, AG, CGA, C2 79 (in Granier, *Aus der Berliner Franzosenzeit,* 300).

Perceiving quickly the advantage they could draw for themselves and their political cause from the minister's personal crisis, these aristocrats sought to turn the new state of affairs to the further discomfiture of the head of their government and the ruination of his program. When, a few days afterward, articles explaining the reform legislation appeared in the newspapers—they had been inspired by Stein, who had the king's permission to undertake a campaign of education on behalf of his legislation[43]—Voss and his ideological confreres represented them as another part of Stein's insurrectionary effort to inflame public opinion. The political and social innovations were portrayed for the French authorities as part and parcel of the scheme to set the countryside ablaze. As they outlined the alleged plot, the people were first to be aroused by clever demagogy to support Stein; then they would be encouraged to rise up behind their benevolent government when the opportunity arose.

With Stein as a self-impeached revolutionary, his domestic program could easily be made to appear tainted to the French. This connection between liberalization of the domestic regime on the one hand, and popular uprising on the other, deliberately underscored by the courtiers for the edification of the French authorities, was a lesson not lost upon them. Henceforth even the domestic legislation undertaken in Königsberg was considered by the French marshals to menace their order in central Europe. Holding this conviction, the minions of Bonaparte became foes of the reform of the Prussian state. Stein's enemies could not have better arranged circumstances to doom his work.[44]

Long before the revelation of Stein's letter, the opponents of Stein in Berlin and the members of the court clique had formed a political

---

[43] Stein, IB, 26 September 1808, and newspaper article, 26 September 1808, *Stein Br.*, II (2), 875–878. See the article on the military and civil reforms from the *Königsberger Zeitung*, 29 September 1808, in Hassel, I, 584–847. This was reprinted in the Berlin *Vossische Zeitung* and the *Spenersche Zeitung* on 6 October 1808.

[44] An example of this sort of attack is the anonymous report to Soult (which could easily have been written by Hatzfeldt or Voss, or a member of their circle) of 7 October 1808, AG, CGA, C2 80. It contains a denunciation of the reforms and Stein's newspaper article of 26 September (see above, note 43), and shows the connection of reform with military action.

connection. With the reformers drawn away to government service in Königsberg, the "old party," which found life under the French occupation tolerable, had easily won control in Berlin.[45] It would have been but one short step for them to have sought out the like-minded party in Königsberg, with whom they had always maintained social relations. But these antagonists of Minister Stein were also rivals of one another. Many among them viewed themselves as the best replacement for Stein, once they had effected his downfall. Kalckreuth sought the job;[46] Voss's friends expected him to be nominated to it;[47] and Zastrow, hoping to make capital of Stein's failure to secure a treaty in the spring, had tried to persuade the king as early as July that he alone possessed the confidence of the French to the extent necessary to secure the final conclusion of a peace treaty.[48]

But whatever their rivalries and differences,[49] personal, moral, or ideological, at least these enemies did hold in common a rationalized disapproval of Stein's domestic program. By contrast, the unlikely alliance[50] they sought in the fall of 1808 with Stein's old antagonist, Beyme, could be founded on nothing better than their common, personal antipathy toward the minister; on jealously, envy, and

---

[45] Stägemann to Frau Stägemann, 24 April 1808, Rühl, *Aus der Franzosenzeit*, 87; Haussherr, *Die Stunde Hardenbergs*, 14.

[46] Emil von Conrady, *Leben und Wirken des Generals der Infantrie und kommandirenden Generals des V. Armeekorps Carl von Grolman*, I (Berlin, 1894), 193. Grolman warned the king in early October on the basis of information he had gotten from his father in Berlin that a cabal of the Kakodämonen with Zastrow and other Berliners had been formed. The king apparently ignored the report. Grolman was already in jail because of his pamphlet.

[47] Stägemann to Stein, 7 November 1808, *Stein Br.*, II (2), 923–925.

[48] Beyme to F.W., 26 July 1808, Hassel, I, 563–564. The French authorities were already spreading the word that Stein would have to go. See Report of French spy to Soult, 30 September 1808, AG, CGA, C2 79.

[49] Conrady, *Grolman*, I, 187–188, 191–193.

[50] "Unlikely" is the proper word. Stein certainly never guessed at the possibility of such a combination at the time. Three years later, however, he wrote to Hardenberg (21 July 1811, *Stein Br.*, III, 556) that a connection between Voss and his party and Beyme (to work against Hardenberg) was a possibility. Eisenhart, in his *Denkwürdigkeiten*, 163, mentions that he saw Beyme at Countess Voss's salons on several occasions in the spring of 1808. He also saw Köckritz there.

malign self-seeking. Yet in this story nothing could have been quite so unexpected as that which actually occured.

Beyme, after his retirement from the court in June, had returned to his estate in Steglitz, near Berlin. From there in late July he forwarded to the king without comment Zastrow's opinion on Stein's inability to make terms with the French.[51] On the surface, it was an innocent act. But on what basis could Beyme, the "Prussian Jacobin," represent (as he surely did by passing along his opinions to the king) the interest of Zastrow, who was so close to the type which had often mocked him as an upstart? Why would he undertake to use his personal influence to forward Zastrow's attack on Stein to the king? This was indeed the second time within a year that Beyme had intervened with the king on Zastrow's behalf.[52] We may assume from these events that whatever antipathies had existed between them before had been smoothed over, at least for the time.

Though the circumstances of the juncture between Beyme and Stein's aristocratic opponents are unclear, we can be certain that such a coalition was attempted. When the flirtation between the former enemies began we do not know. Perhaps Zastrow gave Beyme a reference in gratitude for his approaches to the king on his behalf. Perhaps the violence of Beyme's feelings toward Stein was so well known from his days in Königsberg that no reference was needed. It may be that Voss had already found the occasion to sound out Beyme's opinion since his return to Berlin. In any case, the opportunities did exist. We may also be sure that the negotiations with Beyme had some relation to the campaign against Stein opened at Kalckreuth's tea salon and the factionalism which had developed over the military reforms. Just after the campaign against Stein was mounted in early September, but before Stein's embarrassing letter was known in Königsberg, a Canon Tamm,[53] courier to the members of the

---

[51] Beyme to F.W., 26 July 1808, Hassel, I, 563–564.

[52] Bassewitz, *Die Kurmark, 1806–1808,* I, 463.

[53] In the several sources which mention him the name appears as "Damm" (Chasot to F.W., 12 October 1808, DZA, Rep. 92, F.W. III, B VIIa, 7c); "Jamm" (Report of French spy to Soult, 23 September 1808, Cavaignac, I, 489–499); "Lamm" (Sack to Stein, 23 November 1808, *Stein Br.,* II (2), 986); and "Tamm" (Report of

royal court in Berlin, had been sent by the Kakodämonen with a secret commission to help Beyme win the confidence of the French. Tamm was already well acquainted with one of the most important French agents in Berlin. We do not know his name—it may have been Resident Administrator Louis Edouard de Bignon—but he must have held important social rank in view of his contacts among the highest echelons of Berlin society.[54] Tamm met this mysterious French representative at the home of a certain Madame Obermann, whose "patron" he was.[55] Making no effort to conceal his own political sentiments, he reported the situation in Königsberg as it stood at the time of his departure on the fourteenth of September. He also recounted the gist of a meeting he had had with Beyme since arriving in Berlin.

Tamm claimed to be Beyme's confidant of some years' standing. The ex-adviser, he said, was delighted at Stein's embarrassment because of the letter episode. Beyme was convinced that Stein would be forced out of office, a step the king would finally find the courage to take. Stein's fall would be some consolation for his exclusion, at the minister's behest, from the king's circle. In this likely turn of events Beyme saw, so Tamm reported, the best chance for his own return to power.

French spy to Soult, 30 September 1808, AG, CGA, C2 79). He also appears as "Tamm" of Potsdam in the index of Magnus Friedrich von Bassewitz, *Die Kurmark Brandenburg im Zusammenhange mit den Schicksalen des Gesammtstaats Preussen während der Jahre 1809 und 1810,* ed. Karl von Reinhard (Leipzig, 1860).

[54] The reports were signed "Lully" (?) and were submitted to the French command. It is conceivable, though hardly probable, that "Lully" was Resident Administrator Bignon, who moved in the upper circles of Berlin society.

[55] The nature of Tamm's relation to the lady is unclear. One source calls her "his sister" (Chasot to F.W., 12 October 1808, DZA, Rep. 92, F.W. III, B VIIa, 7c). "Lully" mentioned her as one of his sources of information. He said that she received confidential information from Prussian officers. (L. to Soult, 2 September 1808, AG, CGA, C2 79). To show the difficulty contemporaries had in determining who served whom, it should be noted that a "Widow Obermann" was on a list of distinguished patriots submitted to the king after he returned to Berlin; see Hermann Granier, "Die Franzosen in Berlin, 1806–1808," *Hohenzollern-Jahrbuch,* IX (1905), 42. It is of course possible that she was a double agent, but if so, Chasot did not know her as such and the context in which her name appears in his letter to the king indicates that she was not the source of his report.

From the line of argument Tamm employed we may conclude that his effort was directed toward convincing the French that Beyme might be relied upon as a suitable replacement in the case of Stein's fall. He said that Beyme, in 1805, had been the greatest friend the French had in Prussia. When he had advised the king at that time against the break with France which led to the disastrous war, he had become Hardenberg's enemy. For counseling the king to take up positions the French found desirable, Beyme had been passed some "presents" through Tamm. Keeping this in mind, Tamm advised, the French could see that the future amicable relations between the emperor and the King of Prussia would depend on Beyme being at the king's side. To dispel any lingering doubts about Beyme's friendship for France, Tamm could produce evidence in the form of letters from 1805 which would attest to the ex-adviser's attitude at that time. The French agent seems to have been interested in what he heard, for Tamm agreed to arrange a meeting for him with Beyme at Madame Obermann's in Berlin for the morrow (September 24).[56]

This account of Beyme's astonishing activities, which has generally been overlooked,[57] would scarcely be credible were the general outlines of the evidence not substantially confirmed by another report of the same discussions and by Beyme's subsequent behavior. Indeed, the efficient espionage service of the patriotic circle in Berlin somehow got wind of Beyme's conversations with the French. Count Ludwig Chasot, chief of the Berlin section of the anti-French conspiracy, subsequently wrote all he had heard about them in a confidential letter to the king. Tamm, he said, had been sent to Berlin by Köckritz, with whom he was in constant communication. Köck-

---

[56] Report of French spy to Soult, 23 September 1808, Cavaignac, *La Formation de la Prusse,* I, 498–499 (original in AG, CGA, C2 79). Clausewitz, *Nachrichten,* 453. indicated that Beyme was quite adept at getting "presents" and died a rich man as well as the holder of a title of nobility.

[57] Only Lehmann, *Stein,* II, 598–599, aside from Cavaignac, who originally discovered it, took account of Tamm's report. Ritter has used Cavaignac, *La Formation de la Prusse,* but apparently missed the appendix with the letters from the French archives.

ritz's purpose was to ensure that Beyme would succeed Stein, whose resignation was now thought by his foes to be certain. As for Tamm himself, Chasot reported that he had been in contact with Bignon since the outbreak of the war. From him Soult had heard of the matter and was now eager to find out if Beyme would be a satisfactory replacement for Stein. Tamm had tried to arrange a meeting between Soult and Beyme, but Beyme had discreetly refused any direct confrontation with the French command on the ground that he could not meddle in politics. Since then, Soult had gone off to the Erfurt Congress. In the interim, Tamm was seeking to win the confidence of Soult's secretary. He was still passing Köckritz's messages to Beyme. Thus, for example, Beyme had already learned that Stein had tried to resign when the letter had first been published and that the attempt had been rebuffed by Frederick William. Köckritz had since solicited Beyme's opinion as to what was to be done in the circumstances. This, wrote Chasot, the king could read for himself if he would confiscate the future correspondence between Köckritz and Tamm.[58] Regrettably for the historian and for Stein, he did not; we therefore have no indication of what, if anything, Beyme said. Once again we must take note of the fact that the king, by ignoring and thus tolerating those about him who brazenly conspired against the royal ministry, only encouraged the enemies of the ministers he had appointed.

Chasot's letter adds a second image to complete a stereoscopic picture of the contact between Beyme and Tamm and thereby, incidentally, tends to put Beyme's activities in a somewhat better light. While Chasot's account portrays Beyme as somewhat less enthusiastically pro-French, the revelation of his opportunism remains nevertheless intact. With Stein's fate yet uncertain, it is not much to his credit that he avoided an open meeting with Soult. There is no evidence to show that he also shunned the secret meeting with the French agent that Tamm had arranged. But Tamm, in any case, had significantly overstated the consistency of Beyme's feelings toward the French. So consistent a loyalty to any cause on Beyme's

[58] Chasot to F.W., 12 October 1808, DZA, Rep. 92, F.W. III, B VIIa, 7c.

part would have been entirely out of keeping with his character. Tamm was so concerned with putting the best possible face on Beyme for the French that he had overstressed the point. But the effort itself had the favorite's approval. Tamm could produce Beyme's own correspondence to support his case. This flirtation with the French was only one aspect of the matter. Whatever it shows about Beyme's opportunism or possible disloyalty to Prussia, it can be taken as the major evidence of his connection with the *Hofpartei*. For this developing intrigue we have other bits of evidence as well. Stein's friend Stägemann, who had accompanied Goltz to Erfurt and returned with him to Berlin, also reported that Beyme was in touch with Köckritz and was put up to his activities against Stein by Köckritz. We do not know where he got his information[59] and, it should be noted, he qualified it by stating that this was but one among a variety of different opinions about Beyme. Some persons he had spoken to praised Beyme for remaining quietly in Steglitz; others saw him (rather indefinitely, it is true) as being up to something suspicious.[60] Curious, Stägemann had later gone out to Steglitz to see Beyme for himself, and there he had found him quietly, but unhappily, in seclusion.[61] At about the same time, British agents in Königsberg (who got at least some of their information from Gneisenau) wrote home that Stein, after his resignation, would be replaced by "Zastrow, Beym and that party."[62] Beyme himself, it should be noted, was meanwhile protesting in his

[59] Schleiermacher, who was in the midst of Berlin patriotic activities, saw Stägemann on 17 and 18 October, just after Stägemann's return from Erfurt (Schleiermacher Tagebuch, Schleiermacher Nachlass). Schleiermacher could easily have conveyed the story, having heard it from Chasot, who was leader of his cell of the insurrectionary group. Schleiermacher, after returning from Königsberg, had visited Beyme on 4 October. The purpose of his visit to Beyme, whom he apparently did not know personally, may have been to sound him out on the conspiracy on behalf of the chiefs in Königsberg.

[60] Stägemann to Altenstein, 26 October 1808, DZA, Rep. 92, Altenstein, B43.

[61] Stägemann to Frau Stägemann, 29 October 1808, Rühl, *Aus der Franzosenzeit,* 108.

[62] Drusina to FO, 20 October 1808, PRO, FO, Prussia, 64/78. Internal evidence in Drusina's letters indicates that he got part of his information from Gibson, another British agent, and that both got some of their material from Gneisenau.

letters (far too much to be taken as sincere) that he relished the life
of contemplatation and study which retirement permitted him.[63]
From this we may conclude retrospectively that Beyme's forwarding of Zastrow's complaints in the summer of 1808 had not been an
isolated episode and that this event fits the general plan of his actions that we have discussed. True, we cannot know for sure that he
did not sincerely wish to advance Zastrow's claim rather than promote an oblique attack on Stein from a place of relative safety. Such
devotion to Zastrow would, however, be difficult to conceive of
coming from Beyme. And we may now add with some confidence
that the complaints he had made against Stein in the fall of 1807
and the spring of 1808 and the cabal which the queen believed him
a part of can be placed into a pattern of maneuvers which had as
its purpose toppling the Stein ministry and securing his own return to power.

To explain Beyme's relation with the aristocratic opponents of
Stein we need postulate no more than an arrant marriage of convenience of the government's diverse opponents. Whereas the courtiers
knew for themselves that the king had long since accustomed himself to ignoring their complaints against Stein and his program,
Beyme was well known to all as the apple of the king's eye.[64] If his
majesty could be convinced that he could replace Stein with Beyme,
his own dilemma over the succession would be resolved. Beyme was
traditionally identified with the party of progress which the king
was resolved to back. With the aid of the friends of the French in
Berlin, Beyme would gain the confidence of the French authorities.
The Kakodämonen could also give him the reference of their group
of the aristocracy. Such a recommendation would be important to a
man so often belabored because of his base origin. Once in office, he
would owe his political debts to the courtiers. Perhaps they actually
anticipated sharing ministerial authority with him. In any case,
Stein, the chief architect of their travail and the driving force behind

---

[63] Beyme to Karl von Schroetter, 4 August 1808, "Briefe des Grafen von Beyme,"
944; and 7 December (falsely dated November) 1808, *ibid.*, 947.

[64] Stägemann to Altenstein, 26 October 1808, DZA, Rep. 92, Altenstein, B43:
Beyme's return was "the wish of the king's heart."

the reforms, would be out. As for Beyme, the proofs we have compel us to accept Tamm's explanation, partial and simplistic though it may appear: Beyme was possessed by an overweening hatred of Stein which stemmed from his removal from his place of influence at the minister's insistence. Stein's fall and his own return to the king's side offered fair embrocation to his psychic wounds. Of course he mistrusted Voss, Zastrow, and Kalckreuth, as he in turn was mistrusted by them. But in this instance, they did for him the devious and risky work while he, as his refusal to meet with Soult reveals, remained in the shadows of discretion.

We must of course reconcile this estimate of Beyme as a conniving opportunist in this affair with the general outline of his labors over the years for the King of Prussia. The reader will recall the denunciation of Beyme's "Jacobinism" recorded by Metternich a few years before. Not a trace of this sentiment seems to have remained, not even the vocabulary of radicalism. Rather, his letters from this period—few exist—are filled with banal generalizations about man's destiny which parallel the language and tone of Fichte's utopian moral and educational self-improvement schemes.[65] He was already the philosopher's patron and a sponsor of the project of the university in Berlin in which Fichte hoped to see some of his plans worked out. Probably he like Fichte had made the ideological passage from emphasizing improvement of the collective unit to establish the bases for individual betterment to stressing self-perfection through education for a better society. The latter pursuit almost anyone could applaud and many did, for it epitomized the intellectual spirit of the times in Prussia. Such a program, to be sure, was infinitely less dangerous to purse and place than Stein's bold attack on protected and established privilege.

A brief review of Beyme's ambidexterity on matters affecting the alignment of Prussia's foreign policy in the several years of crisis surrounding Jena will confirm the estimate of him, originally produced by Gentz, as an opportunist who masked a rather ruthless quest for power behind a facade of progressivist philosophical twad-

---

[65] "Briefe des Grafen von Beyme," *passim*.

dle. Before the war which brought about the collapse of the Prussian state Beyme was found among the supporters of the French alliance; after the war began he was the most strident of patriots. In the spring of 1808 he had accused Stein of being too yielding in the negotiations with the French; [66] in the fall of the same year he allowed Tamm to represent him as France's greatest friend in Prussia and, as we shall see, denounced the insurrection plan.[67] By the spring of 1809 he was to be equally violent as a proponent of war with France,[68] though he simultaneously portrayed himself to the French ambassador as pro-French.[69] By the spring of 1810, he was to advocate supplying troops to Bonaparte in Spain in order to win French friendship.[70] In view of this, about the most (or least) that might be said for Beyme, based on the total representation we have assembled, is that he was an adroit dissembler. How else, one might ask, could he have remained so long in power among the knaves and fools at the Prussian court?

Yet it must be added, in the name of caution, that we have described Beyme almost without reference to the historical circumstances in which his choices were made. It is certainly true that his connections with the Francophiles did gain for him the confidence of the French,[71] which was later to be important in his recovery of power. But in the light of other facts of the personal and political situation of the time, Beyme's supple manipulations do seem somewhat less reprehensible. First of all, we may be certain that he had learned very quickly that Napoleon had ordered that the King of

---

[66] See above, Chapter II, and Ritter, *Stein*, 245. On his anti-French position, see Salzer, *Eisenhart Denkwürdigkeiten*, 163–170.

[67] See below, Chapter VI.

[68] Gaede, *Preussens Stellung zur Kriegsfrage*, 84; Stern, *Abhandlungen und Aktenstücke*, 78; Lehmann, *Scharnhorst*, II, 264.

[69] Alfred Stern, "Documents sur le premier empire," *Revue historique*, XXIV (1884), 324. Stein had advocated a similar two-faced policy toward France in the summer of 1808, but this plan fits no pattern of duplicity.

[70] Leopold von Ranke, *Denkwürdigkeiten des Staatskanzlers von Hardenberg* (Leipzig, 1877), IV, 277.

[71] Davout to French ambassador in Berlin, 8 January 1809, Davout, *Correspondance*, II, 343.

Prussia not be allowed to return to his capital until Stein left the government. He may have given credence to the reports he heard from Königsberg that Stein would be forced out whatever might happen. We have no evidence that he actually tried to influence the king directly against Stein at this particular time. It was also not unreasonable for him to seek to use the chance offered by the aristocrats to earn the blessing of the French before he was called to political office. We have already seen to what extent a role in the government of Prussia depended on the favor of Napoleon. And it might be recalled here in extenuation of Beyme that even Hardenberg sought to ingratiate himself with the French for private purposes at this time and was to return to office in 1810 only after Napoleon's consent had been secured.[72] Bearing these circumstances in mind, Beyme's actions can be seen as a relatively legitimate part of the struggle for succession rather than an outright cabal against the government in alliance with enemies of the Prussian state.

But in late September, while Stein's enemies were seeking to facilitate his fall and arrange the succession among themselves, he was still in office in Königsberg, though much reduced in influence and prestige. Foreign Minister Goltz and Tsar Alexander were, as has been noted, dedicated to winning a pardon from Napoleon for him on the ground that the king could not dispense with his services. There was good reason to think they might succeed. Bonaparte, to all appearances, was too seriously in need of Alexander's friendship to refuse consideration to his plea for Stein.[73] And if he could be persuaded to grant the pardon, then all the efforts of the disparate coterie of Stein's enemies to bring down his reform government would come to nought.

The evidence available provides only a fragmentary picture of the proceedings at Erfurt with respect to Minister Stein, but what does

---

[72] Hardenberg to Davout, 17 November 1808, Cavaignac, *La Formation de la Prusse*, I, 502; Hardenberg to Davout, ? December 1808, AAE, CP, Prusse, 1808, 242, p. 477.

[73] Vandal, I, 431.

clearly emerge shows that Count Goltz, after being subjected to an initially violent outburst against Stein by Napoleon, got some indication that Stein could remain in or near the king's entourage. In view of the fact that Napoleon had actually been warned in advance by his agents in Berlin that such a plea would be made, we can ascribe his apparent hysteria to his taste for the dramatic. He had undoubtedly decided in advance that he would relent when he believed it to be worth his while. We do not know what the actual *quid pro quo* of the guarantee for Stein was. In this case, it may have been no more tangible than an unspoken promise of the tsar's continued good will.

As it turned out, Alexander was also given to understand by Bonaparte that, while Stein would have to give up the conduct of foreign affairs (as he had already done) once and for all, he could continue to manage Prussia's financial affairs. Foreign Minister Champagny, in a separate conversation with Goltz and Stägemann, amplified Napoleon's remarks to Alexander by saying that Stein could remain as finance minister, or, at the very least, as the king's private financial adviser. This he appears to have represented as the view of the emperor.[74] Champagny himself opined that Stein's embarrassment would put him on his good behavior and would increase his desire to pay off the reparations specified by the treaty.[75]

Several circumstances might have caused Bonaparte to tender the tsar his word on Stein's reprieve. The first, of course, was Napoleon's eagerness to preserve Alexander's friendship in what apparently would be a time of troubles. Bonaparte was seeking to stabilize, not upset, the peaceful condition of central Europe.[76] He could hardly

[74] Tatischeff, *Alexandre Ier et Napoléon*, 456–457; Goltz to Stein, 10 October 1808, *Stein Br.*, II (2), 888–889; Stägemann to Altenstein, 10 October 1808, DZA, Rep. 92, Altenstein, B43; Hassel, I, 276.

[75] D'Aubier to Goltz, 4 December 1808, DZA, Rep. 63, 88, No. 598.

[76] Vandal, I, 440; Caulaincourt, *Mémoires*, I, 273–274. The conciliatory attitude Napoleon had taken toward Brockhausen and Prince William in the interview of 15 September (Prince William to F.W., 15 September 1808, Hassel, I, 489–492; Brockhausen to F.W., 16 September 1808, DZA, A.A.I., Rep. 1, No. 1234) apparently reflected his new pose. It may have been in this interview that Bonaparte was first presented with the idea that Stein's presence in the government was necessary to pay the reparations. So Brockhausen argued, in any case.

afford to drive the Prussian king over the brink of despair and into the arms of the Austrian war party. For all his arrogance and disdain of the Germans and his undoubted awareness that Frederick William was anything but decisive, even he could not have estimated the extraordinary limits of the king's tolerance. Finally, he could see that the garrisons which, by treaty, he would leave behind in the fortresses (Glogau, Küstrin, and Stettin) astride the Oder River spine of post-Tilsit Prussia could effectively keep the Prussians on the tether. The loyalty of the Warsaw Poles and the King of Saxony to France would firmly reinforce from the east and south the security system which he was attempting to construct to guard central Europe during his absence in Spain.

The final accord between the two emperors at Erfurt was nevertheless difficult to achieve. When completed, as it turned out, a good share of the concessions had been made at the expense of the hapless Prussians, whose cause, entrusted to the tsar, whose first concerns were elsewhere, and to the ineffective Goltz (it was Goltz who unaccountably told Soult and almost everyone else he met in Berlin that the king would ask through Alexander to be allowed to keep Stein),[77] was least well represented.[78] Harsh reparations, abated only slightly in return for a cession of further territory to Westphalia, and a strict limit on the size of the Prussian army were the fundamental clauses agreed to by Alexander just as in the convention of the eighth of September. But Stein's withdrawal from the government was neither demanded nor conceded. Alexander, on a return visit to Königsberg while in transit to St. Petersburg, brought instead the promise that Stein could remain among the king's advisers. During his visit, Alexander seems to have purposefully marked Stein out for a great deal of personal attention. Goltz and Stägemann had, in the meantime, stopped in Berlin to negotiate with Daru the final

---

[77] Soult to Napoleon, 28 September 1808, Cavaignac, *La Formation de la Prusse,* I, 500; Report of French spy to Soult, 29 and 30 September 1808, AG, CGA, C2 79; Report of French spy to Soult, 7 October 1808, *ibid.,* C2 80. See also Hatzfeldt Tagebuch, 27 and 28 September (falsely dated August) 1808, APMW, Archiwum Hatzfeldt'ów, No. 743.

[78] Bignon, VII, 12–14; Vandal, I, 440; Ritter, *Stein,* 350.

conditions of the payment of the reparations and the dates of the withdrawal of the forces of occupation. Stein had meanwhile tried to resign for the second time (October 18), again unsuccessfully.[79] He had done this only two days before Alexander arrived bringing final confirmation of the reports that he could retain some place in the government.[80] As a direct result of Alexander's strong support, Stein put forward his name to the king as a candidate for the post of counselor of state in the succeeding administration. The king would have to fill such posts in the new ministerial organization in addition to naming the usual cabinet

[79] Stein, IS, 18 October 1808, *Stein Br.*, II (2), 898–899.

[80] A courier who arrived with Goltz's letter of 10 October 1808 (*Stein Br.*, II (2), 888–889) probably provoked Stein's effort to resign. See also Drusina to FO, 18 October 1808, PRO, FO, Prussia, 64/78; D'Aubier to Goltz, 4 December 1808, DZA, Rep. 63, 88, No. 598; Theodor von Schön, *Weitere Beiträge und Nachträge zu den Papieren des Ministers und Burggrafen von Marienburg Theodor von Schön* (Berlin, 1881), 50; Ritter, *Stein,* 611n21; Hatzfeldt Tagebuch, 13 November 1808, APMW, Archiwum Hatzfeldt'ów, No. 743; Stern, *Abhandlungen und Aktenstücke,* 6–7; Hassel, I, 300n1, quoting Hrubi to Stadion, 23 November 1808, from Wiener Staatsarchiv. The evidence makes quite clear the importance of Alexander's visit and the return of Prince William (on him, see Stein, Autobiographische Aufzeichnungen, 12 July 1811, *Stein Br.*, III, 546–547) for the change in Stein's plans. Stein visited him on 24 October, just after Alexander had left. See Delbrück, *Tagebuchblätter,* 24 October 1808, III, 87. Compare Drusina to FO, 18 and 20 October 1808 (before Alexander's arrival) with 23 October ("Baron Stein's departure is now doubted. It is even said that the Emperor Alexander will give him a knighthood.") and 27 October ("It is now asserted that Stein will remain in office.") 1808, PRO, FO, Prussia, 64/78. See Gibson to FO, 21 October 1808 ("Stein may not withdraw, but merely give up the nominal title of prime-minister"), PRO, FO, Prussia, 64/79. Compare Clausewitz to Marie von Brühl, 20 October 1808 (Clausewitz, *Briefe,* 173) —"Der Minister vom Stein wird vermutlich (darüber ist fast kein Zweifel mehr) das Ministerium verlassen"—with Clausewitz to Marie von Brühl, 27 October 1808 (*ibid.,* 177): "[Stein] hat zwar jetzt die Aussicht, nicht ganz von uns zu scheiden und bloss seine Verhältnisse zu ändern." Davout also heard from his agents in Königsberg that Alexander had given testimonials on Stein's behalf (Davout to Napoleon, 23 November 1808, Davout, *Correspondance,* II, 320–321). There is one other indication that Napoleon had withdrawn his demand (at least for the record) that Stein must leave office—his instructions for the new French ambassador in Berlin, dated October 1808, made no mention that he should press for Stein's withdrawal, although they singled out the following issues as important: Prussian adherence to the disarmament clauses of the final treaty to be signed on 5 November 1808, and Prussia's strict compliance with the rules of the Continental System (AAE, CP, Prusse, 242, pp. 336–337).

ministers for standard portfolios like finance, interior and foreign
affairs; and a place on the council (*Staatsrat*) for Stein would allow
the king to solicit his financial advice. The ministers themselves
Stein hoped to see named from among his most trusted colleagues.[81]

Thus Stein had eased past the great foreign policy crisis of September. He was seemingly confident of an important post in the
government which would follow. He could hope with the same
assurance that his program would be carried on by his successors.
Yet in the month since the publication of Stein's errant letter had
opened up to his enemies the prospect of a successful cabal to bring
down his government, his party, and his system, they had intensified
and organized their attacks upon him. Hatzfeldt and Voss, with
ever increasing frequency, supplied Soult with stories, most of them
fallacious and exaggerated, which were intended to put Stein, his
party, and his legislation in the worst possible light. These supplemented the even more fantastic accounts of the corps of spies maintained at French expense. Soult, still under Bonaparte's orders to
have Stein put out of the Prussian government before the French
occupation ended, had piled up a giant dossier on the minister. He
had one secret contact in Königsberg, a disgraced member of the
Prussian Foreign Service who was related to Zastrow, Legation
Counselor Bielefeld. He attributed his status, that of a prisoner on
parole, to Stein. In revenge for the wrongs he thought had been done
to him as well as for pecuniary reward he turned over to a French
go-between much personal information on Stein. Most of what he
wrote he apparently got from Köckritz, but we cannot say whether
or not that foolish old courtier knew what would become of the information he supplied.[82]

We may gain some idea of the lengths to which Voss and his
allies would go to bring down Stein when we understand that it was
Voss, the chief Prussian representative in Berlin, who malevolently

[81] Stein, IB, [October, 1808], *Stein Br.,* II (2), 910–912.
[82] Report of French spy to Soult, 21 and 29 September 1808, AG, CGA, C2 79. On
the identification of Baron Bielefeld, see F.W. to Louise, 10 June 1807, *Briefwechsel
Luise–F.W.,* 329 and n. 3; and Ranke, *Hardenberg Denkwürdigkeiten,* II, 239, and
III, 442.

linked Stein to J. A. Sack, his own predecessor as leader of the
negotiating commission; it will be recalled that the French had
caused Stein to put him out of office as a notorious Francophobe the
previous spring. The day after Hatzfeldt and his friends learned that
Goltz and Alexander had been charged with seeking a reprieve for
Stein they appeared before Soult's deputy, General St.-Hilaire, to
denounce such an idea as an incalculable evil for Prussia. They asked
that their words be conveyed to the Emperor Napoleon.[83] Any lurking suspicions that Canon Tamm had simply played the role of
honest broker in seeking to bring Beyme to the attention of Soult
should be dispatched by the treasonable indictment of the King and
Queen of Prussia which he, a Prussian subject and still officially
employed as a courier, supplied to Soult in late September. Tamm
said that neither the king, who acted out of ignorance, nor the queen,
whose chief motive was her hatred of France, was unaware of the
sinister happenings in Königsberg.[84] Not inaccurately, he revealed
that the Prussians were already negotiating with the Swedes, the
Austrians, and the English. The French had gotten a similar report
a month before from another Prussian, a Counselor Rühl, recently
returned to Berlin from Königsberg. Rühl had attacked Goltz at
that time as the author of the French discontents. He said that Goltz
passed the intelligence he got from the capitals of Napoleon's enemies through his wife directly to the queen. Her majesty, served by
the violently anti-French (octogenarian was not part of his descrip-
tion) Countess Voss, he denounced as the soul of the opposition to
France in Königsberg.[85] Tamm subsequently made the same charge.
Unfortunately, we can only speculate upon the causes which brought
Tamm and Rühl to undertake their acts of treason.

Voss, Hatzfeldt, Beyme and Zastrow, Tamm and Rühl in Berlin;
Kalckreuth, Köckritz and Bielefeld in Königsberg—with such a
party of desperate political foes, time servers, and traitors against

---

[83] Soult to Napoleon, 28 September 1808, AG, CGA, C2 78.
[84] Report of French spy to Soult, 30 September 1808, AG, CGA, C2 79.
[85] Soult to Napoleon, 31 August 1808, AG, CGA, C2 79. Spelled "Ruhl" in the
French copy.

him, and to back him only a king who preferred to avert his gaze from impending disaster, how long could Stein's or, for that matter, any responsible ministry have endured? One visiting patriot, aghast at the exchange of gossip and information he had witnessed at court, wrote to his superior to admonish complete silence on all political topics, for "one can learn anything and everything here."[86] Inflated with government secrets and hortatory misinformation by some of the very highest officials and former servants of the Prussian government, it is scarcely to be wondered at that the French authorities in Berlin, shaken by the Spanish affair, had become possessed by the specter of imminent popular uprising and passed their fears along to Bonaparte. In the eyes of those Prussians who supplied and enhanced this intelligence, where did preventing evils to the monarchy by devious methods end and treason begin?

To these disparate enemies of Stein, his fall from power and the end of his influence was the first step, *sine qua non,* toward the refounding of the political strength of the pro-French and antireform parties in Prussia. But at least Stein knew something of his open enemies and was warned about others associated with them; to a certain extent he could counteract their intrigues. At the very same time, a far more dangerous group with its main strength among those he had once counted as his friends and allies in Königsberg was already preparing to rise up against him. Against the secret machinations of the latter group, he was to be found defenseless.

[86] Röder to Götzen, 13 September 1808, Vaupel, 583.

V

THE PLOTS THICKEN

"Everything has been tried to bring about Stein's fall, [but] the goal has not been attained," Scharnhorst observed late in October.[1] Indeed, it seemed that Stein's position was stronger than at any time since the letter affair had become a public scandal. Using the new prestige which Alexander's return visit had won him, he struck back directly at his personal foe, Voss, as he had struck against Kalckreuth in September. New reports of Voss's subservience to the French party had recently come to Königsberg.[2] On the first of November, Stein asked the king to replace Voss with Voss's own predecessor, Sack, in Berlin. He noted blandly that the commission for negotiation with the French which Voss headed would, at the end of the occupation, come to the end of its useful life in any case.[3] The king agreed to the suggestion.

The news of the nomination of Sack[4] and the naming of Count Chasot[5] to be commandant of the city of Berlin at the conclusion of the occupation then presented the mortified Voss with a splendid opportunity to work upon outraged French sensibilities. The French had not forgotten that Sack had been excluded from his post at their insistence in the spring. Chasot (who, as we know, though the king

---

[1] Scharnhorst to Götzen, 27 October 1808, Scharnhorst, *Briefe*, I, 350.

[2] Most recently in Stägemann to Altenstein, 26 October 1808, DZA, Rep. 92, Altenstein, B43.

[3] Stein, IB, 1 November 1808, *Stein Br.*, II (2), 914.

[4] On Sack, see Bassewitz, *Die Kurmark, 1806–1808*, I, 440.

[5] On Chasot, see Heinrich Ulmann, "Graf Chasot inmitten der preussischen Erhebungspartei im Jahre 1811," *Forschungen zur brandenburgischen und preussischen Geschichte*, XIV (1901), 141–150. On the duel between Chasot and the French officer in July see Agnes von Gerlach to Leopold von Gerlach, 9 July 1808, Schoeps, *Aus den Jahren preussischer Not*, 357–358. On Voss and his friends as enemies of Chasot see Sack to Stein, 23 November 1808, *Stein Br.*, II (2), 986.

did not, was leader of the Berlin cell of the insurrectionary organization) was already notorious. He had killed a French officer in a
duel in July after the Frenchman had insulted the King of Prussia.
Tamm and Voss were undoubtedly able to make certain that the
French recalled these facts.[6]

Faced with the prospect of being replaced by one of his bitter foes,
Voss redoubled his efforts to convince the king that Stein in office
was a standing offense to the French. He supplemented his daily
supply of special reports with articles from the pro-French Berlin
papers.[7] According to Stein, the king received forty-two messages
from Voss in one day's post.[8]

Apparently throwing all caution aside, Voss became an open enemy of the head of the government. Petitions from as far away as
East Prussia attacking Stein and protesting the alteration in the relation of peasant and landlord as well as the reorganization of the
military were delivered to him. The idea, apparently, was that he
would forward them to the king.[9] So bold and powerful had he and
his party become in Berlin, in fact, that he was mentioned there
openly as Stein's successor.[10]

Chance then delivered to Voss a golden opportunity to strike a
blow against Stein. Count Goltz and his party, en route to Königsberg, were forced to stop in Berlin in order to negotiate the details
of the final settlement with Daru. Goltz had some knowledge—how
much is uncertain—that Stein had gotten at least an oral reprieve at
Erfurt. In his own letter to the minister, which followed his inter-

[6] Davout to Napoleon, 23 November 1808, Davout, *Correspondance*, II, 320–321;
Sack to Stein, 23 and 26 November 1808, *Stein Br.*, II (2), 984–986, 994–996.

[7] Stern, *Abhandlungen und Aktenstücke*, 18.

[8] Stein's marginal note to Sack to Stein, 23 November 1808, *Stein Br.*, II (2), 985.

[9] Circular letter (probably a counter-petition to that of Stein's friends) of the
nobles of Kreis Mohrungen (in East Prussia). An attack on Stein's proreform articles
(presumably those of 26 September and 29 September 1808) is in DZA, Rep. 92a,
Voss, B5. See also the nobles of Kreis Mohrungen to Stein, 17 November 1808,
ibid.

[10] Stägemann to Stein, 7 November 1808, *Stein Br.*, II (2), 933–934; Nagler, IB,
28 November (falsely dated 8 November—see Chapter VI, note 6, below) 1808,
ibid., 925–927.

view with Bonaparte, he had reported that Stein would have to leave the ministry, but could remain near the king as a private adviser. He evidently did not know that Alexander and Prince William had carried a definite promise that Stein could stay in some official capacity in Königsberg. But this difference between Alexander's and Goltz's view of Stein's future was really only one of degree; just how officially could Stein continue to advise?

Goltz had been convinced by what had transpired in Erfurt that Prussia must henceforth rely on Alexander's magnanimity—a conviction evidently underscored by the tsar's assurances that what Prussia gained at Erfurt was the result of his intercession—and integrate itself completely in the French system in Europe. This predisposition coupled with his uncertainty about Stein's future thus made him ready to be worked upon by Voss and the Francophiles as well as by the French command.[11]

Since the first of November, Marshal Davout, who bore the ominous title Duke of Auerstädt, had directed all French forces in Germany. Fresh from the command in Warsaw and Breslau, he was determined, and perhaps ordered directly, to crush all manifestations of anti-French feeling.[12] His zealous forwarding of the wildest sorts of rumor as verified evidence has already been noted. Maybe during his long tour of duty in Warsaw, so recently liberated from Prussian *Ordnung,* he had been pumped full of the long-standing hatred of Slav for Teuton. Whatever the explanation, he had been overexcited in his dealing with the Prussians in Silesia and overcredulous in assessing any report of unrest. He now promised the tortures of

[11] See Goltz to Stein, 10 October 1808, *Stein Br.,* II (2), 888–889, and Hassel, I, 276, on Goltz in Erfurt and his attitude of dependence on Alexander. For Stein's rebuttal of the argument for dependence on France see Stein, IS, 18 October 1808, *Stein Br.,* II (2), 899. An example of the contact beyond the routine meetings with the French authorities was the attendance of Goltz and his party at a dinner and parade given by Davout, the French commandant in Berlin, on 6 November. Voss was also invited: see *Vossische Zeitung* (Berlin), 8 November 1808. The convention had been signed by Goltz and Daru on 5 November (Haussherr, *Erfüllung und Befreiung,* 243).

[12] Davout to Napoleon, 29 October 1808, Davout, *Correspondance,* II, 315; Davout to Prince de Neufchâtel, 1 November 1808, *ibid.,* 316.

hell-fire to those Prussians who were considering emulating the Spaniards. Their towns, he warned, would suffer the fate of the Spanish city of Burgos, which, for its support for the Spanish insurgents, had been cruelly razed and given over to rape and pillage only a short time before.[13] The fate of resisting Spaniards was, of course, graphically registered by Goya.

Davout identified Stein, on the basis of what he had read of the seized letter, as "the sheet anchor of Prussia." Probably spurred on by Voss and his party, he now steadfastly insisted to Goltz (in spite of the emperor's assurances to the contrary to Alexander) that Stein must withdraw completely from every connection with the Prussian government before the evacuation could take place.[14] This insistence recalled Napoleon's original order to Soult of the tenth of September, but completely reversed what Alexander and Goltz had been told in Erfurt. If Davout had heard what the two emperors had agreed with respect to Stein he evidently chose to ignore it. With Napoleon off to Spain and the tsar now far away in St. Petersburg, matters between Prussia and France were being disposed in Berlin. And Davout seems to have had his own view of how Franco-Prussian relations should be conducted.

There is another equally plausible explanation of Davout's seemingly unilateral renunciation of the promises given at Erfurt. Bonaparte may have told Alexander one thing, Davout and Daru another. Nothing about Napoleon's word had ever been sacred. He had often made treaties only to break them immediately. True, he could no longer act in the case of Stein as brazenly as he did at the height of his power in 1807, when he demanded point-blank Hardenberg's resignation. Could it be that this time he thought it best to concede

[13] Lehmann, *Stein*, III, 10n1, quoting *Moniteur*. The same threat was made by Davout in Leipzig (Hatzfeldt Tagebuch, 16 December 1808, APMW, Archiwum Hatzfeldt'ów, No. 743). See below, Chapter VI.

[14] Davout to Napoleon, 22 September 1808, Davout, *Correspondance*, II, 294; Bassewitz, *Die Kurmark, 1806–1808*, II, 376; Stägemann to Stein, 7 November 1808, *Stein Br.*, II (2), 923–925; Stein to Stadion, 13 January 1809, *ibid.*, III, 20–23; Stern, *Abhandlungen und Aktenstücke*, 10n1, quoting Hrubi's report of 23 November 1808, in Wiener Staatsarchiv.

the point Alexander wanted, obtain some counterconcession, then withdraw his dispensation later through his generals? With Alexander gone, the King of Prussia would yield as he had on numerous occasions. In the confusion of the situation, blame for the change would fall on his marshals and could even be put by him, if explanations were later necessary, upon them. Napoleon could imagine (and he was correct) that without Alexander present, Frederick William would do as little as he had done in July 1807, when Bonaparte had singlehandedly reversed the treaties of Tilsit and Königsberg for his own benefit. There is additional evidence that this was Napoleon's method, for within two weeks of the termination of the Erfurt negotiations, Daru, on Bonaparte's orders, again increased the reparations the Prussians were to pay. Still later, in December, in a fit of pique, the emperor proscribed and outlawed Stein, asking no one for approval.[15]

By the seventh of November, only a week after Davout took over the Berlin command, Stein had heard unofficially that the French were making his withdrawal from office a condition for ending the occupation of Berlin.[16] With this he saw his newly restored hope of remaining in office vanish. He reckoned that Goltz, whom he estimated as too docile, would officially present Davout's demands in Königsberg on his return. He immediately offered his resignation for the third time within two months.[17] In seeking to resign at this time, Stein had one other motive. On the preceding day the king had decided to postpone issuing the stirring reform proclamation

[15] See below, Chapter VI. Note that Stein's withdrawal was not mentioned in the treaty of 5 November 1808.

[16] Davout took over his command on the first of November. On the same day the removal of Stein as the *conditio sine qua non* for the French evacuation was known to the Austrian chargé in Königsberg (Hassel, I, 300, quoting Hrubi to Stadion, 1 November 1808, in Wiener Staatsarchiv). Hrubi's information must have been derived in a roundabout way from the letter of Stägemann to Altenstein, 26 October 1808 (DZA, Rep. 92, Altenstein, B43), or perhaps from Nagler's report of his journey to Berlin (see below, text at note 48). Stägemann's letter to Altenstein would have arrived in Königsberg on 1 November. Stägemann's letter of 7 November 1808 (*Stein Br.,* II (2), 923–925) probably conveys information derived from the meeting he and Goltz had with Davout on the sixth of November.

[17] Stein, IB, 7 November 1808, *Stein Br.,* II (2), 920.

Stein had written out until the new ministry (in which it had been planned that Stein would be a counselor) could give its assent. His immediate withdrawal at this time would serve, so the minister must have decided, to hasten the cause of reform. The sooner he left office, the faster a new cabinet could activate the reform proposals.[18]

Meanwhile, Stein's friends had already opened a campaign to counteract the work of the Kakodämonen. Because Goltz had not yet arrived in Königsberg to report directly, Stein's future was not yet certain in the eyes of his partisans. Poems calculated to win public support for "Ur-Granit Stein" appeared in the Königsberg newspapers.[19] (Professor Süvern, the Fichtean and lecturer on the art of statecraft, was the author.) Petitions in support of the minister and his program were circulated for signatures; a number bearing the names of many citizens including some important nobles came in from Königsberg, Braunsberg, and Kreuzberg, all in East Prussia.[20] Some effort was also made to discredit Goltz as a diplomat and thereby impeach what he would report upon his return. Stein's caustic comments on Goltz's personal weaknesses in his own letter of resignation of the seventh were a part of this attempt.[21] But such efforts were useless. King Frederick William was hardly willing to face renewal on Stein's account of the uncertainty which had characterized the months before the convention. Hence he would not follow one plan suggested to him: that he insist that Napoleon either confirm or deny what Goltz had been told by Davout.

---

[18] F.W. to Stein, 6 November 1808, *Stein Br.*, II (2), 919; compare Ritter, *Stein*, 357.

[19] In *Stein Br.*, II (2), 908.

[20] The petitions had been circulated by Hans von Auerswald according to a report to Nagler, 10 December 1808, DZA, Rep. 89a, L, 14½, Bl. 24. One is printed in *Stein Br.*, II (2), 913–914; others are in DZA, Rep. 89a, L, 14½. See above, note 9.

[21] Stein, IB, 7 November 1808, *Stein Br.*, II (2), 920. See also Nagler, IB, 28 November (falsely dated 8 November—see below, Chapter VI, note 23) 1808, *ibid.*, 925–927. On Goltz see Gneisenau to Götzen, 24 November 1808, Vaupel, 727; Gneisenau to Stein, 14 January and 15 February 1809, in Karl Griewank, ed., *Gneisenau: Ein Leben in Briefen* (Leipzig, 1939), 104, 107–108. See below, Chapter VI, note 11.

By this time Stein was showing obvious signs of emotional strain from the uncertainties about the reform programs to which he was wholly dedicated yet saw imperiled by his prospective fall from power and influence. The uncertainty seems to have weakened his self-possession.[22] We cannot wholly blame him; in the environment of dishonesty and treachery at court bearings would have been difficult to find. He knew there were traitors all about him (though he did not yet know who his most dangerous opponents were), and he began to mistake his friends for his enemies. It must be recognized that his attack on Goltz was neither judicious nor fair. He even began to suspect the completely loyal Stägemann simply because he wrote from Berlin what Goltz had heard from Davout. Stein wanted tact on many occasions; [23] the fusty political air of Königsberg in November surely did nothing to repair that frailty.

But, as we know, hesitation was the king's second nature. Beyond this, he did not want Stein's withdrawal from the ministry, when it came, to be taken for a repudiation of the reform movement, which, as he well knew from the number of attacks on it from the side of Voss and the courtiers, was at a critical stage.[24]

He faced a further quandary; if Stein must go, who could replace him? The king could not employ Voss and the Kakodämonen as long as he was committed to reform. Ex-minister Baron Karl August von Hardenberg, whom he esteemed, was under Napoleon's orders not to come within forty German miles of the royal headquarters. Beyme would have been his first choice, yet Beyme was (as far as he knew) opposed on personal grounds by everyone. But the real cause of the king's procrastination at this time was known

---

[22] See below, Chapter VI. Stein seems to have been moving at the time to the more religious attitude and violent patriotism which ultimately led him to take service with Alexander in order to fight Napoleon. See Ritter, *Stein,* 384.

[23] Radziwill, 293, 297. Schön in his biographical sketch of Scharnhorst recounts some incidents of Stein's behavior (Schön Nachlass, No. 61, pp. 12–13). See also Niebuhr to Moltke, 15 January 1809, in Dietrich Gerhard and William Norvin, eds., *Die Briefe Barthold Georg Niebuhrs,* I (Berlin, 1926), 530; and Beyme to Karl von Schroetter, 14 October 1807, "Briefe des Grafen von Beyme," 941.

[24] D'Aubier to Goltz, 4 December 1808, DZA, Rep. 63, 88, No. 598.

only to a few insiders: he was awaiting secret advice from a quarter Stein did not suspect.

Here I must digress to account for the interim activities of former chief minister Hardenberg. His story and that of his friends Altenstein and Karl Friedrich Nagler bear most on the remaining history of the Stein government in Prussia. Both Altenstein and his brother-in-law, Nagler, had come into the civil service in Ansbach-Bayreuth, a territory that had fallen to Prussia in 1792. There they served under Hardenberg when he administered the area for the king. After Hardenberg left office in July 1807 Altenstein and Nagler remained in Prussian employ. In Riga, in September 1807, Altenstein and Hardenberg had collaborated in turning out the Riga *Denkschriften,* lengthy memoirs on governmental organization and reform. Both programs strikingly illustrated the attitude of the enlightened civil servant toward organization of the state. Altenstein's memoir was, in addition, overlaid with a thick and almost impenetrable veneer of Fichtean philosophy.[25] Soon thereafter, Altenstein returned to the seat of government, becoming one of Stein's chief aides in the early days of the reform government. Both he and Nagler continued to hold Hardenberg's esteem but were from that time regarded as members of Stein's party.[26] Nagler, in fact, seems to have been privy to, and perhaps involved in, the insurrection plot. In August 1808, at the height of the conspiratorial fever, Stein proposed him for the important job of con-

[25] On Altenstein see Eduard Spranger, "Altensteins Denkschrift von 1807 und ihre Beziehungen zur Philosophie," *Forschungen zur brandenburgischen und preussischen Geschichte,* XVIII (1905), 471–517. On Hardenberg see Hans Haussherr, "Hardenbergs Reformdenkschrift Riga 1807," *Historische Zeitschrift,* CLVII (1938), 267–308; and Haussherr, *Die Stunde Hardenbergs,* 24–25.

[26] Haussherr, *Erfüllung und Befreiung,* 209. On Nagler see Haussherr, *Die Stunde Hardenbergs,* 26–27; and Schön Tagebuch, 29 November 1808, Schön, *Papiere,* II, 47. A popular view of Altenstein as Stein's right-hand man is Agnes von Gerlach to Marie von Raumer, 9 December 1808, Schoeps, *Aus den Jahren preussischer Not,* 364. British agent Gibson, who got some of his information from Gneisenau, considered Altenstein as Stein's "confidential friend" and Nagler as being in Stein's party in September (Gibson to FO, 24 September 1808, PRO, FO, Prussia, 64/79).

fidential agent to Vienna to make arrangements there for the combined attack on France.[27] Hardenberg, who could not return to the court because he was anathema to Bonaparte, took up quarters in Tilsit, at the far end of Prussia. There in the provincial town he fidgeted and devoted himself to his personal memoirs. An active statesman who enjoyed and profited from life at court—the facts that he owed his office in 1807 to Alexander's, and in 1810 to Queen Louise's, intercession, testify to his effectiveness as a courtier—Hardenberg was utterly unhappy in his enforced retirement. His political career appeared to be destroyed; his fortune was slowly dissolving through the neglect of his estates in French-occupied Germany.[28] But he was afraid to return to the zone of French control lest he fall victim to the fate of the Duke of Enghien.

From Tilsit, Hardenberg corresponded actively on personal and political matters with Altenstein and Nagler. Flatteringly, the two former subordinates continued to solicit his opinions and advice on matters of government even during his exile. Nagler was now handling the queen's personal correspondence. His wife had also been installed in her majesty's retinue. Both had, in consequence, access to inside gossip and sources of information. Both had won some influence with Countess Voss. Through her they subsequently secured the confidence of the queen.[29] Thus Nagler was in a position to furnish Hardenberg with news and insights into the conduct of political affairs at court. This exchange of letters with Altenstein and Nagler became the main source of Hardenberg's political information. What he witnessed of affairs in Königsberg he witnessed through their eyes; what they neglected to report remained by and large beyond his ken.

Hardenberg's letters to Altenstein and Nagler from this period

---

[27] On Stein's confidence in Nagler see Stein, Denkschrift, 11 August 1808, *Stein Br.*, II (2), 811. See also Princess Wilhelm to Prince Wilhelm, 25 August 1808, Wuppermann, 144; and Ritter, *Stein,* 356.

[28] Hardenberg to Altenstein, 11 June 1808, DZA, Rep. 92, Altenstein, B14.

[29] *Allgemeine Deutsche Biographie*, XXIII, 233–236. On Nagler's wife see Stein, Autobiographische Aufzeichnungen, 12 July 1811, *Stein Br.,* III, 548.

reflect his preoccupation with financial stability of the state; this, after all, was the major domestic and foreign problem Stein faced. One theme constantly recurred in his letters: only the end of uncertainty about the future of the state could bring about the re-establishment of credit and confidence in the government.[30] He appears to have worried at one and the same time about the fiscal soundness of the state and the closely related problems of his own neglected estates in the west.

As early as February 1808, just after his return to Prussia, Hardenberg had sought Stein's permission to transfer his residence from Tilsit to Marienwerder, just across the Vistula from the French-occupied area of West Prussia. At the same time, he seems to have hoped that Stein would intercede with the French and with Jerome of Westphalia to win him permission to return to "Germany" (as East Prussians often called the Reich proper). Through Nagler, Stein had asked Hardenberg to remain in Tilsit in order not to annoy the French unnecessarily. He was about to embark on the Berlin negotiations and he obviously feared the effect of Hardenberg's presence so near the French zone of occupation. He proposed that Hardenberg work through Sack in Berlin or his own brother to obtain the passports he needed.[31] If Hardenberg fretted over Stein's unhelpful answer, there is no evidence of it. He knew that success in Stein's plan to bring about a treaty with the French would best ensure a quick return to the west. But after this time Hardenberg no longer corresponded with Stein, and he carried on his campaign to leave his place of exile through the medium of his correspondence with his former aides, Altenstein and Nagler.[32]

Hardenberg nevertheless remained completely loyal to Stein. He supported the "policy of fulfillment" Stein took up toward the ob-

[30] Hardenberg to Altenstein, 23 April, 9 July, and 14 September 1808, DZA, Rep. 92, Altenstein, B14.

[31] Stein to Nagler, 19 February 1808, *Stein Br.,* II (2), 661.

[32] See the Altenstein to Hardenberg and Nagler to Hardenberg correspondence (in DZA, Rep. 92, Altenstein, B14, and *ibid.,* Hardenberg, K57) for the spring and summer of 1808.

ligations to France as the best possible approach remaining to the half-occupied nation.[33] He occasionally criticized some specific actions taken by Stein, but never attacked the minister generally. He regretted, for example, Stein's long stay in Berlin because there the minister could not keep in touch with affairs in the temporary capital.[34] He thought Stein's appointment of Voss, his old enemy, dangerous and foolish.[35] But the exile of Beyme from the court won his complete support, for he mistrusted the favorite as much as Stein did.[36] The nature of the reform program that Stein was attempting got his general assent, although he probably disagreed with some of the details. Thus he counseled Altenstein to urge firmness on Stein in dealing with the military reforms and care in drafting the new organization for the government,[37] in both cases advice honestly given and sincerely meant.

In this correspondence between Königsberg and Tilsit appears the first evidence of a widening gulf between Stein and Altenstein. The long-standing community of interest had permitted Altenstein and Nagler to confide discontents to Hardenberg which they dared not openly confess.

Stein had relied on Altenstein greatly at the beginning of the reform period, but after the first minister's return from Berlin (which Altenstein had welcomed),[38] an estrangement had grown between them.[39] Theodor von Schön later claimed that the cause of this was nothing more than an ancient grudge.[40] We may speculate, however, that Stein had begun to seek advice elsewhere, turning from Al-

---

[33] Hardenberg to Stein, 24 February 1808, *Stein Br.,* II (2), 666–667.

[34] Hardenberg to Altenstein, 23 and 30 April 1808, DZA, Rep. 92, Altenstein, B14.

[35] Hardenberg to Altenstein, 21 May and 14 September, DZA, Rep. 92, Altenstein, B14; Hardenberg Tagebuch, 20 May 1808, *ibid.,* Hardenberg, L29.

[36] Hardenberg to Altenstein, 11 June 1808, DZA, Rep. 92, Altenstein, B14.

[37] Hardenberg to Altenstein, 11 June 1808, DZA, Rep. 92, Altenstein, B14.

[38] Hardenberg to Altenstein, 11 June 1808, DZA, Rep. 92, Altenstein, B14; Altenstein to Stägemann, 17 May 1808, Rühl, *Aus der Franzosenzeit,* 97–98.

[39] For background material on Altenstein's and Nagler's opposition to Stein see Lehmann, Stein, II, 592–593; Hassel, I, 292. See also note 26, above.

[40] Schön Nachlass, No. 61, p. 12.

tenstein to depend more on Schön, Schroetter, and Stägemann and on the military reformers who were proponents of the insurrection.[41] Though a convinced opponent of Napoleon, Altenstein had no interest in the latter adventure or in any other plan which sought to capitalize on popular passions. By the fall of 1808, he was admitting opposition to Stein's scheme to end patrimonial justice. Stein and Altenstein had also come to disagreement on the ministerial reorganization plan. Altenstein preferred a strong "Premierminister" as the king's chief adviser whereas Stein now wanted equal departmental ministers and ultimate advisory authority to the king given to a general council of state.[42]

But in spite of agreement with Altenstein on many of the principles and proposals dealing with leadership and organization of the Prussian government, Hardenberg gently though firmly resisted the opportunities to attack Stein offered by Altenstein's persistent innuendo and criticism. Hardenberg, purposefully ingenuous, counseled him to swallow his unhappiness and hurt pride to work with Stein for the programs they all supported. To Altenstein's increasingly direct complaints he replied generally or evasively or pinned the cause of the discontents on the French occupation.[43] It is patent that Altenstein's purposes—to gain Hardenberg for an ally in his disagreements with Stein—were not lost on the shrewd ex-minister.[44] But for one reason or another, either because he disagreed with Altenstein's judgment about Stein's conduct of affairs, or because he was unwilling to risk Stein's displeasure if his comments became known, Hardenberg brushed aside the rather persistent cavils. Not an iota of evidence exists showing Hardenberg's conscious disloyalty to Stein before he learned of the seizure of Stein's fateful letter by the French.

---

[41] Hassel, I, 291–292; Ritter, *Stein,* 239; Hardenberg to Altenstein, 24 April 1808, DZA, Rep. 92, Altenstein, B14.

[42] Ritter, *Stein,* 230–231, 239–250.

[43] Hardenberg to Altenstein, 24 and 31 August, 7 and 14 September 1808, DZA, Rep. 92, Altenstein, B14.

[44] Hardenberg Tagebuch, 5 September 1808, DZA, Rep. 92, Hardenberg, L29; Hardenberg to Altenstein, 7 September 1808, *ibid.,* Altenstein, B14.

As soon as the letter episode opened, however, Hardenberg took up a markedly different stance toward Stein. He jumped to the conclusion (incorrect, as we have seen) that the affair had brought about the harsher peace terms Prince William had signed. He was sure, though he had no recent evidence for his assumption, that Prussia could not pay the sums imposed upon her by the new convention. He agreed at first with Nagler, whose original resolve was to temporize until the results of Alexander's intercession for remission of the harsh financial terms became known.[45] The later news that Napoleon had showered presents and testimonials of friendship on Prince William before the prince's departure stilled some of his first apprehension.[46] We may indeed surmise from the fact that Hardenberg gradually came over to join the proponents of ratification that he had cooler second thoughts on the treaty's terms. He must also have observed that the ratification of the convention promised him a return to his own estates in the west before the onset of winter made travel difficult. If Prussia could meet the financial conditions of the treaty, domestic stability and the refounding of credit, both his ardent wishes, would be attained.

Now we may see the importance of Nagler's newsmongering. Nagler had gone to Berlin in late September and had returned in early October.[47] The object of his journey I cannot discover, but while there he must have met those who insisted that the French would force Stein out. Hardenberg had heard the same rumor by the seventeenth of October, just in time for Nagler to have sent him the information after his return to Königsberg.[48] This would seem to establish the fact that it was Nagler who was one of the first to bring this report back to Königsberg.

It was at this time that Nagler himself seems to have decided to work behind Stein's back to hasten his fall and to promote his re-

[45] Hardenberg Tagebuch, 26 September 1808, DZA, Rep. 92, Hardenberg, L29.
[46] Hardenberg Tagebuch, 30 September 1808, DZA, Rep. 92, Hardenberg, L29.
[47] Countess Voss, *Sixty-nine Years at the Court of Prussia,* 151. In 1807 Nagler had been named to the official Prussian delegation in Berlin. See Bassewitz, *Die Kurmark, 1806–1808,* I, 440.
[48] Hardenberg Tagebuch, 17 October 1808, DZA, Rep. 92, Hardenberg, L29.

placement by Altenstein. The background of this decision, aside from the rather obviously increasing hostility between Altenstein and the chief minister, is wholly obscure. As is the case with so many of Stein's contemporaries, Nagler's figure is almost lost in the shadows of history. If we knew more of him, we could perhaps follow him through the events which helped to form his resolution to act against the head of his government. Was his change of allegiance the consequence of some personal demand for influence which grew out of his newly acquired importance inside the royal entourage? Or was his decision to conspire against Stein the result of a calculating assessment of the momentary configuration of circumstances in October 1808? One set of facts would tip the balance in favor of the latter explanation: his associations in Königsberg before his trip were among the patriots, as far as can be determined.[49] His secret, but increasingly active, opposition to Stein seems to have developed suddenly out of the opinions he fetched home from Berlin. Did he then, like Beyme, decide early that Stein was out and thereafter concoct his schemes with that notion firmly fixed in his mind?

Hardenberg, of course, remained innocent of the knowledge of the causes of Nagler's change of heart. He did not detect the new posture in the political news Nagler supplied. But in Nagler's letters to him, none of the details of the French hostility toward Stein were missing. And Hardenberg heard that he, too, a violent Francophobe in Napoleon's eyes, had also been implicated as a plotter in the uprising plan. Nagler was undoubtedly the source of this story.[50] By repeating this canard Nagler managed, whether or not intentionally, to convey to Hardenberg the impression that Stein's indiscretion had revived French hostility toward him. We need not doubt that this increased Hardenberg's annoyance with Stein and his bungling. Even before this, Hardenberg himself had come to judge Stein's embarrassment as a "frightful accident" and "extremely imprudent."

[49] See, for example, Schleiermacher Tagebuch, 23 September 1808, Schleiermacher Nachlass; and above, note 26.

[50] Hardenberg confided his thought to his diary on 17 October 1808 (DZA, Rep. 92, Hardenberg, L29), just in time for him to have read this in a letter from Nagler, who returned on the fourteenth from Berlin.

In his estimation, if the minister sought to remain in office he would menace the conclusion of a treaty of peace. In such circumstances, Bonaparte could be expected to behave with small-minded rage, "as he did toward me." [51] He had assumed in his own case that Bonaparte's proscription was irrevocable.[52] Viewing Stein's position as identical with his own, he concluded that the option put to the minister would be to resign or be forced out. Hardenberg, far removed from the political scene and supplied with even fewer facts than the government in Königsberg possessed, simply could not understand that the circumstances of the previous year existed no longer. What Napoleon could accomplish by fiat at Tilsit he could not attain in a Europe revived by Spain's example. We have already seen how Stein's withdrawal from his offices to return to an advisory capacity in financial affairs was, at least officially, the small balm for his wounded ego which Napoleon settled for at Erfurt.

Unconversant with all this, and with the assurances Alexander later gave to Frederick William, Hardenberg had adopted the conviction that Stein must withdraw. This he wrote in a letter to Altenstein as if it were settled fact.[53] Perhaps he really longed, though he could never admit it to himself, to see the compromised troublemaker out. Stein and his foolish letter may now have loomed before him as the main obstacles to peace and his own return to the west. In any case, Altenstein read Hardenberg's conclusions just a few days before Nagler returned from Berlin with his own new plans.[54] No doubt he was quick to tell his colleague, who was now prepared to develop his own plans about the succession to Stein, of Hardenberg's views. Nagler, with his connections, was correctly placed to insinuate Hardenberg's private opinions on Stein's position into the court.[55]

[51] Hardenberg Tagebuch, 26 September 1808, DZA, Rep. 92, Hardenberg, L29; Hardenberg to Altenstein, 8 October 1808, *ibid.*, Altenstein, B14.

[52] Hardenberg to Stein, 24 February 1808, *Stein Br.*, II (2), 666. On the banning of Hardenberg, see Bassewitz, *Die Kurmark, 1806–1808*, I, 407.

[53] Hardenberg to Altenstein, 8 October 1808, DZA, Rep. 92, Altenstein, B14.

[54] Countess Voss, *Sixty-nine Years at the Court of Prussia*, 151.

[55] Radziwill, 295; See Stein, Autobiographische Aufzeichnungen, 12 July 1811, *Stein Br.*, III, 548.

The queen, we know, had originally supported Stein through the letter affair with her special appeal to Alexander. By the time Stein's ministry had run its course, she had become his enemy. This change of heart we may attribute most of all to the constant disparagement of Stein by the court cabal to which were later added the insinuations of Nagler and perhaps of Altenstein as well. Certainly one other key to understanding the alteration of her opinion toward her former favorite is to recognize her increasing awareness of the difficulties which had overcome the Prussian state since Stein's misadventure. Equally important was the role played by Hardenberg. Altenstein and Nagler knew that the queen would give attention to Hardenberg's views. They had had ample opportunity to gauge her trust in the fallen minister and his political considerations. Hardenberg, with his courtly manner and bearing, his conciliatory attitude and his posture of personal devotion to her, was the opposite of the bluff, direct Stein.[56] Knowing this, Nagler must have realized that he could use Hardenberg's private opinions to destroy Stein by making them known to the queen. We may surmise that he did so sometime in late October and that the queen carried Hardenberg's words to the king.[57] If this is correct it would explain part of the hardening of the king's attitude toward Stein after the departure of Alexander. This state of affairs had baffled Stein, who attributed it to Goltz and his news from Berlin.

So far we have been speculating about the exact course of events, though the existing evidence supports our line of thought. The remainder of the story, by contrast, is clear. Nagler, with the connivance of Altenstein (who daily was a guest at Stein's table),[58]

---

[56] Radziwill, 294. The queen's esteem for Hardenberg (at Tilsit) was expressed thus: "Ne cédez pas [Hardenberg], au nom de Dieu, ce serait le premier pas vers l'esclavage" (Louise to F.W., 30 June 1807, in Paul Bailleu, "Die Verhandlungen in Tilsit," *Deutsche Rundschau*, CX (1902), 206). See also Louise to F.W., 27 June 1807, *ibid.*, 43.

[57] Radziwill, 293.

[58] See Ritter, *Stein*, 581n3. Ritter used the Tagebuch of Staatsrat von Rhediger from the Breslau archive; I have not seen it.

arranged with the masterful touch of an old conspirator to use Hardenberg himself, as his opinions had already been used, against Stein. Since the summer, Hardenberg had planned to meet with Altenstein and Nagler somewhere between Königsberg and Tilsit.[59] Circumstances had never permitted the meeting. But in October, after Erfurt, Hardenberg, seeing the treaty being finally arranged, prepared to leave Tilsit before winter set in to move to his estate in the Mark Brandenburg. Altenstein and Nagler eagerly took over the advance preparation of the journey. They had already been entrusted by him, since Stein's rebuff in the same matter, to secure for the ex-minister and his equipage the requisite passports. Beyme joined in, obviously at their behest, to make use of his new good relations with the French to secure the necessary documents for his ostensible enemy—proof that the brothers-in-law in Königsberg were in communication with Beyme, though the correspondence between them has been lost. Beyme, we may surmise, was seeking to mend fences all around. It would be particularly important to him, if a change in the placement in the ministries were impending, to have more friendly relations with the influential ex-minister. At last the long-postponed meeting between the three friends, Altenstein, Nagler and Hardenberg, was arranged for Hardenberg's stopover on the way west near Königsberg.[60] The whole trip was kept a tight secret, for the Napoleonic injunction that Hardenberg remain at least forty miles from the court had not been withdrawn.

The plans for the secret rendezvous were carefully laid. With boldness and cunning, Nagler and Altenstein plotted a surprise which they concealed from everyone in Königsberg but the king and queen. In secret, the royal party would be brought together with Hardenberg during his passage near Königsberg. There is no indication that Hardenberg was informed in advance of all the details of the scheme. There is, indeed, some reason to doubt that he was told

[59] See the Altenstein to Hardenberg and Nagler to Hardenberg correspondence (in DZA, Rep. 92, Altenstein, B14, and Hardenberg, K57) for the summer and fall of 1808, passim.
[60] Hardenberg to Altenstein, 8 October 1808, 24 October 1808, DZA, Rep. 92, Altenstein, B14; Nagler to Hardenberg, 29 October 1808, ibid., Hardenberg, K57.

of the planned meeting itself until just before it occurred. To each side Altenstein and Nagler could argue that absolute privacy must be maintained lest both parties appear to be conspiring against the French in violation of the prohibition. The logic of this seemed manifest. Away from their court and other eyes—behind a screen, as it were—the king and queen could hear for themselves Hardenberg's views of Stein and the make-up of the government to replace his. It was not the French alone, however, who would be deceived. The mask of silence, as the brothers-in-law knew, would hide the plot from Stein and his friends just as well.

Full of guile, the two disloyal bureaucrats planned to use the testimony of their half-informed, half-misled ex-chief against the head of the ministry he had helped name. Hardenberg's political opinions were already completely familiar to Altenstein and Nagler; [61] moreover, he had supplied them with a paper outlining his point of view on internal affairs in which we may assume he also made suggestions for places in the new ministries.[62] They undoubtedly surmised that Hardenberg would be overwhelmed by the emotional impact of the meeting with his sovereign and the queen and flattered by the attention which his advice still commanded. His gratitude to them would reach far. And the king, who since the letter episode had no one on whom he could rely, would doubly value the suggestions of Hardenberg, especially when they were supported by the queen's high regard for the exiled baron.

On the tenth of November, only a few days after Stein had heard that the French commanders were now insisting on his withdrawal, Hardenberg passed incognito through Königsberg. Just before his departure from his inn on the shore of the Pregel River outside the city, Altenstein and Friedrich von Schladen, the Prussian ambassador in St. Petersburg and a confidant of the two schemers, opened

---

[61] Hardenberg to Altenstein, 24 October 1808 (DZA, Rep. 92, Altenstein, B14): "With regard to Stein and the measures under consideration I agree with you completely." Hardenberg's innocence in the preparation of the plot is suggested by the fact that he had at first been against keeping the visit secret. See Hardenberg to Altenstein, 2 November 1808, *ibid*.

[62] Hardenberg to Altenstein, 5 November 1808, DZA, Rep. 92, Altenstein, B14.

to him the prospect of meeting later that very day with the king and queen. At this time he was probably reassured that what Nagler had hinted and what he had assumed was true: the French had demanded Stein's resignation. The same afternoon on the road between Königsberg and Preussisch Brandenburg where he had planned his original rendezvous with the counselors,[63] he met with the royal party, accompanied by Nagler.[64] At first sight, the king and Hardenberg began to weep. There in the frosty air of the gray November landscape Hardenberg easily worked his old charm on the king and queen.[65] Another meeting with the king, who was again, it should be noted, to be accompanied by the queen, was planned for the next day. That evening Altenstein, who had guessed or learned what opinions the king would solicit from Hardenberg—it will be recalled that either Nagler or his wife was able to get information directly from the queen or through Countess Voss—supplied Hardenberg with a letter of advice.[66] It began with an effusive statement of the esteem the brothers-in-law held for Hardenberg. In the preamble, Altenstein recorded at some length his own unselfish devotion to what he always called "the good cause" (*die gute Sache*).

What Hardenberg said to the king and queen on the next day, Altenstein reported, would be of great importance in the final determination of affairs. Hardenberg should, he advised, put forward ideas on reorganization of the government, on the conduct of affairs past and future, and on placement in the ministries. The last was extremely important for, Altenstein surely knew, Stein had proposed him for a relatively unimportant position in a list of ministerial candidates that he had presented to the king in October.[67] To Hardenberg, however, Altenstein disclaimed personal interest; rather, "the

[63] Hardenberg to Altenstein, 5 November 1808, DZA, Rep. 92, Altenstein, B14.
[64] Hardenberg Tagebuch, 10 November 1808, DZA, Rep. 92, Hardenberg, L29.
[65] Radziwill, 295; Hassel, I, 294.
[66] Hassel, I, 294; Altenstein to Hardenberg, 10 November 1808, DZA, Rep. 92, Hardenberg, K30.
[67] Stein, Aufzeichnungen zum Organizationsplan [October 1808], *Stein Br.*, II (2), 910–912. See Altenstein's complaint in Nagler, IB, 28 November (falsely dated 8 November—see below, Chapter VI, note 23) 1808, *ibid.*, 925–927; and Altenstein to Hardenberg, 10 November 1808, DZA, Rep. 92, Hardenberg, K30.

good cause" was his sole concern. But in this document, Altenstein's purposes clearly emerge through his circuitous bureaucrat's German. First of all, Hardenberg should take a firm stand against the effort by Stein "to stir up the people" (*die Bearbeitung des Volkes*), by which Altenstein meant such things as seeking popular support for the reforms.[68] All institutions, he complained, were being turned upside down in an effort to outdo the French in popularity. From such methods, which included the use of secret societies (that is, the Tugendbund, which Altenstein knew Hardenberg had been against from the outset),[69] dangerous and unknown consequences might emerge.

These remarks, as well as Hardenberg's attitude toward the petitions being signed on Stein's behalf,[70] show how closely Altenstein's thinking paralleled Hardenberg's. Altenstein had by letter and undoubtedly in conversation as well been able to estimate the exile's opinion before he made his proposals. Both thought of governing correctly as the work of wise absolutists directing steady change toward definite goals.[71] Altenstein plainly wanted to slow the work of reform to a bureaucratic pace, a mode of operation congenial to himself as well as to the personal requirements of the king. If Hardenberg made an appeal of this sort to reasonable moderation it would point up the contrast between Altenstein's cautious approach and Stein's revolutionary incitements.

Altenstein must have heard that Beyme and Schön had already been mentioned for places in a new ministry. He asked Hardenberg to take a definite stand against them. The king longed for Beyme, said Altenstein, but the French would take umbrage at his nomination. Altenstein made Beyme out to be a supporter of Stein's radical "French" (that is to say, "revolutionary") system. Obviously no one

---

[68] See the article prepared by Stein and approved by the king in the *Königsberger Zeitung*, 26 September 1808, in *Stein Br.*, II (2), 876–878; on the military reforms in the *Königsberger Zeitung*, 29 September 1808, see Hassel, I, 584–587.

[69] Hardenberg to Altenstein, 27 July 1808, DZA, Rep. 92, Altenstein, B14.

[70] Hardenberg Tagebuch, 28 October 1808, *ibid.*, Hardenberg, L29.

[71] See above, note 25; and Simon, *Failure of the Prussian Reform Movement*, ch. iv. The Riga *Denkschriften* of Altenstein and Hardenberg are in Winter, 302–566.

outside the Kakodämonen knew about Beyme's most recent change of political views, for Beyme, as we know, was doing his utmost to ingratiate himself with the French and to dissociate himself from the compromised Stein. In any case, Altenstein ran on, delivering what he undoubtedly regarded as the *coup de grâce,* Beyme was untrustworthy. He would usurp the king's confidence and would then alienate the king from the rest of the ministry. All this, of course, was nothing new to Hardenberg, who had thought the same thing of Beyme for a long time. Altenstein also had a positive suggestion: instead of allowing the role of trusted adviser to fall to Beyme, why not let Nagler (who had done so well already) win the king's confidence? From this position he could accomplish something for what he termed "our" views. The king now trusted him, as did the whole court. From a good post (as, for example, Vice-General Postmaster) he could be on the lookout for cabals.

As for Schön, Altenstein continued, he had recently won a much greater place in Stein's confidence; Stein himself had proposed him as his own replacement as Minister of Finance, the very post Altenstein was ultimately to take.[72] He was, Altenstein charged, completely a dependent of the "radical" system (the same, undoubtedly, as Stein's "French" system), more devoted to the people than to the king. Though (Altenstein probably meant "because") he was Stein's candidate, the king was not for him; and in his case, Hardenberg's condemnation would surely be decisive.[73]

Altenstein's counsel was followed directly by Hardenberg in his conversation with Frederick William and Louise at Kallgen on the eleventh. In a report covering the conversations which he submitted formally from his stopping place at Braunsberg a day later, Hardenberg noted that he had argued that Stein's complete withdrawal was a first necessity. His ostensible grounds for expressing this view were Goltz's opinion that the financial agreement and the withdrawal of

---

[72] See Schön Tagebuch, 30 November 1808, Schön, *Papiere,* II, 50.
[73] Altenstein to Hardenberg, 10 November 1808, DZA, Rep. 92, Hardenberg, K30. The king's judgment of Schön, dating from 1810, is in Paul Haake, "König Friedrich Wilhelm III., Hardenberg und die preussische Verfassungsfrage," *Forschungen zur brandenburgischen und preussischen Geschichte,* XXVI (1913), 540.

the French were contingent upon Stein's retirement. He had then suggested that the succeeding ministry should be made up of Altenstein in finance, Goltz in foreign affairs, and Count Alexander von Dohna, who would hold the portfolio of interior. Dohna, an East Prussian Junker known to be of liberal persuasion, was then chief of the provincial court administration in Marienwerder, the seat of government for the rump of West Prussia remaining outside the French occupation. Nagler had been suggested for a post as aide to Dohna; the two opponents, Scharnhorst and the conservative Hinrich Christoph von Lottum, were to continue their work in the war ministry. Chancellor Karl Wilhelm von Schroetter, the brother of the East Prussian Provincial Minister, was nominated to take the post of Minister of Justice.[74]

Hardenberg recommended definitely that Beyme not be re-employed. To give satisfaction to the king's feelings for him (and to reward him for his service to Hardenberg?), the favorite was recommended as a candidate for elevation to noble status and was to receive the Order of the Red Eagle. Following Altenstein's prescription almost to the letter, Hardenberg attacked the "incautious and ill-timed agitation (*Bearbeitung*) of the people," by which he appears to have meant not only the campaign in favor of the reforms being conducted in the popular press, but also the Tugendbund's incitement of public virtue and national spirit. All of this, he warned, might result in revolutionary activity if it were not halted.[75]

At this point Hardenberg, his service to Altenstein and Nagler, and, as he understood it, to the monarchy, performed, drove off to Marienwerder on the Prussian side of the Vistula to await the French evacuation or permission to cross into the French zone. There he wrote his request to Davout to be allowed to return to his estate near Berlin. Beyme, we may presume, had already paved the way for French acceptance. The nature of Hardenberg's appeal gives some indication of the state of his mind at this time; it must also

---

[74] What Hardenberg had in mind by proposing the division of the war office between Scharnhorst and the conservative Lottum, who were more often than not opponents, is unfathomable.

[75] Hardenberg, Denkschrift, 12 November 1808, Hassel, I, 567–575.

have reflected the attitudes he held when he advised the king. The French, he said, need have no qualms about allowing him to return. The new relation between France and Prussia had no more stalwart champion or firmer supporter. Had he not, he inquired rhetorically, once resigned in order to alleviate an embarrassment in French and Prussian relations?—a line of argument which sounds very much like that Tamm had made on Beyme's behalf. Hardenberg's adjustment to the new order in Europe appears to have been as complete as Beyme's.[76] Could Hardenberg's evident new loyalty to France have been a move for tactical purposes only? Perhaps, but he stayed with the system until 1813, when circumstances made the French alliance no longer tenable for Prussia. Hardenberg, whatever might be said of him as minister before 1807, seems to have learned to lean with the wind in foreign affairs. The taste for power and influence, like that for the good food and wine and elegant company he craved, could not easily be forgotten.

A stopover in Marienwerder permitted Hardenberg the opportunity to seek out Count Dohna to discuss the ministerial post with him. This chance, we may suppose, had not escaped Altenstein's and Nagler's attention. Dohna had little to recommend him for his post aside from an outspoken liberalism (Schön bitterly confided to his diary his conviction that neither Altenstein nor Dohna would have come into office had they not been "Baron" and "Count" respectively).[77] Stein's support for Dohna, for whom he also had contemplated the interior ministry,[78] had apparently been based on esteem for his well-meaning, positive attitude and his patriotism; Altenstein and Nagler, on the other hand, wanted him as a coworker because of his malleable character. He would easily serve as their foil.[79] Harden-

---

[76] Hardenberg to Davout, 17 November 1808, Cavaignac, *La Formation de la Prusse,* I, 501–502. Hardenberg's new point of view was duly noted by the French diplomatic authorities; see Hardenberg to Davout, ? December 1808, AAE, CP, Prusse, 1808, 242, p. 477.

[77] Schön Tagebuch, 30 November 1808, Schön, *Papiere,* II, 50.

[78] Stein, Aufzeichnungen zum Organisationsplan [October 1808], *Stein Br.,* II (2), 910–912. On Dohna see Haussherr, *Die Stunde Hardenbergs,* 23–24.

[79] So Ritter, *Stein,* 359–360, suggests. But he does not take note of the fact that Stein had originally proposed Dohna.

berg found Dohna completely overcome by the unexpected honor he had received and somewhat reluctant to take on the task, which he justly considered as beyond his powers. Hardenberg's purpose was to persuade Dohna that he should work hand in hand with Altenstein and Nagler. His views and theirs should be one in ministerial affairs, Hardenberg told him. To this adjuration, Dohna most solemnly gave his promise to Hardenberg while honest tears came to his eyes.[80] The edifice of power built by the bureaucrats, probably engineered by Nagler, thus appeared secure.

Hardenberg's stay in Marienwerder also coincided with the return of Goltz and Stägemann to Königsberg with the information on Stein provided by the French authorities in Berlin. They also carried the final terms negotiated for the financial settlement and the termination of the occupation. Theirs was the report which, as we have seen, the king was awaiting. Goltz and his party had left Berlin on the ninth of November on what was normally a five-day journey by coach to Königsberg.[81] But Goltz did not, for some reason, hasten his journey in keeping with the urgency of the report he carried. The gist of his discussions and the outline of the convention he had evidently sent ahead. It is apparent that he did not know that the timing of the change of administration would in part depend on his personal report of the conversations with the French authorities. Hardenberg saw Goltz in Marienwerder at least once, on November 16. But not until three days later, on the nineteenth, had Goltz completed the one-day trip from the Vistula to the seat of government.[82]

The meeting of Goltz and Hardenberg was probably of little consequence in the circumstances, except to ease any last doubts Hardenberg may have had about his recent advice to the king to part with Stein. Goltz, we may assume, told Hardenberg directly that the French demanded Stein's ouster. At the same time, Goltz was able to learn from Hardenberg that the king would continue to

[80] Hardenberg to Altenstein, 27 November 1808, DZA, Rep. 92, Altenstein, B14.
[81] Stägemann to Frau Stägemann, 8 November 1808, Rühl, *Aus der Franzosenzeit*, 109; *Spenersche Zeitung* (Berlin), 10 November 1808.
[82] Hardenberg Tagebuch, 16 November 1808, DZA, Rep. 92, Hardenberg, L29; Bassewitz, *Die Kurmark, 1806–1808*, I, 557, 560.

make use of his own services. Goltz must also have taken comfort from the fact that the controversial matter of Stein's dismissal had already been settled with the king. The tidings he bore would therefore present nothing wholly upsetting. Goltz, we may suppose, would not have wished to make an enemy of Stein.

At this point it is surely logical to ask why Hardenberg undertook these assignments on behalf of Altenstein and Nagler in which his own reputation, now at such a high point at court, was deeply involved. We have already noted his hasty, though honest, conclusion that Stein's case paralleled his own and that Napoleon would insist on the removal of Stein as he had once demanded his own exile. This conviction had probably been strengthened by the advance information Nagler and Altenstein had given him about what Goltz and Stägemann had learned in Berlin. But his letters indicate that in the back of his mind also lay a subconscious longing for peace and security. While arguing that Prussia needed a period of tranquillity he may, without quite realizing it, have been considering the fact that his own fortunes also required a period of quiet and fiscal stability. Stein was thus more than a simple obstacle to the French evacuation of Berlin. His insurrection plan, if carried forward, would mean chaos and profound uncertainty. Even the reforms, which now involved direct appeals to the people, could be seen as dangerously unsettling. Altenstein had argued this point and Hardenberg had been receptive to it. The same outlook, it should be remarked, was shared by Voss and the conservatives. Friendship with France was the demand of the hour. Only this would bring peace and stability to Prussia. In contrast, the patriots, with their demagogic insurrection scheme, called for gambles and a renewal of parlous times. To Stein, Scharnhorst, and Gneisenau, who had made their original choice before the news of Napoleon's decision for a treaty with Prussia had arrived, the alternatives had appeared to be different. But even now, a long-term adjustment to alliance with France and a damping down of popular reform seemed to them too high a price to pay for quietude. In the final analysis, the profound differences in outlook between Hardenberg and Stein's party stemmed from a fundamental inclination deep within the individual personalities. Where Hardenberg was predisposed to caution, Stein and his friends tended toward boldness.

But even more than his feeling for the expedient, the hope of material gain, and a fundamental difference in temperament had carried Hardenberg to what was really a personal betrayal of Stein.[83] By nature vain, he relished the succulent flattery which Altenstein and Nagler heaped upon him. That his memoranda were well received by the conniving brothers-in-law and by the royal couple was no doubt a satisfaction to a minister-in-exile so long without power. The very fact that the interview with the king and the queen extended to a second day at their request apparently goaded his vanity. Hardenberg had always been a cavalier and a man for the ladies.[84] Hence the very presence of the lovely Louise and her rapt, if moony, attention to his observations—the same coquette, it should be remarked, she had played before to Stein, Napoleon, and Alexander —no doubt increased his longing to return to the king's service. Can we doubt that the receptivity of the king and the ministers-to-be to Hardenberg's ideas and memoranda fostered his hope that his counsel would be often sought in the future? Can we doubt that the role of secret adviser to the new government was hinted at by Altenstein and Nagler, if not directly opened to him? Why else had he submitted the memoranda and his plans to Altenstein and Nagler before and after the meetings with the king and queen? Here was the opportunity for a new entree to power and influence: a temporary restitution of his political fortunes, an ultimate return to the spotlight of political action. Schön later said Hardenberg told him that had been his reason,[85] and we have no cause to question that report. If he seized the occasion to betray Stein, can we not surmise that he thought it in his own best interest as well as that of the state to do so?

[83] Compare Haussherr, "Stein und Hardenberg," 277.
[84] See Walter M. Simon, "Prince Hardenberg," *Review of Politics*, XVIII (1956), 88–99; and the interesting comparison in Simon, *Failure of the Prussian Reform Movement*, ch. iv, and Haussherr, "Stein und Hardenberg," *passim*.
[85] Pertz, *Stein*, II, 295.

But if this was his calculation, the situation worked out differently than Hardenberg had hoped. Altenstein and Nagler, as we shall see, gave increasingly less attention to Hardenberg's reports in the months that followed. Within a year and half, Hardenberg, disgruntled, worked for the fall of the bureaucrats as he had once worked against Stein. Can it be that Hardenberg decided, when he later inquired of himself why he had acted as he did to bring about the fall of Stein and his replacement in the king's council by Altenstein and Nagler, that he had been gulled? A Hardenberg would scarcely appreciate the dupe's role. Was the removal of Altenstein and Nagler that he effected in 1810 his revenge?

This is to jump ahead of the story, however. It is necessary to return to Stein and the court to observe the denouement of the plot as it looked to those who were not in on the secret of Hardenberg's meeting with the king and queen. In simple chronology, events had gone as follows: about the sixth of November Stein, as we know, had heard rumors from Berlin that the French authorities there were demanding his complete removal from all connection with the government. The next day he had tried to resign, but on the tenth, the very day of the first meeting with Hardenberg, the king had again declined to accept his resignation.[86] On the thirteenth, however, the more definite French demands which came forth from Goltz's talks with Davout became an open secret at court.[87] The gist of Stägemann's letter of the seventh, which reported these conversations, was that Stein could not remain in any capacity.

We may be sure that both the king and Stein gleaned from Goltz's and Stägemann's letters from Berlin some indication of the date of the French withdrawal. The very fact that Goltz made such a leisurely journey to Königsberg, stopping over for some days at his estate while en route, is a certain proof that he had already forwarded

[86] Stein, IB, 7 November 1808, Stein Br., II (2), 920; F.W. to Stein, 9 November 1808, ibid., 933.
[87] Delbrück, Tagebuchblätter, 13 November 1808, III, 96, which may refer to the arrival of Stägemann's letter to Stein of 7 November 1808, Stein Br., II (2), 923–925.

the outline of the terms he had agreed upon with Daru on November 5. Now that the French evacuation of Prussia to the Elbe was set for the first week of December, Stein and the king could estimate the number of days remaining to the ministry.[88] The news of Stein's resignation, they could calculate, would have to be in Berlin by the first of December. Assigning the last five days in November to the dispatch of the news to Berlin, Stein had approximately ten to twelve days more of political life. To this knowledge we may account the furious preparation of reform legislation in the last ten days of Stein's ministry; it was a last-ditch effort to enact as much as had been worked out of the new legislation before the impending end. Stein and his aides strove to put actual drafts of reform edicts in the king's hands for his quick ratification. They enjoyed considerable successes.

There is every indication that this drawing out of the tenure of the Stein ministry to its last possible moment was calculated by Stein and the king. It does not simply represent his majesty's usual tendency toward procrastination. Committed to reform, yet only too familiar with the chief political theme of Stein's open enemies, the king had feared from the onset of the letter affair that Stein's dismissal would be taken as an indication that he wished to reverse the reform movement. He wanted it made evident that Stein was leaving only because of French pressure, not because the king had turned against his legislative program.[89]

Between the seventeenth and the nineteenth of November the new ordinances for the organization of town government with popularly chosen officials were submitted.[90] The outline of the new central administration, on which Stein placed so much emphasis, followed on the twenty-fourth,[91] the same day his resignation was accepted.[92] But in spite of this emphasis on the reorganization plan for the ministry

[88] Bassewitz, *Die Kurmark, 1806–1808*, I, 557, 560.

[89] D'Aubier to Goltz, 4 December 1808, DZA, Rep. 63, 88, No. 598.

[90] Stein to Friedrich von Schroetter, 17 November 1808, *Stein Br.*, II (2), 945; KO to Stein and Friedrich von Schroetter, 13 November 1808, *ibid.*, 937–939.

[91] Stein, IB, 24 November 1808, *ibid.*, 987.

[92] KO to Stein, 24 November 1808, *ibid.*, 988.

and cabinet, the king accepted it only to postpone its pronouncement. A new government would come in, he said. Its opinion must first be heard.[93] But as we know already, Altenstein, scheduled to succeed Stein, was at odds with him on the question of the organization of the administrative cabinet. Stein's plan, with its council of advisers and equal ministries, was thus destined to be shunted aside. Altenstein and Nagler delightedly reported to Hardenberg this frustration of Stein's proposal as the first result of their work against his program.[94] Altenstein seems to have had a different scheme, which was never enacted for reasons which shall be made clear later. Under it, he planned to assume the role of chief minister, a post Stein judged him incompetent to hold.[95] In this, as it turned out, Stein was right, even though Altenstein never got the full responsibility he wanted.[96]

But before Stein could finish his last work in peace, his enemies on every side, uncertain as to the king's reasons for holding him in office, set up ever louder claques to shout him down. From Berlin came a tide of rumors suggesting that Voss would be Stein's replacement.[97] Yet Frederick William's method of operation, which was indirect as well as closemouthed, combined with Stein's feverish activity in the last week of his ministry, gave no one a hint of the final decisions the king had taken. The rumors of Voss's succession undoubtedly were spread by Voss himself as well as by his friends in Berlin and Königsberg. We have already noted how he had made himself responsible for reporting to the king the French displeasure with Stein. We may be sure that Voss had the complete cooperation of Davout in his efforts to attain a post in the ministry. Each seems to have fed on the other's rage against the government in Königsberg. Davout's suspiciousness, as we have seen, had always been unhindered by reference to canons of common sense; we may ascribe

---

[93] F.W. to Stein, 24 November 1808, *ibid.,* 987.

[94] Altenstein to Hardenberg, 25 November 1808, DZA, Rep. 92, Hardenberg, K30; Nagler to Hardenberg, 25 November 1808, *ibid.,* Hardenberg, F1.

[95] Schön Nachlass, No. 61, p. 37.

[96] Ritter, *Stein,* 248–249.

[97] Sack to Stein, 23 November 1808, *Stein Br.,* II (2), 984–986; Nagler, IB, 28 November (falsely dated 8 November—see below, Chapter VI, note 23) 1808, *ibid.,* 923–925.

much of his behavior to his arrogance and his insecurity. Voss, by this time, had simply allowed his passion to unhinge him; his forthcoming replacement by the patriots Sack and Chasot, as ordered by the king, must have been the final blow to his political sense of balance. We must recall that Voss had no knowledge of what was going on in Königsberg except for what he heard from his friends among the Kakodämonen; reports from that source would have been no help in bringing about a rational assessment of his political position. Now putting aside any fiction of loyalty which he might have maintained before, he began to participate openly with Davout in an active cabal against the head of his own government.

Before we recount the fantastic last acts of the tragicomedy played out in Berlin in November, thus bringing the chronicle of events on that scene up to the point where we left affairs in Königsberg, we must point out again how successful Voss, if not the facts of the situation themselves, had been in bringing the French command in Berlin over to opposition to the internal reform of Prussia. The connection between liberal reform, insurrection, and revival of Prussian military power had become as clear to Davout and the other French authorities as it was to Gneisenau. Thus they added the power of France which they wielded to the opposition to Stein's reform program.[98] The potential danger from such schemes to the French as well as to local landowners had already been established by the small peasant uprising in Silesia.

In addition, the same campaign on the part of Stein's friends which produced the poems on his behalf in the Königsberg newspapers added more evidence for Voss's campaign against Stein and his measures. In an article which appeared on the eighth of November in Berlin's *Spenersche Zeitung,* French-controlled and censored, we may detect the hand of Voss or one of his supporters as well as

---

[98] One English agent in Königsberg had also surmised that the French would oppose reform in Prussia for the same reason. See Alexander Gibson, Memorandum, "The Misfortunes of Prussia," December 1808, in PRO, FO, Prussia, 64/79. On Daru, Napoleon's intendant-general, who shared this view, see Sack to Stein, 23 November 1808, *Stein Br.,* II (2), 984–986.

the views of Davout. Those visionaries (*Schwärmer*—like Professor Süvern) who supported Stein were indicted as no better than the English agents Friedrich von Gentz and August von Kotzebue. They were accused of planning to lead Prussia from the principles of Frederick the Great. (This argument against Stein's reforms had been drearily repeated by his opponents, but it sounded incredible indeed coming from a French source.) In order to ridicule Stein personally, the letter episode was recounted once again.[99] In this article we see the beginning of the direct and open attack on Stein's domestic program which Davout mounted in the French-controlled press.

Like Voss's, Davout's wrath against the patriot-reformers had been brought to a new height by the naming of Sack and Chasot. This news arrived at the same time as a new incident broke over which the Königsberg government had no control. It proved to Davout, as it should to us, the extent of the hostility on the part of the ordinary Prussian citizen to the French. The coastal population near Memel had manhandled and mistreated the crew of a French privateer operating out of Danzig, the French-controlled "free city." The privateer had seized an American vessel just off the coast and had put ashore at Memel. There the French crew had been set upon by the local populace. The French consul claimed that the emperor's flag had been dishonored by the townsmen and by the Prussian soldiers sent to rescue the crew from the mob.[100] There were other incidents at the time involving the movement of couriers (that this was an issue after Stein's affair could be foreseen), the communications of the Saxons and French with their troops in the Grand Duchy

[99] *Spenersche Zeitung* (Berlin), 8 November 1808. The edict lifting compulsory membership in certain guilds in East and West Prussia was also published in the *Vossische Zeitung* on 10 November 1808.

[100] Voss to Daru, 11 November 1808, AAE, CP, Prusse, 1808, 243, pp. 341–343. See also Voss, IB, 14–15 November 1808, *Stein Br.,* II (2), 939; Goltz to Davout, 25 November 1808, DZA, Rep. 63, 88, No. 598; Goltz to F.W., 2 January 1809, DZA, Rep. 92, Nagler, 45. On Davout's unhappiness because Stein was still in office see Davout to Napoleon, 23 November 1808, Davout, *Correspondance,* II, 320–321.

of Warsaw, and authentic accounts of the secret rearmament of the Prussian fortresses in Silesia.[101] But it was the affair at Memel that put Davout well beyond reason.[102]

Davout's state of mind and his desire to strike out at the subversives about him led directly to the charges placed against Stein's friend, Chamberlain Troschke, and the Prussian privy councilor, Theodor Anton Schmalz. Bielefeld, the traitor under house arrest in Königsberg who supplied the French agents in Berlin with much of their information, had reported that Stein had secretly transferred to Troschke the title of his estate near Birnbaum (Międzychód), in the Grand Duchy of Warsaw. Troschke was arrested, and the news of the faked sale was turned over to the Polish authorities so that Stein's properties could be confiscated.[103] Thus Davout was at last able to attack Stein personally.

Schmalz's case was entirely different. He had been one of the very few Berliners inducted into the Tugendbund. Although he had resigned officially shortly afterward, he continued to receive literature from the headquarters in Königsberg, which he forwarded to the remaining members. His association with the "Frères vertueux" was sufficient in itself to make him a suspected person. But in early November he received a commission from Stein's adviser in Königsberg, Theodor von Schön, to write a pamphlet in favor of the elimination of patrimonial justice in the countryside. Like Stein and the king, Schön was interested in seeing the reform program popularized. Schön already knew Schmalz to be an opponent of these antiquated forms of justice. When Schmalz accepted the commission, Schön advised him to "sweeten the pill in honey," that is, to carry out his task in a way least offensive to those who might have some feeling of opposition to the measures.

[101] AAE, CP, Prusse, 1808, passim.

[102] Goltz to F.W., 2 January 1809, DZA, Rep. 92, Nagler, 45; D'Aubier to Goltz, 4 December 1808, DZA, Rep. 63, 88, No. 598.

[103] Report of French spy, 21 September 1808, AG, CGA, C2 79; Königliches Sächsisches Publikandum, Warsaw, 13 January 1809, Stein Br., III, 18–19; Autobiographische Aufzeichnungen Steins, 12 July 1811, ibid., 551–552. Compare Ritter, Stein, 617n29.

Schmalz prepared the pamphlet and submitted the corrected printer's copy to the censor appointed by the French, the Berlin pastor Hauchcorne.[104] Hauchcorne took immediate umbrage at the "revolutionary" notions advanced by Schmalz, who, it is true, set down some rather extravagant claims for a Prussian professor. But the spirit of the document was not far from that of the proclamation which Stein himself had worked out and submitted to the king in October. The French authorities got the printer's proof from Hauchcorne and seized upon it as more confirmation of the supposed plot to work up the people by means of popular legislation. Schmalz was immediately arrested.[105] Among his papers was found Schön's letter of commission.

The local press, following the official French account, reported that Schmalz had been jailed because he accepted the orders of persons in Königsberg close to the king who held "demagogic ideas" of agitating the people. Such words and phrases as "public freedom," "equality," and "removal of special privileges" had been used. Woe, the article continued, to the land which imitated the revolutionary excesses of France! Not every nation could expect to have the good fortune to find a Napoleon to make an end to chaos. Any monarch, so ran the final injunction, who wanted to end the threat to the public safety posed by such demagogues would get rid of those around him who recommended such a publication.[106] Sack, who sent word of Schmalz's imprisonment to Stein, pointed out that the connection between the French marshal's fear of an uprising, Stein's domestic policy, and the arrest of Schmalz was obvious.[107]

With Schmalz in jail, his letter from Schön with its reference to the "honeyed pill" was recalled. Someone, and it may well have been Davout himself, then set out to weave it into the whole cloth out of which his final indictment of Stein was to be manufactured.

[104] Bassewitz, *Die Kurmark, 1806–1808*, II, 367–368.
[105] Schleiermacher in his Tagebuch (in the Schleiermacher Nachlass) records 12 November as the date of the arrest.
[106] *Vossische Zeitung* (Berlin), 26 November 1808, quoting the French *Telegraph* of 25 November 1808.
[107] Sack to Stein, 23 November 1808, *Stein Br.*, II (2), 984–986.

The reader will remember that the arrest of Koppe, the Prussian courier, had netted the French several other letters, some of them personal in nature, from completely innocent parties. One such was the letter from the queen's chatty old confidante and Nagler's friend, Countess Voss, to Baron Wittgenstein. This had also been sent on to Paris with a copy of Stein's inculpating letter. A forgery was now, in mid-November, produced purporting to be extracted from the original. General St.-Hilaire, who gave the counterfeit to Davout, reputedly had learned of its existence from Voss. In it, the octogenarian dame advised the artful baron that if the Prussians really wanted to imitate "the brave people of the south," they must make use of "the chocolate of health." Going on, the fabricated letter asserted that the whole court took delight in a parrot which had been trained to repeat the phrase "The devil take the French." This letter bore the date, August 16, 1808, and was nothing more than a remanufactured version of the completely innocent note seized from Koppe.[108]

Davout, possibly gullible, but more likely malicious, actually asserted that Schön's "honeyed pill" and Countess Voss's "chocolate of health" were evidences of a widespread plot afoot to poison the Emperor Napoleon. Schmalz remained behind bars because he could not explain (in French) to his jailers just what Schön had meant by

[108] Who falsified the letter? Davout reported that he got it from General St.-Hilaire, who got it from the person who had given the tip on Koppe (Davout to Daru, 14 November 1808, AAE, CP, Prusse, 1808, 243, p. 297; Davout to Napoleon, 23 November 1808, AG, CGA, C2 81, also in Davout, *Correspondance,* II, 323). St.-Hilaire said he got the tip from Voss, which, if true, would suggest that Voss gave the original information on Koppe (Daru to Napoleon, 14 November 1808, Granier, *Aus der Berliner Franzosenzeit,* 306). I found only an extract from the counterfeit in AG, CGA, C2 81. The original of Countess Voss's letter of 16 August 1808 is there, in C2 79. As for the falsification, we can account for it as follows: if it was Davout's work, the intent was presumably twofold. First, it would serve to demonstrate to Bonaparte the correctness of Davout's harsh policy toward the Prussians. Second, it would convince the King of Prussia that the intrigue against France was still underway and that Davout knew about it. Davout, we may guess, seized on the forged letter because he saw that it was addressed to Wittgenstein, who was already suspect to Bonaparte for his earlier involvement with Stein. Davout would hardly have known that the writer of the original letter was an eighty-year-old dowager. Stern, "Documents sur le premier empire," 310, writing for a French readership, refuses to impugn the French marshal's reputation.

his singular phrase.[109] Wittgenstein, now twice implicated, was jail-ed, his dwelling searched, and his papers seized, in spite of his scoundrelly effort, of which more shall be heard, to blame the whole matter on Stein.[110]

In the name of this fantasy, Davout ordered Chamberlain D'Au-bier, who but five days earlier had come to Berlin as a courier from Königsberg, to return to report the mortifying news of Countess Voss's perfidy against Bonaparte to the Prussian king and to demand an explanation. The respectable, if gossipy, old countess was sub-jected to the indignity of hearing the special courier's report to the king of what purported to be her account of language from a par-rot's mouth which could scarcely have crossed her lips. If that good lady swooned, we may forgive her, but she at least was quickly able to clear up the matter to the satisfaction of her royal mistress.[111] D'Aubier reported to Königsberg on the same day, the nineteenth, that Goltz arrived with his own definitive report of the French con-ditions. A letter from Voss, written on the fifteenth, arrived at the

---

[109] On the arrest of Schmalz I have followed the account given by Schön (Schön Nachlass, No. 61, pp. 23–24). In a letter to the king, 2 December 1808 (Schön Nachlass, No. 27), Schön admitted commissioning the pamphlet, but left out the "honeyed pill" story.

[110] Wittgenstein's connection with Marshal Bernadotte got him out of jail quickly. Bernadotte mocked his colleagues in Berlin for spinning out this fantasy: "Ces gredins à Berlin font un tort infini à l'empereur" (*Stein Br.*, II (2), 943–944n). The conse-quence of Wittgenstein's effort to cast the blame on Stein was the outlawing of the minister. See below, Chapter VI, and Gerhard Ritter, "Die Aechtung Steins," *Nas-sauische Annalen*, LII (1931), 1–17. Ritter, who did not use the French archives, missed two letters written by Wittgenstein which were precedents for the effort he made in November. These letters, protesting his own innocence, were deliberately sent through the regular post in order to have them fall into French hands. In them, Wittgenstein argued the case for himself and sought to put the blame on Stein (where, at least in the case of the August letter, it belonged). See Wittgenstein to Privy Counselor Faudel (in Berlin), 16 and 20 September 1808, AG, CGA, C2 79. In November, Wittgenstein used the same technique, but sent the same sort of letter in two copies through the regular mails to Stein. See Wittgenstein to Stein, 22 Novem-ber 1808, *Stein Br.*, II (2), 981–984. A rather different, if inexact, account is in Bassewitz, *Die Kurmark, 1806–1808*, II, 368–369. See also Ritter, *Stein*, 363.

[111] Delbrück, *Tagebuchblätter*, 19 and 20 November 1808, III, 100–103; Hermann Granier, "Der angebliche Vergiftungsbrief der Oberhofmeisterin Gräfin Voss," *Hoh-enzollern-Jahrbuch*, XVI (1912), 100.

same time. In it, Voss once more dredged up every bogey to influence the king against Stein and his party: Schmalz's incendiary pamphleteering was connected with the Tugendbund; the opposition of the French marshals toward Stein and Sack and toward the "revolutionary" reform program was grimly recounted again, and Schön's role in the preparation of Schmalz's nefarious incitements of the canaille was added for good measure. To these was joined Voss's own credulous repetition of the absurd charge of regicide directed by Davout against Countess Voss.[112]

Although the "poison letter" episode was more farcical than anything else, at least it revealed to the king the lengths that he would have to go to allay Davout's rage. He now knew as well that the French (Davout's outrageous opinion had to be taken for Bonaparte's insofar as Königsberg knew it) had connected the reform movement with the anti-Napoleonic forces. And this pointed up the risk of proceeding too quickly with reform at the same time as it underscored the warnings against "revolution" directed against Stein by Altenstein, Nagler, and Hardenberg. If Prussia were to implement the policy of peaceful relations with Paris which the king hoped to develop from the convention, he would, so it appeared, have to temper his domestic program accordingly.

On the twentieth, it was heard at court, and attributed to what either Goltz or D'Aubier had told the king, that Stein's withdrawal was as good as certain.[113] The end of the French occupation of Berlin was set for December 3, and Goltz was preparing to confirm in a letter to Voss that Stein would be out by that date.[114] The last phase of the struggle for succession had begun.

[112] Voss to F.W., 14–15 November 1808, *Stein Br.*, II (2), 939–944; but in her diary Countess Voss wrote that Voss had privately communicated to her that he really did not believe the story (Granier, "Der angebliche Vergiftungsbrief," 100). D'Aubier, in spite of the fact that he was close to Voss and the Francophiles in Berlin, demonstrated a fair amount of objectivity in his later reports dealing with Stein. See his letters dating from this period to Goltz in DZA, Rep. 63, 88. D'Aubier also carried Voss's letter of the fourteenth and fifteenth to Königsberg (see Voss, IB, 14–15 November 1808, *Stein Br.*, II (2), 939).

[113] Delbrück, *Tagebuchblätter*, 19 and 20 November 1808, III, 100–103.

[114] Goltz to Voss, 24 November 1808, Stern, *Abhandlungen und Aktenstücke*, 32–33.

V I

THE TRIMMERS
COME TO POWER

Just over a week passed between the return of Goltz to Königsberg and the official publication of the names of the ministers who were to replace Stein's government. In this critical period the struggle for the succession would finally be resolved. Stein, we know, sought to use the time to bring to completion those items of reform legislation which could be quickly finished. Simultaneously, he tried to rid the court of some of his enemies there and to fill the posts in the next administration with men who would carry on the work he had initiated. The goal of all these efforts was to make certain, if possible, that the termination of his ministry would not betoken the end of his legislative program and the final frustration of his work. Such was the irony of his situation that he found himself nominating some unlikely candidates for key ministries and, in the end, his program had to be entrusted to men more likely to frustrate than to fulfill it. But Stein, as we shall see, was not the only one to be balked by the unfolding plots; his conservative enemies and, to some extent, even Hardenberg and his friends, were to be little more successful than was he.

He developed the attack on his aristocratic foes in connection with a general attack on frivolity in the court—the reader will understand that such an antagonism between Stein and the courtiers must have been of long standing. The question which aroused Stein's notorious temper on this occasion had actually been posed by Alexander. On his return visit to Königsberg, he had invited the king and queen to visit him in St. Petersburg. Frugal, Stein was vehemently against the trip on the ground of necessity for economy.[1] But the queen be-

[1] Stein, Denkschrift, 22 November 1808, *Stein Br.*, II (2), 979–981; Nagler to Hardenberg, 25 November 1808, DZA, Rep. 92, Hardenberg, F1. Voss and the

held enthusiastically the prospect of a temporary change from the bourgeois austerity of Königsberg to the dream-world joys she imagined awaiting in imperial St. Petersburg. Egged on by Schladen and Nagler (the latter had Hardenberg's advice that the king's whim should be flattered in this "unimportant matter"),[2] she lightheartedly urged the king to an affirmative decision.[3] Stein, who at this particular moment had cause to be especially irascible, angered the queen by his stubborn opposition to the trip. Well before this, the minister's Teutonic severeness had become an uncomfortable partner to the queen's harum-scarum femininity. Now, it appears, she was unwilling to make an effort to close the gap between herself and the minister. In her mind, he no longer served as the best hope for the salvation of the kingdom, though a simple, uncomplicated thought on the matter as calculating and direct as this doubtlessly had never crossed her mind. Instead, we may postulate the following growth of the estrangement which had arisen between her and the minister. Gradually, following the letter affair, Stein's stature, as viewed through her eyes, had declined. Nagler, as we have seen, was responsible for bringing about one part of this change of attitude, and the courtiers for another. Then, with his combination of personal charm and advice seemingly grounded on bitter personal experience, Hardenberg had easily been able to win her to the view that Stein could and must be replaced. Along with the ministerial halo, the sanction for the economic restraint which Stein and his program embodied had been eroded. For Louise, the trip to Russia appeared as a first step, not to be postponed, toward the recovery of the courtly life which had disappeared with Jena, a first ecstatic release from the straitened circumstances of provincial Königsberg. The return to Berlin, which was set for the end of the visit abroad, would be the second.

Francophiles were also against the trip to St. Petersburg because they feared it would cause the French to suspect a secret undertaking between Russia and Prussia (AAE, CP, Prusse, 1808, 242, p. 438).

[2] Hardenberg to Altenstein, 27 November 1808, DZA, Rep. 92, Altenstein, B14.

[3] Clausewitz to Marie von Brühl, 20 November 1808, Clausewitz, *Briefe,* 174; Radziwill, 297–298; Stein, Autobiographische Aufzeichnungen, 12 July 1811, *Stein Br.,* III, 548.

We may suspect that the queen's anger against Stein on this occasion doubled because his attack on the Russian journey came in conjunction with a simultaneous indictment of Countess Voss. That venerable dame, so recently maligned by the upstart Davout, Stein included in his bill of charges along with Köckritz, the queen's own court chamberlain and the marshal of the royal court. He accused them of indiscretions in matters of state which hampered the conduct of government affairs. These, he charged, occurred at the countess' own salons, where gossip and inside information were exchanged about the work of government which were then passed directly to the French consul.[4] This agonized denunciation of the witless courtiers was the harassed and resentful minister's final recorded outcry against the indolence, vacuity, and inanity of the court circle, where idle minds concocted tales and intrigue and where French agents overheard the innermost secrets of the Prussian government.

From this indirect exchange with Stein on the subject of the Russian journey and the indiscretions of her friends, the petulant and unstable queen gained a sudden violent dislike for the minister whom she had once so completely idolatrized.[5] Before long she could, being completely honest to herself, as it appears, blame the whole disastrous situation into which Prussia had fallen since Jena on Stein's letter.[6] In December, she was indeed to take personal credit before the French consul in Königsberg for having brought about the minister's fall.[7] We may realistically view this act as motivated at least in part by the queen's shallow conception of the state's needs. She would win French gratitude for the Prussian royal house by a histrionic display directed against the fallen minister. Yet so great was her pique at the fallen Stein that the statement truly reflected her satisfaction at his departure. Of the queen we may justly state

<hr/>

[4] Stein, Denkschrift, 22 November 1808, *Stein Br.*, II (2), 979–981.

[5] Lehmann, *Stein*, II (2), 589–590; Gneisenau to Götzen, 24 November 1808, Vaupel, 727.

[6] Louise to her brother George, 21 and 28 February 1809, *Königin Luise: Briefe*, 401.

[7] It appears that she tried the same gambit earlier: Clérembault (the French consul in Königsberg) to Davout, 25 November 1808, AG, CGA, C2 81, reported that Stein had resigned, thanks to the firmness of Louise and Goltz on the issue. See Haussherr, *Erfüllung und Befreiung*, 252; Cavaignac, "La Saisie de la lettre de Stein," 77.

that, if she shared but little of the prime responsibility for bringing down the Stein government, she delectated in the event itself and must take at least a major part of the blame for unwittingly bringing about the appointment of his personal foes as his successors.[8] Stein's attack on the court fools at this time might easily be judged by some as indiscreet. Stein was rarely given to discretion, and here we have a clear example of the tongue once again serving the enemies of the man. His bluff outspokenness, which often verged on outright rudeness, had not only won him many enemies, it also on occasion earned the disapprobation of his friends.[9] But it is hard to see what might have been changed at this late date had he chosen bland discretion over forthrightness; his fate, as he well knew, was already certain. Thus his attack on the Kakodämonen and the court gossips may realistically be viewed as a last honorable, yet despairing, effort to free the government of the dangerous baggage which hindered the conduct of affairs.

Finally on the twenty-fourth of November Stein took his last official action, handing in the plan for the reorganization of the Prussian central administration, which he considered to be the crux of his whole reform program. At the core of the central government five functional ministries were to be established. He still included a *Staatsrat* or council of state, the idea he had first adopted in October, but no longer put in his own name for the post which had originally been planned for him. Both he and the king were certain that

[8] Compare Schön Nachlass, No. 61, pp. 27–28, with Schön, *Papiere*, IV, 582. In the manuscript (of his biographical sketch of Scharnhorst cited here) Schön wrote that the demand of Napoleon (that is, of Davout) was "unterstützt durch eine Kabale der Königin." On several occasions that I have noted the editor of the printed edition of Schön's papers amended the text or omitted sections. Here in the printed edition he obviously sought to protect Louise's reputation by eliminating the reference to the queen and substituting "Hofcabale." Schön wrote in his Tagebuch (30 November 1808, *Papiere*, II, 52): "What a woman can accomplish!" See also Radziwill, 294–298. Compare the account of the growth of the antagonism between Stein and her majesty in Klatt, 76. The queen remained Nagler's patroness for some time. In the spring of 1810 she tried to bring him and Wilhelm von Humboldt into the chief ministries to replace Dohna and Altenstein. See Boyen, *Erinnerungen*, II, 55.

[9] See Chapter V, note 23.

the French would allow no position, advisory or other, to him. For the most important posts of Minister of Finance and Minister of the Interior in the new ministry he now suggested Altenstein and Dohna.[10] In view of the fact that he had first thought of Stägemann and Dohna and later of Schön and Dohna for these positions, it is clear that he had since learned in some way of the king's wish to employ Altenstein and Dohna.[11] His nomination must therefore show him putting a good face on his acceptance of the royal decision. At this point he obviously did not know why the king wanted Altenstein; of the latter's bad faith Stein had no notion.[12] It may be that he hoped by his ready agreement to the king's choices to win his majesty over to his own candidates for the other positions. He now wanted the king to offer lesser ministries to Schön, Stägemann, and Wilhelm von Humboldt.

Altenstein, it will be recalled, had anticipated Stein's suggestion of Schön in his instructions to Hardenberg for the meeting at Kallgen. Stein's earlier lists show that the estrangement which grew up between Stein and Altenstein had been accompanied by a progressively greater dependence of Stein on Schön. This Altenstein obviously recognized. But in view of the fact that the king was not in favor of

---

[10] Stein, IB, 24 November 1808, *Stein Br.*, II (2), 987.

[11] Stein, Aufzeichnungen zum Organisationsplan, [October 1808], *Stein Br.*, II (2), 910–912; Stein, Autobiographische Aufzeichnungen, 12 July 1811, *ibid.*, III, 550; Schön, *Papiere*, II, 52. Compare Ritter, *Stein*, 359–360. The question why Stein dropped Stägemann may possibly be answered by noting that Stein had begun to mistrust him because he forwarded the news Goltz learned in Berlin (see above, Chapter V, at note 23). On the seventeenth of November, Baroness Stein, in Berlin, had written to her husband to warn him not to trust Stägemann. The reason for her warning is unknown. See Stern, *Abhandlungen und Aktenstücke*, 8–9n2.

[12] Altenstein and Stein were still publicly regarded as sharing the same political views: see Agnes von Gerlach to Marie Raumer, 9 December 1808, Schoeps, *Aus den Jahren preussischer Not*, 364. Stein apparently did not have the same suspicions of Altenstein as he had of Nagler: see Hardenberg to Altenstein, 22 December 1808, DZA, Rep. 92, Altenstein, B14; Schön Tagebuch, 30 November and 3 and 10 December 1808, Schön, *Papiere*, II, 52, 54, 61; Stein to Stadion, 13 January 1809, *Stein Br.*, III, 20–22; Gneisenau to Stein, 14 January 1809, *ibid.*, 24–25. Even much later Stein put the blame on Nagler: see Stein, Denkschrift, 12–13 September 1810, *ibid.*, 405 and n; Stein, Autobiographische Aufzeichnungen, 12 July 1811, *ibid.*, 548.

Schön, as Altenstein had confidently noted, Hardenberg had had no difficulty in removing him from consideration for the post.[13] In addition, Schön had recently become a candidate unacceptable to the French. The "honeyed pill" affair had presumably convinced Davout that Schön was part of the conspiracy of regicides to poison the emperor. At the very least, as far as Davout and the French were concerned, Schön had incited the publication of Schmalz's revolutionary tract.

The same day Stein submitted his reorganization plan he asked for and got his leave.[14] Although the king had to avoid bestowing honors on Stein for his service,[15] it was obvious that he regretted the necessity to remove the minister, the second chief of administration he had disengaged at Bonaparte's insistence.

The day after Stein resigned Altenstein was called in by the king and offered control of the state finances. He feared at first that his majesty meant that he should only hold the post provisionally. He modestly protested that, although an official title as such was quite unimportant to him, without the title as well as the responsibility of office, "the good cause" would not be advanced. To deprive Altenstein of proper recognition was not the king's intent at all. In fact, we may attribute this small but interesting misunderstanding to the king's usual indecisiveness, which led to a refusal to come down to cases with Altenstein. A few days later, as we shall see, Altenstein did get his title as well as the perquisites of the office. In the meantime, Hardenberg, alerted to the situation by Altenstein, had once more volunteered to come to his rescue by taking a stand with the king in favor of Altenstein's receiving the title of Minister of Finance. But even then Altenstein and Nagler were not secure on the course on which they had embarked. First of all, they were eager to see Stein leave Königsberg and his former sphere of influence as soon as possible. They undoubtedly feared he might learn of their handiwork. They were also fearful that Dohna, whom neither appeared to

---

[13] Altenstein to Hardenberg, 10 November 1808, DZA, Rep. 92, Hardenberg, K30.
[14] KO to Stein, 24 November 1808, *Stein Br.*, II (2), 988.
[15] F.W. to Scheffner, 4 December 1808, *Stein Br.*, II (2), 999–1000.

know very well—his name seems to have been put forward to them originally by Hardenberg—would not prove amenable to their leadership. But on this they could remain at ease; Hardenberg, as we know, had already convinced Dohna of his responsibility to stand together with the other two.[16] And the honest, well-meaning Dohna did not have as yet any suspicions about the role the others had carved out for him.

In spite of the summoning of Altenstein to take control of the finances on the twenty-fifth, the make-up of the entire ministry had not been finally decided even by that date; Altenstein himself had gotten the impression that everything was still quite uncertain. In these confused circumstances, at a time when the behind the scenes struggle for place was at its height, Stein appears to have learned for the first time of Nagler's duplicity. We can only assume that Stein's conversations with the king about his original list of names gave him some hint of Nagler's plans to become a key adviser, although from the wings rather than from the center of the stage. But though Stein may not at first have connected Altenstein with Nagler's treachery, the prospect of the devious Nagler achieving influence over the conduct of affairs as the wages of betrayal would have been grounds enough to cause Stein's unhappiness. As he saw it, there was no one in the new ministry who could offset the evil Nagler might accomplish. Thus there would no longer be anyone on whom Stein thought he could rely to be the driving force which could carry on with his work.[17] His hopes for a continuation of his program seemed fated to be dashed.

For these reasons alone, we must assume, Stein acted precipitously, with a hope born of despair, on an astonishing suggestion made by Scharnhorst and Schön. The three must have taken stock of the

[16] Nagler to Hardenberg, 25 November 1808, DZA, Rep. 92, Hardenberg, F1; Altenstein to Hardenberg, 25 November 1808, *ibid.*, Hardenberg, K30; Hardenberg to Altenstein, 27 November 1808, *ibid.*, Altenstein, B14; Hardenberg Tagebuch, 27 November 1808, *ibid.*, Hardenberg, L29.

[17] On Dohna's weakness—apparent at the time—see Stein to Schön, 26 November 1808, *Stein Br.*, III, 5–6; Schön Tagebuch, 30 November and 3 and 8 December 1808, Schön, *Papiere*, II, 52, 54, 56.

situation sometime late on the twenty-fourth or early on the twenty-fifth after putting together whatever evidence they were able to gather on Nagler's perfidy.[18] Then Stein returned to the king with the proposal that the Ministry of Justice with the title of *Grosskanzler*, an honorary judicial rank not usually conveyed, be offered to none other than Stein's old foe Beyme.

Bewildering though the selection of Beyme may first appear in the light of his past relation with Stein, it must be recalled that the minister had no way of knowing of Beyme's ancient and recent flirtations with the French and with the Kakodämonen; nor did he appreciate the violence of Beyme's personal feeling toward him. Of course he did know that Beyme was untrustworthy, but, as he must have reasoned, it would be of utmost importance to have in office a man to whom he still credited a passionate zeal for reform. Beyme's patriotic fervor of 1806 was undoubtedly recalled in his favor. And his success in obtaining the king's ear, as Stein knew from past experience, could be counted upon to undo the fainaiguing of all his enemies. In effect, he could insulate the king from Nagler as well as from the courtiers. Goltz, whom Stein now despised for his role in bringing about his resignation, would likewise be rendered innocuous through Beyme's nomination. In the eyes of the reformers, Beyme possessed the force of character which they estimated as a prime requisite of the chief adviser of Frederick William III. They believed that Beyme, acting for the first time in an official ministerial capacity, would be forced to take responsibility as well as operate openly; neither of these had he ever been compelled to do as a counselor-in-cabinet (*Kabinettsrat*). Schön thus justified his suggestion of Beyme by arguing: "Even if Beyme were a Satan, he is at least a man; and he cannot do evil if we can watch him in the open." [19] The king, of course, as the reformers (now, ironically,

---

[18] Schön, according to Dohna, was possessed by a violent hatred of Altenstein, some of which is apparent in his Tagebuch, 30 November and 10 December 1808, *Papiere,* II, 52, 61. See Dohna to Merckel, 1 April 1809, Linke, "Der Geschäftsbericht des Ministers Grafen zu Dohna," 3.

[19] The post of Minister of Justice was not mentioned in Stein's Aufzeichnungen zum Organisationsplan of October (*Stein Br.,* II (2), 910–912), nor was it men-

having reduced themselves to scheming) anticipated, delightedly seized the chance to take back his favorite.

Although we cannot be certain that Nagler's role in bringing about the fall of the government was known to Stein as early as the moment of his proposal of Beyme for the ministry,[20] the secrecy and suddenness of the nomination tend to bear out the hypothesis. Beyme's letter of appointment was sent on the twenty-fifth, though neither Altenstein (who saw the king) nor Nagler knew of the naming of their future colleague on that date.[21] Thus the suggestion of Beyme's name must indeed have been a last-minute affair, for Nagler, with his inside sources of information, would otherwise have found out within a few days what had been done. But since he still

---

tioned in the list he submitted to the king at the time of his resignation (Stein, IB, 24 November 1808, *ibid.*, 987). See also Schön Tagebuch, 30 November 1808, Schön, *Papiere*, II, 52. Only a few weeks later Schön seems to have been less certain that his action had been wise, for he confided to his Tagebuch that he suspected that Beyme, who had not yet arrived in Königsberg, was chiefly inspired by his hatred of Stein and the inordinate ambitions of his wife (19 December 1808, *ibid.*, 63). But Stein gave out a more favorable view of the situation in a letter to Merckel, 23 December 1808, *Stein Br.*, III, 4–5. On Stein's hatred for Goltz see Gneisenau to Stein, 14 January 1809, *ibid.*, 24–25. Niebuhr suggested that Stein, in appointing Beyme, had simply shown once more his propensity to appoint his enemies to office: Niebuhr to Moltke, 15 January 1809, *Niebuhr: Briefe*, I, 530. The king's letter of nomination to Beyme is in J. D. C. Preuss, *Friedrich der Grosse: Eine Lebensgeschichte*, III (Berlin, 1833), 531–532, and is quoted by Bassewitz, *Die Kurmark, 1809–1810*, 630–631.

[20] Schön, in his Tagebuch, 30 November 1808 (Schön, *Papiere*, II, 52), suggests that Stein must have found out who was untrue to him. On 25 November, just the day after Stein's resignation, Nagler wrote to Hardenberg (DZA, Rep. 92, Hardenberg, F1) that Stein was departing in a tizzy, blaming everything on Goltz. Moreover, "real anger and hatred" were already directed at himself. On 3 December, Schön confided to his Tagebuch that Stein must know about Nagler, so great was his bitterness toward him (*ibid.*, 54). Stein called him the "seichter, listiger und gewandter" Nagler (Stein to Schön, 26 December 1808, *Stein Br.*, III, 6), recalling later (Stein, Autobiographische Aufzeichnungen, 12 July 1811, *ibid.*, 548) how Nagler, out of an apparent concern for Stein's welfare and that of the kingdom, had used every opportunity in the fall of 1808 to persuade him to withdraw from the government and leave Königsberg.

[21] The secret was well kept (probably because the king alone knew it): Gneisenau, in a letter to Götzen of 24 November 1808, could supply no information about the successors of Stein (Vaupel, 727).

remained uncertain as to the king's final disposition of the ministries, Nagler soon began to fear that the plans discussed by the king at the meeting with Hardenberg two weeks before would not be carried out. Now that he had learned in some way that Stein had found him out he unmasked himself to enter the fray openly for the first time.[22] In a letter dated the twenty-eighth,[23] addressed to the king, Nagler was emboldened to ask that Stein be dropped immediately. At the same time he defended Goltz from the charges which Stein and his friends had made to discredit him and his report from Berlin. Goltz, Nagler argued, was an honorable man; what he said of the French stand against Stein must be accepted. In contrast to his praise for Goltz Nagler accused Stein of outright hypocrisy: Stein had privately assured Altenstein he would support him for the ministry, but instead was promoting another (Schön?).[24] Stein, Nagler charged, was working feverishly to enact his program before the benefit of the new ministry's advice could be obtained. Meanwhile, the name of Voss as Stein's replacement was on all lips. Consequently there was confusion and frustration everywhere. The new measures being issued, such as that for the organization of the city governments, were bound to be associated with Stein and thus compromised domestically as well as in the eyes of the French.[25] Hence, he argued, Stein

[22] Nagler to Hardenberg, 25 November 1808, DZA, Rep. 92, Hardenberg, F1.

[23] *Stein Br.,* II (2), 925–927. This letter is dated 8 November in the Botzenhart and Hubatsch editions of Stein's correspondence, but the sense of the letter as well as internal evidence show that it must be of a later date. First of all, Nagler complains of the extent of the hostility toward Goltz, which did not develop until later. Nagler mentions that he is writing on the date of the promulgation of the new city government ordinances, which were published on 28 November in the *Königsberger Zeitung.* Moreover, Nagler writes as if the king and he already know who has been selected to replace Stein; this information neither Nagler nor the king could possibly have shared until after Hardenberg's visits of 10 and 11 November. Finally, Nagler notes that the announcement of Stein's resignation (which had occurred on the twenty-fourth) appeared in the paper on the day of his writing. Lehmann, *Stein,* II (2), 598n2, and Hassel, I, 292–293n3, both date the letter 28 November.

[24] For Goltz's disclaimer that he had worked against Stein see Goltz to F.W., 9 January 1809, DZA, Rep. 92, Nagler, 45. See also D'Aubier to Goltz, 4 December 1808, DZA, Rep. 63, 88, No. 598. Nagler may refer to Stein's Aufzeichnungen zum Organisationsplan [October 1808], *Stein Br.,* II (2), 910–912. The date of the promise to Altenstein, if there was one, I cannot establish.

[25] See above, Chapter V.

must be replaced without delay by Altenstein and Dohna. In conclusion he begged the king's leave to make public that very day the names of the new ministers.[26] This he was apparently allowed to do and thus he and Altenstein found out for the first time of the appointment of Beyme to the Ministry of Justice.[27]

When Beyme, still in Berlin, heard of his nomination he must have been astonished at the news of this improbable turn of events.[28] Though he did not at first know the circumstances of his election he must have quickly realized, when he did learn, that Stein had acted out of despair. Thus because he had come in under such peculiar circumstances, he had no responsibility to Stein. True, Beyme was obliged to some small degree to Voss and the court party for the assistance they had rendered earlier in winning him the confidence of the French. And we may speculate that Altenstein and Nagler, once they had recovered from their surprise, found the occasion to tell the king that Beyme was an impossible choice because he was anathema to the French. (They had put Hardenberg up to the same story in November.)[29] But the Kakodämonen were happily on hand to give him a countervailing testimonial if it were necessary; Beyme, they could report, was held in the highest esteem by the French authorities in Berlin.[30] Of course, whatever aid the courtiers might have given him would have been small in comparison with the help Stein had rendered, and Beyme came off owing nothing in political debts to the nobility as a whole. Though Voss and his own friends were later to seek to capitalize on their relation with

[26] Clausewitz to Marie von Brühl, 27 November 1808, Clausewitz, *Briefe,* 187, shared with her the opinion that Stein had fallen because of the work of Goltz and Voss, but even at this date, though he obviously was aware of the general information spread at court, he had nothing to say about the composition of the new ministry. Delbrück, the court tutor, did not note the names of the new ministers until 29 November (Delbrück, *Tagebuchblätter,* III, 107).

[27] Schön Tagebuch, 29 and 30 November 1808, Schön, *Papiere,* II, 52.

[28] On Hardenberg's consternation at Beyme's nomination see Hardenberg Tagebuch, 18 and 20 December 1808, DZA, Rep. 92, Hardenberg, L29; Hardenberg to Altenstein, 15 December 1808, *ibid.,* Altenstein, B14.

[29] Altenstein to Hardenberg, 10 November 1808, *ibid.,* Hardenberg, K30.

[30] Davout to French Ambassador in Berlin, 8 January 1809, Davout, *Correspondance,* II, 343.

Beyme,[31] apparently quite without success, the majority of the nobles continued to regard him as a *roturier,* a commoner, to whom the king should never have tendered such an eminent post.[32] To the incoming ministers, including the calculating brothers-in-law, he had no private obligations. He would find out soon enough, if he did not already know, that they had opposed his nomination. And since Altenstein wanted to assign to Nagler the role Beyme had traditionally played as the king's confidant, a conflict within the government had become inevitable. But even if that had not been so, Beyme soon found other reasons to oppose his new colleagues: he heard within a few days that an intrigue had already been undertaken to displace him before he ever got to Königsberg.[33]

Such a cabal, if it truly existed, could only be explained as a vain attempt by Altenstein to restore the conditions that he and Nagler had so carefully arranged. The wily brothers-in-law and Hardenberg himself had been completely nonplused by Stein's eleventh-hour act. Their masterfully conceived scheme to upset Stein and replace him themselves had been effectually subverted. In the flexible government structure which Stein had proposed, which included the cabinet of equal ministers each with access to the king, Beyme as Minister of Justice would enjoy a status equal to that of any of the others. Thus the situation Altenstein had described as the worst of all possibilities in his advice to Hardenberg of the tenth of November would develop. Beyme would come to a post of independence and win his old influence with the king. Then he could easily interpose himself between the king and Nagler and Altenstein. Here I am compelled to agree with Altenstein's earlier line of thought in his letter of advice to Hardenberg. What had Stein accomplished by the nomination of Beyme? little more than the reopening of the struggle for power which Hardenberg, Altenstein, and Nagler had thought closed. He had undone the plotters only to re-establish on a more permanent basis the system of cabal and personal intrigue.

[31] Hardenberg to Altenstein, 1 January 1809, DZA, Rep. 92, Altenstein, B14.

[32] Report of a French spy from Berlin, 19 December 1808, transmitted in Davout to Napoleon, 29 December 1808, AG, CGA, C2 82.

[33] Beyme to Karl von Schroetter, 26 and 30 December (both falsely dated November) 1808, "Briefe des Grafen von Beyme," 948–949.

As soon as the French evacuated Brandenburg in early December, Hardenberg crossed the Vistula and took up residence at his estate near Müncheberg, east of Berlin. Stein too had decided to go directly to Berlin, where his family continued to reside, as soon after his resignation as possible. Nagler, meanwhile, had been included in the party planned to accompany the king and queen to St. Petersburg. Thus in late December, only Altenstein and Dohna remained behind in the temporary seat of government.

In this state of affairs Hardenberg, who had advised Nagler and Altenstein to agree to the trip to St. Petersburg as a matter of "no importance," was in a position to learn why Stein had characterized the journey as frivolous. While the king was away little final action toward reform could be taken even if a will to act had existed. Hardenberg, in consequence, now found himself chafing at the absence of action in Königsberg. He sensed that things were going poorly. Altenstein was manifestly not initiating the reform legislation and the changes on which they had agreed. Delay, he warned his former subaltern delicately, allowed the opposition to organize its strengths once more against the ministry.[34]

Hardenberg, it will be recalled, had not opposed to the same extent as Altenstein the ministerial reorganization scheme which Stein had presented on the day of his resignation. He presumably thought that a strong personality could easily rise to become the king's chief adviser though in title only the equal of his fellows. Thus while Altenstein regarded the postponement of these innovations by the new ministry as a great victory, Hardenberg saw inaction as valueless or harmful. Moreover, whereas Altenstein does not seem to have wanted Stein's name connected with any further program, Hardenberg was more concerned with the effectiveness of the administration than with the distribution of the credit. He had obviously made the false assumption that Altenstein held a similar view. Here we have a second indication that Hardenberg's stand in favor of Altenstein had been based on misunderstanding: in the first instance, as we have seen, he had been certain that Bonaparte would force Stein to

---

[34] Hardenberg to Altenstein, DZA, Rep. 92, Altenstein, B14; Hardenberg Tagebuch, 20 December 1808, *ibid.*, Hardenberg, L29.

withdraw (this, as we have established, cannot be asserted with any degree of certainty); in the second, he had staked his own reputation on the belief that Altenstein and Nagler would quickly move forward the fundamental reform program while, at the same time, asking his advice and eliminating the revolutionary overtones. Hence a misunderstanding of his former subordinates' aims as well as a misconception of their abilities underlay Hardenberg's most critical decisions in November and December.

Soon after arriving in Berlin in his customary elegant style on the sixteenth of December, Hardenberg was visited "dans le plus grand incognito" by Stein, who had arrived only a few days before.[35] The meeting between the two exiled ministers had undoubtedly been prearranged. They were closeted together for some time. It is fair to assume that Stein at this time did not know the role Hardenberg had played in his fall, and that he did not imagine that Hardenberg had been led to cast himself as a sort of "gray eminence" behind Altenstein and Nagler. Stein told him of the earlier meeting he had had with Beyme on the eve of Beyme's departure for Königsberg.[36] From Stein Hardenberg learned for the first time who had recommended Beyme to the king and thereby frustrated the plans he had arranged with Altenstein and Nagler. Hardenberg hid his annoyance—he could hardly hazard a reproach to Stein which might reveal the scheme to which he was a party. Privately, however, he

[35] Stein's arrival on the twelfth of December was announced by the *Vossische Zeitung* (Berlin, 13 December 1808), reprinted in *Stein Br.,* II (2), 1000. The meeting between Stein and Hardenberg was reported by a French agent to Davout, 16 December 1808 (annex to Davout to Napoleon, 25 December 1808, AG, CGA, C2 82). This is confirmed by a report on German affairs in AAE, CP, Prusse, 1808, 242, p. 471; and by Stein's account of Hardenberg's attitude toward him and Schön (Stein to Schön, 26 December 1808, *Stein Br.,* III, 5–6). Hardenberg and Stein met once again on the twentieth of December. See Hardenberg to Altenstein, 22 December 1808, DZA, Rep. 92, Altenstein, B14. The French thought the first meeting to be quite significant and Davout had a report written about it and published in a Hamburg newspaper. See Goltz to F.W., 26 January 1809, *ibid.,* Nagler, 45; and *Stein Br.,* III, 87n28. Compare Haussherr, "Stein und Hardenberg," 277, who makes an important point of his erroneous supposition that Stein and Hardenberg did not meet.

[36] Report of a French spy in Berlin, 13 December 1808, transmitted in Davout to Napoleon, 25 December 1808, AG, CGA, C2 82.

discounted Stein's belief that Beyme would take over the leadership of the reform movement.[37] During his own meeting with Stein, Beyme, like Hardenberg, must have smiled secretly at his sincerity. Because of Stein's faith in his zeal for reform, Beyme found himself carried into an office and station more important than any he had held before. Though lachrymose because of his unwillingness to give up the life of contemplation he had come to love, he had naturally accepted the post. He protested that he had been driven reluctantly to his affirmative decision because of his sense of duty and feeling of obedience to the king. Then by the time of Stein's first visit, he had become the cynosure of political attention. He found himself courted by letter from Königsberg and personally in Berlin, for the manner of his nomination, as we have seen, had left him singularly unencumbered in choosing his future political course. Karl von Schroetter, his predecessor in the justice ministry, had written to him to beg him to hurry to Königsberg to take the lagging reforms in hand.[38] Schön later was to write in the same vein: Beyme must hasten to Königsberg to give a spur to the reform movement. Only Beyme, Schön implied, could save the situation. But Beyme's reply, which dodged both the issue of the trip to Königsberg and that of the reforms, deliberately missed the point: things, he wrote with a disingenuousness that must have infuriated Schön, must progress "according to the law" [39]— the "law," of course, which Schön had hoped Beyme would help improve. This interesting exchange of letters clearly mirrors Schön's sincerity and Beyme's lack of commitment. Platitudes were the main stock of Beyme's arsenal of ideas and the essence of the "moderate" position which he (like Altenstein) probably imagined he held.

[37] Hardenberg Tagebuch, 20 December 1808, DZA, Rep. 92, Hardenberg, L29.

[38] Beyme to Karl von Schroetter, 7 and 26 December (both falsely dated November) 1808, "Briefe des Grafen von Beyme," 947, 949.

[39] Beyme to Schön, 25 December (falsely dated October) 1808, Schön, *Papiere,* I, 83–84; Schön Tagebuch, 19 and 30 December 1808, *ibid.,* II, 63, 65; Hardenberg to Altenstein, 1 January 1809, 3 January 1809, DZA, Rep. 92, Altenstein, B14. Scharnhorst was also eager for Beyme to hasten to Königsberg and told the king so (Scharnhorst, IB, 10 December 1808, Vaupel, 772).

Though Beyme had once actually started off for Königsberg, he had turned back when he received a letter from the king urging him to remain temporarily in Berlin. He could, Frederick William had written, be more valuable there by representing symbolically the king's plan to return to his capital at the conclusion of the journey to St. Petersburg.[40] In dead earnest in his hope that Beyme would take command of the languishing reform movement, Schön had then even connived in an attempt to frustrate the king's intention by delaying the sending of the letter.[41] But in spite of his efforts Beyme got it en route and followed the king's order to go back, even though he believed initially, as Schön apparently did also, that the change of plan reflected the success of his foes who were seeking to keep him away from the king and from taking up his new post.[42]

A few days after his visit from Stein, Hardenberg himself made the pilgrimage to his former enemy Beyme to see just what the favorite did intend in Königsberg. Beyme confided to him sententiously that he was bringing the king proofs of extreme revolutionary tendencies he had discovered. These, he warned, were extraordinarily dangerous and, if they did not have the approval of the king— Beyme appears not to have known to what extent the machinations he had learned of had the king's consent—they would be illegal.[43] The dangers which Beyme wanted to report were undoubtedly the Tugendbund and aspects of the conspiracy for armed action against the French, which really was connected with the former in some areas as well as in the minds of the anti-Stein aristocrats. No doubt the "working up" of the people as epitomized by Schmalz and his pamphlet was also among the scandals Beyme proposed to denounce. On these matters at least Hardenberg could, on behalf of his colleagues in Königsberg, put Beyme's fears to rest. Altenstein, he

[40] The king's intention to return to Berlin at the end of the Russian trip was announced in the *Vossische Zeitung* (Berlin) on 24 December 1808. The king ultimately decided to heed Stein's advice and did not return to his capital until December 1809. See also Beyme to Karl von Schroetter, 26 December (falsely dated November) 1808, "Briefe des Grafen von Beyme," 949.
[41] Schön Tagebuch, 10 December 1808, Schön, *Papiere*, II, 58.
[42] Beyme to Karl von Schroetter, 26 and 30 December (both falsely dated November) 1808, "Briefe des Grafen von Beyme," 948–949.
[43] Hardenberg to Altenstein, 22 December 1808, DZA, Rep. 92, Altenstein, B14.

could swear, had used the very same vocabulary in discussing them. And both he and Hardenberg himself had earlier spoken to the king in the same sense as Beyme now proposed.[44] The general tone of Beyme's interview with Hardenberg confirms the reports Schön and Altenstein had begun to receive as well as the information reaching Hardenberg from Christian Friedrich Scharnweber, another of his former administrative colleagues. To these observers it appeared that Beyme was still taking his cues from Voss with a view to pleasing the French. Some in Berlin believed him to have fallen completely under the influence of the chief of the French party.[45] There is no way to account for Beyme's reported subservience to Voss at this juncture except to speculate that he still did not know that it was not the Kakodämonen who had won him his new place. It may be that he was reluctant to shift his political stance until he was more certain of his position.

Hardenberg saw his major task in this conference with Beyme as winning the parvenu's support for his friends in Königsberg; without it, he feared a renewal of the war of clique and cabal which had marked the last months of Stein's administration.[46] For what it was worth, Beyme was prodded into giving Hardenberg at their meeting what amounted to a guarantee of good behavior. Such promises, like tears, he had in plenty. He pledged not to go beyond the limits of his own office, and he volunteered to work together with Altenstein and Dohna in a friendly manner. But he would not commit himself except in generalities. Nor did he mention to Hardenberg his suspicions of his new ministerial colleagues, though Hardenberg heard privately that Beyme was complaining bitterly in other quarters that Nagler was seeking to usurp his position with the king.[47] As Beyme appeared in Hardenberg's final shrewd estimate, he was savoring his newly won influence to the fullest. He had

[44] Hardenberg to Altenstein, 22 December 1808, DZA, Rep. 92, Altenstein, B14.
[45] Hardenberg to Altenstein, 22 December 1808, DZA, Rep. 92, Altenstein B14; Scharnweber to Altenstein, 11 December 1808, *ibid.*, Altenstein, B35; Schön Tagebuch, 10 December 1808, Schön, *Papiere,* II, 61.
[46] Hardenberg to Altenstein, 22 December 1808 and 1 and 3 January 1809, DZA, Rep. 92, Altenstein, B14.
[47] Hardenberg to Altenstein, 1 January 1809, DZA, Rep. 92, Altenstein, B14.

heard all views but had given nothing more in return than a few commonplace hopes and some pious wishes for the retention of Voss.

Before the year was out, Stein, with touching naiveté and honorable persistence, was to return to visit Beyme several times in Berlin. He even prepared for him a special report on what was most vital among the reforms not yet promulgated: extension of self-government to the rural communes, preparations for the summoning of the estates, and elimination of patrimonial justice in the countryside.[48] Stein, who put no faith in Altenstein and Dohna, urged him to take over the state's rudder for himself. Hardenberg, to the contrary, had implored him to cooperate with the other ministers.[49] To be sure, a regrettable situation, but one which stemmed naturally enough, as we have seen, from Hardenberg's wish to preserve his own influence through his own agents on the one hand, and from Stein's and Schön's correct assessment that Altenstein himself could not effectively conduct affairs on the other.[50]

By the end of the year Hardenberg himself was far less confident of his own judgments than he had been when he counseled the king in November. The legislative inaction in the temporary capital had persisted in spite of his constant prodding. Initially Hardenberg, as we have seen, could comfort himself by putting the blame on the king's absence. He had for some weeks now taken pains to overlook the fact that the brothers-in-law did not write to him and that his confidential memoranda were being ignored and, insofar as he

---

[48] Stein to Beyme, 2 January 1809, *Stein Br.*, III, 8–9. The king was also in favor of ending patrimonial justice and continuing other legal reforms and gave the formulation of legislation in this department over to Beyme; see F.W. to Beyme, 25 November 1808, in Preuss, *Friedrich der Grosse*, III, 531–532. Stein expressed himself satisfied with the new administration (Stein to Merckel, 23 December 1808, *Stein Br.*, III, 4–5), but excluded Nagler from his praise (Stein to Schön, 26 December 1808, *ibid.*, 5–6).

[49] Hardenberg to Altenstein, 1 and 3 January 1809, DZA, Rep. 92, Altenstein, B14. Confirmation of Stein's visits to Beyme is in Bassewitz, *Die Kurmark, 1806–1808*, I, 630n.

[50] Schön Tagebuch, 29 November 1808, Schön, *Papiere*, II, 47; Schön Nachlass, No. 61, p. 37.

knew, not passed on to the king.[51] Obviously he was not being allowed to fulfill the role he had been given to understand that he would play. He recalled to the brothers-in-law that he had been instrumental in their succeeding to the government and that he had, therefore, taken personal responsibility for what might happen. Gradually his letters filled with hints that he found the absence of action incomprehensible. Only through speed, he wrote, could the necessary changes be made, confidence regained, and the inevitable intrigues frustrated. In this connection, he warned them that they would have to watch Beyme carefully.[52] Then once again he returned to an old theme: lack of faith in the state and the decline of confidence in the government's ability to act will ruin the national credit.

By the end of the year, Hardenberg, isolated in Berlin, having heard nothing from his friends since his stay in Marienwerder in November, could no longer repress his own doubts about the ministry which he had helped promote. His formerly flourishing correspondence with his ex-disciples had become a one-way exchange. He wrote to Altenstein directly and openly of his concern but, for the record, he still contrived to put the blame for his complaints on misunderstandings caused by time and distance. These, he said apologetically, tend to alter one's opinion.[53] Had new insights, derived from his meetings with Stein and Beyme, caused him to reassess his actions of November? Did he now regret his previous advocacy before the king and queen of the proposals made by Altenstein and Nagler? He did not say so directly at this time—he obviously could not in the circumstances—but his carefully wrought phrases now poorly masked his deep dissatisfaction.

"One mad head (*unsinniger Kopf*) is now crushed; the rest of

[51] Hardenberg to Altenstein, 22 December 1808 and 1 January 1809, DZA, Rep. 92, Altenstein, B14.

[52] Hardenberg to Altenstein, 22 December 1808 and 1 January 1809, DZA, Rep. 92, Altenstein, B14.

[53] Hardenberg to Altenstein, 22 December 1808 and 1 January 1809, DZA, Rep. 92, Altenstein, B14.

the nest of vipers (*Natterngeschmeiss*) will dissolve in its own poison"—thus one conservative, Junker York von Wartenburg, greeted the news of Stein's fall.[54] Their enemy fallen, the *Hofpartei* intended that one of its own would succeed him. Their most formidable candidate had been Voss.[55] There is little doubt that he would have been acceptable to Königsbergers and Berliners of like political views.

We have already seen how Voss had taken the news of his replacement by Sack as license to assault his enemies without restraint. In report after report to the king he had openly sought to discredit Stein and those about him.[56] In this campaign, which occupied most of the month of November, Voss had had the complete cooperation of Davout, whom he described to the king as "a true friend of Prussia." [57] By this time, of course, there was little of a positive nature the Prussians could have done at which the French authorities would not have taken offense. As the French had correctly divined, the appointment of Sack and Chasot was a reflection of the powerful anti-French sentiment in Königsberg. The nomination of Ewald Georg von Massow to be Minister for Silesia they had considered similarly offensive.[58] These charges Voss conveyed servilely to Königsberg. The same sort of information he sent also to the Prussian ambassador in France.[59] In effect, he made himself the mouthpiece of the French authorities in Berlin rather than of the government he was supposed to represent. He encouraged French annoyance rather than seeking to calm it. He scattered their opinions helter-skelter wherever he thought they would be influential. They, for

---

[54] 26 November 1808, Droysen, I, 162.

[55] Stägemann to Stein, 7 November 1808, *Stein Br.*, II (2), 923–925; Nagler, IB, 28 November (falsely dated 8 November—see above, note 23) 1808, *ibid.*, 925–927.

[56] See Voss to F.W., 14–15 November 1808, *Stein Br.*, II (2), 939–940; and Stein's marginal note on Sack to Stein, 23 November 1808, *ibid.*, 985.

[57] Stern, *Abhandlungen und Aktenstücke*, 22–23, 33–34, quoting Voss to Goltz, 24 November 1808, and Voss to F.W., 4 December 1808, from the former Preussisches Geheimes Staatsarchiv.

[58] Davout to St.-Hilaire, 1 December 1808, DZA, Rep. 63, 88, No. 598.

[59] Voss to Brockhausen, 17 November 1808, Granier, *Aus der Berliner Franzosenzeit*, 307.

their part, had come to know they could rely upon him and they praised him in their letters to Bonaparte.[60] The very extravagance of the charges Voss made against Stein and his friends ultimately reduced his authority even in Frederick William's eyes.[61] To the causes which led to the discrediting of Voss we may add his repetition of the charges of regicide directed by Davout against the queen's dear friend, Countess Voss. The weight of her majesty's opinion in the king's council has already been noted. Thus if the courtier party counted on Voss to succeed Stein, they were foredoomed to disappointment. The proud king would cooperate reluctantly with the French, but he would not succumb to an attitude of servility. His common sense could not be stretched sufficiently to cover Voss' estimation of Davout as Prussia's "true friend."

But irrespective of the king's ultimate unwillingness to hear their complaints, Voss and his party had done much to pull Stein down. To their agitation with the French authorities in Berlin we have been able to attribute much of the violence which came forth against the minister from that direction. Indeed, had Voss served his office by representing Stein's cause tactfully instead of by seeking to undermine him, Goltz might have returned to Königsberg with far different opinions. The majority of Davout's suspicions could have been reduced to their intrinsic absurdity by an artful, responsible diplomat in Voss's place. An able representative might have deftly outlined to the choleric marshal the contrast between his own opinions and the more pacific utterances of Napoleon and Champagny, to which might have been added a strong representation of the tsar's support for Stein. But Voss was of a far different stripe; his aim was to bury Stein politically, not to praise him. The tragic element of this story lies in the fact that it was Stein himself who had put Voss in the office from which he conducted his intrigues, just as he had once

---

[60] Davout to St.-Hilaire, 1 and 2 December 1808, DZA, Rep. 63, 88, No. 598. See what is apparently the fragment of one of Voss's reports to the king from November in concept form in DZA, Rep. 92a, Voss B7.

[61] See Gneisenau to Götzen, 24 November 1808, Vaupel, 727.

sought to employ the scheming Nagler and, so recently, had reposed an equally undeserved trust in Beyme. Voss continued to work against Stein's friends even after the minister's fall. When Sack arrived in Berlin, he found himself once again, thanks in part to Voss, persona non grata with the French. This status enabled Voss to refuse to turn over his office to Sack on the ground that he could not operate because of the hostility of the French.[62] Though he yielded up his place after the French evacuation in December,[63] he continued his epistolary attacks, turning his effort against Schön and Scharnhorst. These charges reached the king about the same time as attacks on Scharnhorst by the *Hofpartei* (which may not have been merely coincidental). The king informed Scharnhorst and Schön of the indictment,[64] but to this complaint Voss seems to have gotten no response.

Voss's own fall from his position of political influence was soon to be almost complete. By February 1809, just two months after the fall of Stein, Voss was to lament to his spiritual confrere, Prince Hatzfeldt, that he no longer had any influence whatsoever in government. He felt himself a pariah, now thoroughly at odds with the spirit which dominated the new government of Altenstein, Dohna, and Beyme. He had taken as a personal affront (as it was meant) his replacement by his old adversary, Sack.[65] Obviously the liaison which he had had with Beyme, which was reported as still in being while Beyme was in Berlin in December, had been of short duration. Once in Königsberg, Beyme, we may suspect, perceived the depth of Voss's disgrace and the real balance of political forces. At that point he forgot the vows that linked him to the aristocrats in Berlin and Königsberg.

[62] Sack to Stein, 26 November 1808, *Stein Br.*, II (2), 995; Voss to Brockhausen, 2 December 1808, Granier, *Aus der Berliner Franzosenzeit*, 314–315; Schön Tagebuch, 10 December 1808, Schön, *Papiere*, II, 61; Stein to Princess Radziwill, 22 December 1808, *Stein Br.*, III, 3.

[63] Stern, *Abhandlungen und Aktenstücke*, 33–34, quoting Voss to F.W., 4 December 1808; Stein to Merckel, 23 December 1808, *Stein Br.*, III, 4–5.

[64] Schön Nachlass, No. 61, pp. 35–38; Schön, *Papiere*, I, 47.

[65] Voss to Hatzfeldt, 10 February 1809, APMW, Archiwum Hatzfeldt'ów, No. 673. Yet Goltz, in January, paid tribute to Voss for his help in exonerating Wittgenstein (Goltz to Voss, ca. 9 January 1809, DZA, Rep. 92, Nagler, 45).

As for Davout, his work in Prussia, and against Stein and his party, was not yet done. We have noted his unique capacity for describing any trace of Prussian animosity toward France as a major intrigue. This faculty was strengthened by the animus, which he shared with his master, against all Prussians and against Germans in general. Dresden, Prague, Leipzig, Berlin, the whole of Silesia —there was hardly a place where he had not espied new phantoms of subversion.[66] Nor did he leave Berlin at the beginning of December (in accordance with the treaty with the Prussians of the previous month) before he had once more sought to exercise the Napoleonic technique of unilaterally altering terms once agreed upon. Since the withdrawal of Stein had been arranged so that the news would be in Berlin several days before the scheduled evacuation by the French, the actual condition—Stein's resignation—for the evacuation of the Prussian capital conveyed by Davout to Goltz had never been put to the test. But once Davout had learned of Stein's demission, he said this was not in itself enough. To propitiate the emperor, Stein would have to leave Prussia and with him must go all his "creatures," those Prussians, like Sack and Scharnhorst, holding his political views. Davout threatened to carry Sack away a prisoner anyway; the marshal claimed him as a rebellious subject of the King of Westphalia.[67]

This bold threat to Sack was a flagrant example of the arrogance on the part of the French which would soon turn against them the opinion-making public all over occupied Europe. The same interview which had included the direct threat to Sack had begun as a lecture that Davout intended to conduct for the men whom he regarded as leaders of patriotic opinion in Berlin. With Sack, who was unwilling to accept docilely the slurs on Prussia and its king Davout so freely cast, the harangue quickly turned into an argument. Davout's warnings became a tirade. Both men began to shout simul-

[66] Davout to Napoleon, autumn 1808, Davout, *Correspondance,* II, *passim.*
[67] D'Aubier to Goltz, 4 December 1808, DZA, Rep. 63, 88, No. 598. Davout had an additional cause for anger: two Prussian ships, forced by a storm to put into Danzig, were found to be carrying dispatches which were offensive to the French: see the concept of a report written by Voss (?) after a meeting with Davout in DZA, Rep. 92a, Voss B7.

taneously, raising their voices to suit the occasion and the charges. Every time Sack interrupted the marshal, the Frenchman's anger doubled. The coda became a chorus of loud yelling during which neither participant could hear the other.[68]

The argument with Sack was only the first of Davout's parting shots at local patriots. He also called in for a tongue-lashing selected Berlin pastors, actors, and government officials, conservative and liberal, active and inactive, patriots. They were, he assured them, hotheads and mischief makers. Were he in Spain, he would quickly stand them before a wall for the quietus Marshal Victor reserved for Spaniards of their kind. And if, he warned, the Prussians ever did rise in insurrection, it would not be the simple people on whom he would revenge himself. It would be the intellectuals; they would bear the wrath of the French. Cautious, conservative old Otto von Gerlach, whose own suspicion of insurrection was to lead to his denouncing the Berlin patriots to the king, Davout wantonly traduced as a dangerous imbecile. He, Davout, would personally chase him out of town; Chasot, the new Prussian commandant, got a similar threat. As for the future, Davout foresaw more "folly" like Stein's. He would be back in Berlin, he predicted, inside of six months. When he arrived, he would take out his list of malefactors, and his first order would be given to have Sack shot.[69] Davout's performance in Berlin was not unique; within a few weeks he had played the same act for the mayor and journalists of French-allied, Saxon Leipzig.[70]

Goltz and the king were aghast at the French marshal's presumptuous disrespect for the royal authorities and the Prussian citizenry.

---

[68] D'Aubier to Goltz, 21 December 1808, DZA, Rep. 63, 88, No. 598.

[69] D'Aubier to Goltz, 4 December 1808, *ibid.;* Stern, "Documents sur le premier empire," 341–344, quoting a dispatch of Austrian chargé Bombelles of 13 December 1808 (also in Stern, *Abhandlungen und Aktenstücke,* 32–33). See, on the confrontation with Gerlach, Agnes von Gerlach to Marie Raumer, 23 December 1808, Schoeps, *Aus dan Jahren preussischer Not,* 367–368.

[70] Hatzfeldt Tagebuch, 16 December 1808, APMW, Archiwum Hatzfeldt'ów, No. 743.

Both rebutted in sharply phrased messages the accusations which Davout had made and denounced his arrogant behavior. Goltz staunchly denied the authenticity of the letter attributed to Countess Voss.[71] But in spite of this, the sort of charges Davout and Voss had made were still to have their final cruel effect. Thus when Napoleon precipitously issued his infamous order to outlaw Stein a month later, he acted from afar on the basis of information supplied by the French authorities in Berlin. This was composed of little more than the full measure of suspicions cast upon the former minister by the wrathful Voss in late November. Bonaparte, deeply involved in his Spanish troubles, evidently assessed these latest reports of unrest in Prussia uncritically, for they substantiated the evidence of Stein's August letter. Then, at just about the same time, Bonaparte received the news of the incredible affair of Countess Voss's patriotic parrot, another handiwork of Davout's, which was to result in bringing before his eyes yet another indictment of Stein. The rascally Wittgenstein, whom the reader will recall as the intended receiver of Stein's first letter, for the second time had seen himself cast under suspicion as a dangerous schemer through no fault of his own. Even before he knew the circumstances of the second letter, he tried to exonerate himself by putting the blame for the whole affair on Stein, whom he deliberately sought to portray to the French as the chief revolutionary in Germany.[72] It was a technique he had used before,[73] and its use this time, coming to Bonaparte's attention as it did with the full tide of Voss's maleficence, was to result in a personal disaster for Stein. Hence we may judge in the light of this tragic epilogue to Stein's official career that had the king discredited Voss and those at court who supplied him and the French with information long before, as any resolute monarch would have done, Stein might have been spared the pain of the long exile and the loss

[71] Goltz to Davout, 25 November 1808, DZA, Rep. 63, 88, No. 598; Goltz to St.-Hilaire, 13 December 1808, *ibid.*; Goltz to D'Aubier, 15 December 1808, *ibid.*; F.W. to Davout, 17 December 1808, AG, CGA, C2 82.

[72] Ritter, "Die Aechtung Steins," 1–17, *passim.*

[73] See Chapter V, note 110.

of his personal fortune which were the consequences of his proscription by Bonaparte.[74]

Yet even the personal disrepute which Voss had earned in the last weeks of the Stein administration had not fundamentally altered the situation of the parties and factions in Königsberg. The Kakodämonen, only slightly more discreet than Voss, and his equals in unscrupulousness, were still in place around the king and queen. The extent of the influence they still wielded was illustrated by the renewal of their attack, now directed at Scharnhorst, in December. The aged courtier-generals sent in a report of York's discovery of the affair of a French privateer captured by the English after Scharnhorst had refused to allow it to make port at Pillau, off Königsberg. Similar episodes at sea, as we have seen, had only aggravated Davout's rages.[75] The king reproached Scharnhorst for his responsibility in the matter. Scharnhorst, also under attack by Voss, offered to resign. But at the same time he defended himself, noting that the account the king had received had been garbled and that Kalckreuth and Köckritz were merely echoing the French by conducting personal vendettas against him.[76] The king begged for moderation on both sides and for Scharnhorst's tolerance of the old soldiers' faults, which he obviously wished to overlook. Hence Stein's fall and the self-impeachment of the chief of the opposition had not altered in the slightest the nature and terms of the conflict inside the Prussian government. Only the chief personalities had been changed. One group of the king's advisers still sought to ruin another. The king himself had seemingly grown not an iota wiser.

But in spite of the fall and banishment of Stein and their own continued tenure at court, where they could continue their attacks on the remaining reformers, the hopes of his aristocratic enemies to

[74] Stein, Autobiographische Aufzeichnungen, 12 July 1811, Stein Br., III, 551–553.

[75] See Chapter V, note 100, and above, note 67; see also Scharnhorst, IB, 4 December 1808, Vaupel, 759.

[76] Scharnhorst to F.W., 5 December 1808, Scharnhorst, Briefe, I, 355; F.W. to Scharnhorst, 5 December 1808, ibid.; Schön Tagebuch, 8 December 1808, Schön, Papiere, II, 56.

succeed him had gone unfulfilled. Seen through their eyes, in fact, though Stein had been ruined, their work was a failure. As they understood the situation, Stein's policies would be carried on by Altenstein and Dohna. The head "Jacobin" had merely been replaced by others of his own party, for they still viewed Altenstein, ironically, as Stein's right-hand man.

It was, however, soon to be manifest, even to its enemies, that the new government, which the conservative foes of Stein had inadvertantly assisted into office, was dominated by a spirit entirely different from the restless reformism of Stein and his party. Following Altenstein's lead, the new ministry was cautious in its approach to the reform program, and alternately timorous and bold in its attitude toward the insurrection scheme.[77] The excesses involved in both they had once denounced to the king as faults of the Stein administration. In early December the Altenstein-Dohna ministry decided upon an investigation of the Tugendbund (to which Stein had never given much favor) in order to determine if it had really played anything like the role ascribed to it by Voss and the French.[78] On the sixteenth of December, in response to the same sort of suspicion, a prohibition against all other secret societies was issued.[79] At this time, Scharnhorst was ordered to put a definite stop to all preparations for the insurrection against the French though, curiously enough, the new ministry renewed the discussion of war plans with the Austrians.[80] Now, with Stein gone, the originally contingent policy of insurrection could be reversed by the feckless king without encountering the opposition of his first minister.

Looking toward the future, it ought to be added for the record

[77] Rössler, I, 408–412; Alfred Ritter von Arneth, *Johann Freiherr von Wessenberg* (Vienna, 1898), I, 106–121; Gaede, *Preussens Stellung zur Kriegsfrage,* 11–34. Gneisenau, in fact, originally thought that the mood of the new ministry was more favorable to the patriots' plans than it had been under Stein. See Gneisenau to Götzen, 4 January 1809, Gneisenau, *Briefe,* 102.

[78] Paul Stettiner, *Der Tugendbund* (Königsberg, 1904), 27–28.

[79] *Vossische Zeitung* (Berlin), 24 December 1808.

[80] Scharnhorst to Götzen, 29 November 1808, Scharnhorst, *Briefe,* I, 351; Rössler, I, 408; Maximilian W. Duncker, *Abhandlungen aus der neueren Geschichte* (Leipzig, 1887), 275–276.

that the fall of Stein did not stifle hopes for quick liberation. Within six months of the order for the dissolution of the insurrectionary groups, the king and his new ministers were ready to take up the cause of war with France. This decision Frederick William made once again under the spur of transient enthusiasm generated by the initial Austrian successes in the war of 1809 with the French. Only the news of the campaign of Major Schill, who tried to join the Austrians with a Prussian contingent without the king's permission, seems to have turned the king back from the edge of yet another military disaster. For had Prussia entered the war in the spring of 1809, it would have been without any special long-term preparation and without a plan of insurrection behind French lines or even of cooperation with the Austrians. It would have been 1806 all over again. Schill's reckless disobedience, however, raised once again in the king's mind the specter of internal unrest which he feared would accompany any popular war. This prospect apparently so terrified his majesty that he became instantly cautious and shrank from action. Joining the Austrians was forgotten, Prussia remained immobile, and the Habsburgs once more went down to defeat alone before the Napoleonic armies.[81]

Stein's robes of authority, it is clear, had been given over to trimmers, the intriguers who served first of all themselves and only secondarily the ministry and the state which employed them. They fell not upon those who stood for Stein's principles, nor to those who stood up to be counted against them, but to the trimming bureaucrats who stood for moderation (as if this constituted a platform rather than an attribute of character or state of mind) and who sought personal popularity at Stein's expense with the king and queen. In the hands of men like these, what chance had Stein's radical programs? The new ministers were for reform, but for no measure which might cause unrest among the people—as almost any change of consequence in the Prussian situation would. They were for liberation but not for a war which would agitate the populace—as

[81] Gaede, *Preussens Stellung zur Kriegsfrage*, 92; Bailleu, "Zur Geschichte des Jahres 1809," 454–455; Stern, *Abhandlungen und Aktenstücke*, 73.

if such a war were possible in civilized Europe after 1789. Soulmates of his majesty, they, like him, orally espoused progressive ideas and principles, but they were prevented by the bureaucrat's incapacities, a too strongly developed sense of caution and an unwillingness to risk positions of power once gained, from accomplishing their tasks.

Schön, privately reflecting on the political situation as he saw it in early December 1808, just after Stein's resignation, identified three parties struggling for control of the Prussian government: the conservatives, who had gone so far as to manipulate the French when necessary against the domestic changes they feared; a second party, composed of those who loved the king and the nation and who wished to do away with the causes of public unhappiness; and finally, the party of eclectics, whose sole urge was to remain in power. These were, he wrote, that miserable and intriguing group whose term in office, now begun, would not long endure.[82] Schön gave no title to the second party, to which he undoubtedly accounted himself, but Scharnweber, who was, as we have seen, one of Hardenberg's friends, disdainfully named them "liberals." By this label he meant to describe the East Prussian group, which we have identified before as disciples of Adam Smith and Kant. Scharnweber joyfully credited Altenstein with the skill to prevail in the political contests he foresaw in the immediate future over both groups of his opponents: the party around Voss (to which Scharnweber, with some knowledge of the situation in Berlin, still assigned Beyme), and the liberals as well.[83] Though Schön would have approved of the terminology used by Scharnweber, Stein might not have. But irrespective of the controversy over names, Schön's delineation and Scharnweber's classification of the personal alignments captured accurately the essence of the partisan conflict in Königsberg. Stein, during the last months of his ministry, had more and more closely aligned himself with the liberals. Schön had played an increasingly greater role among his civilian advisers; Gneisenau had taken up a similar place

[82] Schön Tagebuch, 10 December 1808, Schön, *Papiere*, II, 59–60.
[83] Scharnweber to Altenstein, 11 December 1808, DZA, Rep. 92, Altenstein, B35.

among his military advisers. Still, Schön's and Scharnweber's remarks give us nothing more than a catalogue of party titles. These
would have been understood by only a few contemporaries, and
recognized by fewer still. Fundamentally the struggle within the
reform group that Schön and Scharnweber descried was between
personalities.

Striking examples of the importance of the conflict of personalities
are afforded by Beyme and Altenstein. As expressed to Hardenberg
in his December interview, Beyme's notion that innovations in government and society must be introduced cautiously mirrored to a
remarkable extent Altenstein's earlier arguments made to the king
on the same subject. There were other similarities between the two
men: both Altenstein and Beyme were civil servants. Both were
convinced Fichteans, patrons of the arts (Altenstein was one of
Kleist's sponsors, Beyme a benefactor of the famous actor-director
A. W. Iffland), and supporters of the plan, then under consideration,
to establish a university in Berlin.[84] Like Hardenberg, each had
accepted as a personal canon of reference the notion that Prussia
was now a link in the French system and that the state must necessarily be operated before a tricolor backdrop for an indefinite period.
Hence a reasonable amount of cooperation between Beyme and
Altenstein might theoretically have been expected. But we have
already seen that, based on their past performances, such ideological
and temperamental unity could be anticipated as being far less deter-
minant for their future relations than their discordant personalities
and conflicting egos. Probably, though this is pure speculation, the
very lack of partisan organization and clearly defined ideological
groupings actually had tended to put excessive emphasis on the
personal nature of the conflicts; factions arose, crystallized, and broke
apart with the shifting fortunes of individuals. Indeed, we should
note how misleading it can be to identify ideological groups precise-
ly because it is even difficult to label individuals meaningfully (for
instance, Scharnweber on Beyme and the *Hofpartei's* estimate of

---

[84] Spranger, "Altensteins Denkschrift von 1807," 471–517; Richard Samuel, "Heinrich von Kleist und Karl Baron von Altenstein: Eine Miszelle zu Kleists Biographie,"
Euphorion, XLIX (1955), 71–76. On Beyme, see above, Chapter II.

Altenstein) with a badge of party. Stein, for example, would not have characterized himself as a "liberal" though his program was supported and sometimes conceived by the liberals which Scharnweber had mocked. Altenstein, whom Scharnweber intended to edify by his mockery of liberals, quite obviously shared the political opinions of Hardenberg, who has usually been considered a liberal.[85] And, to cite the best example, who could have termed Frederick William a liberal even though he supported the reforms Stein had enacted and was proposing to legislate, and was to employ as Stein's successors men who were pledged to carry out programs much like Stein's and whom the minister's established enemies regarded as of his party? This action, as we have seen, reflected the king's own choice in the matter.

From this we may judge that the gravest weaknesses of the king as well as of the men who followed Stein were not in the realm of ideology, but in that of personality. For all his good will and his conviction of the necessity for reform, how could the extensive program Stein proposed be carried out unless the king stood firmly with the ministry which would complete the task? Instead of giving loyal and firm support to the ministers he had employed, he had surrounded himself with toadies, some of them downright ludicrous, and allowed his court to become a hotbed of antiministerial activities. He permitted the queen to maintain in her chambers a scandalous nest of treason against the royal government. When she brought to him the rumors that the intriguers fabricated in the royal drawing room he made no noticeable effort to end the conniving; nor have we any evidence that he ever discounted her silly whims in matters of state as long as they were not labeled as hers.

Thus it is relevant to ask whether, in the long run, any reformer

---

[85] By Walter Simon, for example, in "Variations in Nationalism during the Great Reform Period in Prussia," *American Historical Review,* LIX (1953–54), 309. See also the biographical sketches in Ernst Rudolf Huber, *Deutsche Verfassungsgeschichte seit 1789* (Stuttgart, 1957), I, 121–145, *passim.* He unaccountably puts Beyme, Hardenberg, and Altenstein among the reformers, and Nagler in the "restoration party." Georg Siegrist, *Stein als Staatsmann und sein Gegensatz zu Hardenberg und Metternich* (Basel, 1940), sees Stein as a conservative, Hardenberg as a liberal (128). Helmut Rössler poses the same antithesis of parties artificially in order to sustain his National Socialist interpretation (vol. I, *passim*).

could have carried out a successful program under Frederick William. For though the evidence gathered here is only detailed for the few months before Stein's fall, it is patent that the fundamental attributes of the king's personality which we have discussed did not change much during the rest of his lifetime. We have seen how Stein's enemies had begun to attack him before the consequences of his captured letter were known, and that the king permitted this then and later. Was it unlikely that Stein, as we have seen him operate, would have been guilty of some other fatal miscalculation which his foes could have seized upon to incriminate him with the French and the king? Once the peace treaty had been signed would the urgency of Stein's program not slowly have diminished? Would the king and queen have been able to preserve their tolerance of the sometimes disrespectful minister once his usefulness no longer seemed so great? To be sure, in suggesting that Stein could not long have remained in office even if his incriminating letter had never been written we are speculating about events which did not take place and thus are well beyond the province of history. But we do know that the trimmers who followed Stein, as well as Hardenberg himself, in spite of their much longer tenure of office, were ultimately to be far less successful than he was in bringing about the changes they said they wanted. It is true that they lacked Stein's character, convictions, and force of personality, but they excelled him by far in the courtier's arts and political skills which were requisite at the court of Prussia. Yet when Altenstein, Dohna, and Beyme fell from power in the spring of 1810 and when, in 1819, Hardenberg surrendered his final connection with the stillborn Prussian constitution in order to keep his office, the combination of forces which brought about these changes was the same one that had led to the fall of Stein: external pressure and domestic opponents.[86] Though the parallels with Stein's case are far from exact, it is remarkable that it was the perennial intriguer Wittgenstein who helped undermine Altenstein, and the spiritual heirs of the *Hofpartei,* with the aid of Wittgenstein, who brought Hardenberg, wise in the ways of his

[86] Simon, *Failure of the Prussian Reform Movement,* 49–50, ch. ix, *passim.*

world, to his final surrender of principle in order to maintain his political hold. Thus it is only fair to assess the king, who continued to maintain at his court (if only through inaction) a forum for cabal, with a large part of the blame for the failure to achieve reform in Prussia.

Among the most important underlying causes of Stein's political fall which we have identified was the fact that, as minister, he had never possessed the king's confidence. The resulting estrangement, which was difficult to conceal, gave Stein's foes the possibility of ultimate success in their campaign against him. Yet Stein could not have had his majesty's trust, for they disagreed on the nature of their relationship. The king wanted advisers, whereas Stein wanted to be a prime minister. His majesty wanted ideas submitted for his judgment, not discussed in the give-and-take method of cabinet governments. We have indeed seen how Frederick William, at least in the case of his secretive ratification of the treaty of peace, actually feared intercourse on political matters with his chief minister. One may judge from the general conduct of the affairs we have had under scrutiny how alien he was to the role of constitutional monarch that some, including Stein and Hardenberg, had devised for him. He wanted instead to be absolute monarch over a liberalized state of intelligent, equal, and politically active citizens. He wanted to make the final, correct, and irrevocable decisions between equally attractive alternative proposals presented by responsible ministers who would subsequently accept his decision without demur. He wanted to create a state in which no one would have any special class or privilege— except himself, divinely anointed. My unflattering portrait of the king is, to be sure, drawn from a single brief period, but it reflects the general outline of history's record of Frederick William III. Only the best of fortune (or divine anointment) could have permitted that dullish king to follow in the wake of history without succumbing to the forces arrayed against greater men through the entire forty-three years of his reign.

Were this not the age of Talleyrand, Fouché, Bernadotte, and Bonaparte we might wonder even more at the level of political morality we have discovered: Voss, Prince Hatzfeldt, Kalckreuth, and Köckritz had clearly indulged in behavior which, according to the public morality of today, we would judge treasonous.[87] Altenstein and Nagler seem to have been completely innocent of any feeling of personal loyalty toward the chief of the government which employed them and the ex-chief who helped them. Beyme, if he has not been wholly misjudged, had no fidelity to any principle beyond himself. The underlying purpose of all of them seems not to have extended much beyond the attainment and perpetuation of their own long tenure in office, whatever the arguments they mustered to conceal their aims from themselves and others; these were the "eclectics" Schön wrote about. Who could reconcile the Fichtean faith of Altenstein and Beyme in reason and a "Golden Age" to be achieved by the efforts of men, with their single-minded pursuit of political power? Altenstein, who was not just an unprincipled schemer, may have been ultimately a fool; urged by Nagler, he perhaps succumbed to the temptation of the ambitious man to hold power greater than he could manage. Beyme, on the other hand, unless the record is completely false, was a knave. Did he simply ignore the claims of his Fichtean faith while he engaged in the pursuit of mundane power? Were his professions merely a façade for his quest for power? Or was he insensitive to the inconsistency of his actions and his ideals?

By contrast, Hardenberg seems to have acted without conscious guile in this affair. Where there is evidence that might contradict this it is not impossible to attribute Hardenberg's questionable behavior to erroneous judgments based on inadequate or biased information. He was a sincere partisan of reform; he was conscientiously loyal to Stein so long as he thought that loyalty served the purpose of the reform which he and Stein both desired and, it must regrettably be added, as long as that loyalty did him no personal disservice. Even in helping to turn Stein out he had maneuvered as he did, so it appears, only because he was honestly convinced that

---

[87] Yet Voss was actually to replace Hardenberg as the head of the king's ministry in 1823.

it was necessary. And once Altenstein had taken power, Hardenberg urged him to press on with the program of new legislation. He did not care personally which ministry got the credit for the work (since he had no opportunity to take it for himself), but sought rather the enactment of the legislation itself. His work with Dohna, Goltz, and Beyme had the same purpose: to solidify the ministry so that the work might continue, for he felt that Stein's continuation in office had only menaced the conduct of important government business. Once Stein was out, he reasoned, that business could go on.

Yet his longing to satisfy his personal vanity and his desire to take up again a decisive political role had undoubtedly betrayed his own reason on more than one occasion. Perhaps the extent of his gullibility in this instance hints only at how desperately he wished to find once again his old place at court. Very little of this Hardenberg would have been aware of; he could not have made contemporaneously the same assessment of his motives and acts which the historian seeks to construct retrospectively. Only later Hardenberg must have reproached himself, if only privately, for having so easily permitted himself to be led to serve the purposes of Altenstein and Nagler. The extent of his animus toward the brothers-in-law, which he betrayed only a year later, must have been founded to a great extent on his own belated recognition of the dupe's role which they had cut out for him. This understanding could only have developed from their ignoring him in the post of secret adviser in which he had been encouraged to put himself.[88] While he undermined Stein, who trusted him, in the name of progress, he was himself being hoodwinked by those in whom he reposed a similar, if equally vain, trust. Yet could Hardenberg ever really comprehend how badly he had misjudged the situation which led to his condemnation of Stein? What wry irony that Hardenberg, with his reputation for political craft, was taken in by such second-raters as Altenstein and Nagler! From Stein Hardenberg had successfully concealed both his per-

---

[88] Ranke, *Hardenberg Denkwürdigkeiten*, 216–223, 228, 231; Ernst W. Zeeden, *Hardenberg und der Gedanke einer Volksvertretung in Preussen, 1807–1812* (Berlin, 1940), 85–86; Haussherr, *Die Stunde Hardenbergs*, 80–85.

sonal disloyalty—Stein seems never to have learned of the secret
meetings with the king—and his personal incredulity at Stein's behavior. He judged Stein's letter and the appointment of Voss and
Beyme as cases of enormous political ineptitude. He believed that
Minister Stein had wrought the circumstances of his own political
demise. In his private diary from this period we can read of Hardenberg's growing impatience with Stein. Stein had remained in office,
thereby prolonging the agony of the state. Stein stayed in Königsberg after his resignation, thus giving the impression that he would
continue on as the king's secret adviser—this prospect enraged Davout. Stein had come to Berlin, further embarrassing the King of
Prussia and making it appear as if the notorious agent had merely
transferred the locus of his activity—that was not only provocative
to the French, but compromising to Hardenberg himself so long
as he chose to conduct his own affairs there. How could a clever man
behave so foolishly was the substance of the thoughts on Stein which
Hardenberg in wonder confided to his diary.[89]

Stein, we should now understand, was a man of the type a
Hardenberg could never comprehend; a man of faith as well as of
action. When he took up a program, he did so with a zeal Hardenberg could never muster. The very intensity of his convictions which
he attempted to work out with a characteristic lack of caution and
discretion and his foolish propensity to look for the best in his worst
enemies betrayed him. The same vitality which directed the success
of his programs struck fear into his enemies and rallied them in
desperation against him. His virtues were also his vices, as it appears.
Yet, as we have seen, in our story he was as much the luckless victim
of fate as of his own folly; witness the confused circumstances surrounding the capture of his foolish letter, Wittgenstein's cowardly
posturing to save his own skin, Davout's farcical sensitivity to the
demimonde of espionage and intrigue, and Bonaparte's own arbi-
trary treachery.

---

[89] Hardenberg Tagebuch, 27 November 1808 and 6 January 1809, DZA, Rep. 92,
Hardenberg, L29. The same thing is expressed in Hardenberg to Altenstein, 27
November 1808, *ibid.*, Altenstein, B14.

Hardenberg had neither the same virtues nor the same vices. He possessed neither Stein's pious conviction nor his determination. Hardenberg espoused principles;[90] he believed in reform and progress through political action. But the political tergiversations which mark his earlier and later career, like his behavior in the case of Stein's continuing in office, manifest a desire to hold political power irrespective of its content and purpose. Hardenberg obviously did not share Stein's intense German patriotism, which later became a passion, or his wanton hatred of Napoleon. Stein might easily have become a political zealot. He could have been a dangerous man, were he to seize firmly on the wrong ideas. Hardenberg, by contrast, would tack and furl. Hardenberg would follow the politic course. He did it, for example, in recommending Stein's dismissal. In 1812, he could counsel yielding to the French to the point of supplying troops for the Grand Army's Russian campaign. After 1819, the same formerly enlightened administrator yielded both himself and Prussia up wholly to the Metternichean system; his counsel again, as in 1808, was *raison d'état*.[91]

Between Stein and Hardenberg communication had already broken down in December 1808. Hardenberg, fearful that Stein would discover his duplicity and set off a claque among the liberals which might menace his own political future, was forced to dis-

[90] Hardenberg, for example, objected strongly to Stein's anti-Semitism. But here again his argument was practical: Stein's bitterness toward the Jews was impolitic. Had he given them better treatment, he could have obtained money from them to pay the indemnity (Hardenberg to Altenstein, 1 January 1809, DZA, Rep. 92, Hardenberg, L29).

[91] Simon, *Failure of the Prussian Reform Movement*, ch. xi, *passim*. On Hardenberg from 1810 to 1812 (from the beginning of his administration to the defeat of the Grand Army in Russia) see Ursula Seyffarth, *Zur Aussenpolitik des Staatskanzlers Freiherrn von Hardenberg von 1810–1812* (Würzburg, 1939), 3, 71, 77–79: "Sein [Hardenberg's] Staatsdenken und seine politische Haltung waren von Interessen, nicht von Ideologien beherrscht (77)." See also Haussherr, "Stein und Hardenberg," 279. Haussherr (289) suggests that Hardenberg and Stein might have complemented one another, but I see nothing in Hardenberg's behavior on this occasion to warrant such a conclusion. Siegrist, *Stein als Staatsmann*, effectively states the antithesis, in general terms, between Stein and Hardenberg: "One's strength was the other's weakness and vice versa" (120). He suggests that Hardenberg came to power through "kluges Verhandeln und Intrigue" and was a "feiner Menschenkenner."

semble once again by concealing his true opinions. Hence he and
Stein could come to no agreement on the future of the reforms and
the advice which they should give to the new ministers. Each then
purveyed conflicting advice to Beyme. The augury for future cooperation between them would have been dismal. Still, Stein
continued to be loyal to Hardenberg at the outset of Hardenberg's
second ministry after 1810, just as Hardenberg had been loyal to
him before the news of the letter. Since Stein never forgave his
enemies, we may be certain that he never did learn what role
Hardenberg had played in bringing about his fall.[92]

A "Fronde" now threatens all political action—so Hardenberg
despairingly warned Altenstein just after the turn of the new year,
1809.[93] The conflicting advice which Hardenberg and Stein gave
Beyme had already been succeeded by the conflicting advice which
the divided ministry gave the king. The well-meaning Dohna first
remained loyal to Altenstein and Nagler, true to the pledge he had
given to Hardenberg in Marienwerder. But within a year he too
broke with them completely and reproached them for having misled
him. Long before, in the spring of 1809, both Gneisenau and Schön
had left the government. Stein was far away in Bohemian exile,
ignored; Hardenberg was removed from the seat of government,
increasingly isolated. The aimless, meandering course taken by the
Altenstein-Dohna-Beyme government in foreign affairs as well as
in domestic action attests to the absence of a strong hand and the
presence of divided counsel around the helm of state. But the king
was finally at ease among men of his own caliber, the *frondeurs,*
the lot he deserved, and for the rest of his reign the state of Frederick
the Great and Stein was pulled willy-nilly in the tow of fate.

[92] Haussherr, "Stein und Hardenberg," 277.
[93] Hardenberg to Altenstein, 3 January 1809, DZA, Rep. 92, Altenstein, B14.

BIBLIOGRAPHICAL ESSAY

A monograph which deals with a short series of covert events may call for a vaster bibliography than some historical studies dedicated to more extended inquiries into public affairs. Because conspirators and intriguers consciously leave few traces of their efforts, the researcher must sift a relatively large amount of historical evidence to uncover a few hints and suggestions. Only occasionally is a complete piece of evidence found which may lead toward recovery of the outline of the affair under investigation. Thus it was necessary in the course of this research to visit a large number of archives. Although I discovered in one or two only a few clues (which, however, proved essential to bringing this study to its present state), in the course of this research I inevitably learned much about a number of European archives and their holdings. Because of the paucity of printed primary materials, it seems worthwhile that I should dedicate a major part of this bibliographical essay to pointing out the location of unprinted sources which may assist others undertaking studies in related aspects of the same period of German history.

The abundance of secondary materials dedicated to the Stein ministry which permits the completion of studies like this one also fattens the bibliography. Most of the secondary sources listed below were written to clarify subjects on the periphery of this topic. The researcher is nevertheless obliged to render an accounting of the materials written by his predecessors who in any way contributed to the historical literature on the subject, for he is unavoidably bound to their work, as they were bound to the writings of those who came before them. It is easy for errors passed on to be sanctified as truth by repetition and for myths to be perpetuated unknowingly. In the following paragraphs I have attempted to convey my sense of appreciation for works which appeared, in my judgment, to have been done conscientiously, and which were not construed by some cast of mind or impregnation of ideology twisting the conclusions into agreement with selected facts. I have also tried to identify those studies which did not meet the standards of objectivity that I take to be the accepted criteria for measuring historical writing. Excluded from the following sections are almost all surveys which treat the period, most of them only briefly. As they are built on the monographs and specialized studies I have included, they are only as informed or uninformed as the works on which they had to depend.

I. Manuscript sources and inventories of sources

The fact that I had under consideration a period which has so often been examined previously meant that there were few prospects of finding a vast new cache of unused materials. This was particularly true with respect to the German archives, so thoroughly scrutinized by generations of earlier scholars. As it turned out, the novelty of my work in these archives consisted primarily of scanning with a different eye—that of the foreigner—the same collections often examined before. In the course of this work I did manage to find some documents, even a few whole fascicles, which had not been used with profit by my predecessors. In a number of cases I was able to find a new use for a source often cited before in another connection. But those sections of my study in which I have been able to advance understanding of the Stein era are the product of the concurrent use of both German and non-German archives, the latter mostly unexploited by German historians.

Published catalogues of the Prussian and Reich central archives were issued before the Second World War. They are: Ernst Müller and Ernst Posner, eds., *Übersicht über die Bestände des Geheimen Staatsarchivs zu Berlin-Dahlem,* Mitteilungen der preussischen Archivverwaltung, vol. 24 (Leipzig, 1934); and Ludwig Dehio, and others, *Übersicht über die Bestände des brandenburg-preussischen Hausarchivs zu Berlin-Charlottenburg,* Mitteilungen der preussischen Archivverwaltung, vol. 27 (Leipzig, 1936). But since many of the prewar holdings have since been destroyed or lost, these catalogues in some respects give an inaccurate account of today's collections in the Deutsches Zentralarchiv, Abteilung II, in Merseburg, where the repositories of the former Preussisches Geheimes Staatsarchiv relevant to this period have been housed since being gathered from the places of safety in which they had been stored during the latter part of the Second World War.

A catalogue of the Deutsches Zentralarchiv, Abteilung II, the most important depository for my research, is not yet available. Some idea of the losses as well as what is still available among the *Nachlässe* (personal papers and other literary remains) and other materials in the former Prussian and Reich central archives can be obtained from the inventory published by the West German Bundesarchiv in Coblenz: Wilhelm Mommsen, *Die schriftlichen Nachlässe in den zentralen deutschen und preussischen Archiven*, Schriften des Bundesarchivs, vol. 1 (Coblenz, 1955).

The researcher interested in study in this field should also know that the majority of the holdings of the former Prussian and Reich central archives have been carefully analyzed over the years. Consequently, elaborately annotated handwritten and typed catalogues of the repositories can be used at the archives. Though not always completely reliable, they are on the whole of inestimable value.

I used the following *Nachlässe* (Reps. 92 and 92a) from the former Preussisches Geheimes Staatsarchiv, now in the depository at the Deutsches Zentralarchiv, Abteilung II, at Merseburg.

Rep. 92, Altenstein
A. III, No. 10. "Reformpläne, u.s.w."
A. III, No. 13. "Gutachten Hardenbergs über die Entlassung Steins und das neu zu berufende Ministerium"
B14. "Altensteins Briefwechsel mit Hardenberg, 1797, 1822"
B15. "Korrespondenz mit Hagen, u.a."
B35. "Korrespondenz mit Scharnweber, u.a."
B43. "Korrespondenz mit Staegemann, u.a."
Rep. 92, Friedrich Wilhelm III
B VIIa, 7c. "Akta betr: Innere und auswärtige Politik 1808"
B VI, 22. "Die politischen und militärischen Verhältnisse Preussens 1805–1808"
B VIIa, 8. "Charakteristik der Berliner 1808"
Rep. 92, Hardenberg
F1. "Die politischen Begebenheiten nach dem Tilsiter Frieden, 1808–1810"
K30. "Schriftwechsel mit dem Freiherrn von Altenstein, 1806–1822"
K57. "Hardenbergs Schriftwechsel mit Nagler 1808–1821"
L29. "Tagebücher des Staatskanzlers Hardenberg, IX Theil, 1808–1809"

Rep. 92, Nagler
  45. "Akta betr: Schriftwechsel des Kabinetts und Naglers mit dem Minister von der Goltz während der Reise des Königs nach Petersburg Jan. 1809"
Rep. 92a, Voss
  B4. "Akta betr: die Correspondenz verschiedener Behörden in Königsberg mit dem königlichen wirklichen Geheimen Staatsminister, Herrn Freyherrn von Voss, Excellenz"
  B5. "Akta betr: die Aufhebung der Patrimonialgerichtsbarkeit u. die Stände des Mohrunger Kreises 1808"
  B7. "Bruchstück eines Französischen Briefes (Ende 1808)"

Beyond the personal papers housed in the Deutsches Zentralarchiv, Abteilung II, I examined, or found useful, the following repositories.

A.A.I., Rep. 1
  No. 1064. "Dépêches du et au Sieur de Jacobi"
  No. 1234. "Dépêches du et au Baron de Brockhausen"
  No. 2409. "Dépêches du et au Baron de Schladen"
Rep. 63, 88
  No. 598. "Correspondance . . . sur la conduite du Maréchal Duc d'Auerstadt"
Rep. 77, Tit. XVII
  1. "Akta wegen Verhütung und Bestrafung geheimer Gesellschaften und Verbindungen"
  1½. "Akta den Tugendverein betref."
  2. Vols. I and II. "Akta betr: die Existenz und Aufhebung des unter dem Namen Tugendbund bekannten sogenannten sittlich wissenschaftlichen Vereins"
  3. "Akta betr: die anonym eingesandten Brief und Schriften, mit Beziehung auf geheimen und sträflichen Verbindungen"
Rep. 77, Tit. 520
  No. 21, Bd. 1. "Tagebücher J. A. Sacks aus den Jahren 1808–1809"
Rep. 89a, XXVII
  3. "Akta betr: die in Königsberg in Pr. gestiftete Gesellschaft zur Uebung öffentlicher Tugenden oder das sittlich wissenschaftliche Verein, 1808–1809"

Rep. 89a, XLVIII
1. "Akta betr: Miscellanea 1807–1809"
Rep. 89a, L
5. "Akta betr: das Ressort des Staatsministers Dohna und Grosskanz-
lers Beyme 1808–1809"
11. "Akta betr: Regierungen v. Klewitz, v. Schroetter, Nagler, 1808"
14. "Akta betr: das Ressort des Ministers Freiherrn vom Stein, 1807–
1808"
14½. "Petitionen wegen Beibehaltung des Ministers vom Stein, 1808"

Two other Nachlässe proved useful to my study. The Literatur-Archiv
des Instituts für deutsche Sprache und Literatur at the Deutsche Akademie der Wissenschaften in Berlin contains the Schleiermacher Nachlass,
including Schleiermacher's manuscripts, letters, and *Tagebücher*. Many
of these papers have not been published. The Staatliches Archivlager in
Göttingen, which houses some of the collections of the former Preussisches Staatsarchiv at Königsberg, contains the Theodor von Schön Nachlass, part of which is unpublished. A comparison showed that the
published portions of the latter have been on occasion edited in a number
of small but important ways to obscure or modify the original meaning.
I found volumes 27 and 61 of Schön's reminiscences valuable. A printed
catalogue gives some indication of the contents of those segments of the
Staatsarchiv Königsberg which have now been preserved and which are
available for use in Göttingen. See Kurt Forstreuter, *Das preussische
Staatsarchiv in Königsberg: Ein geschichtlicher Rückblick mit einer
Übersicht über seine Bestände,* Veröffentlichungen der niedersächsischen
Archivverwaltung, No. 3 (Göttingen, 1955).

The following inventories of German archival holdings may also be
useful to those contemplating research in this period of Prussian history:
Karl-Heinz Hahn, *Goethe- und Schiller-Archiv: Bestandsverzeichnis*
(Weimar, 1961); Helmut Lötzke, *Übersicht über die Bestände des
Deutschen Zentralarchivs Potsdam* (Berlin, 1957); Berent Schwineköper,
Gesamtübersicht über die Bestände des Landeshauptarchivs Magdeburg,
Quellen zur Geschichte Sachsen-Anhalts, vol. I in 2 parts (Halle, 1954);
Sächsische Akademie der Wissenschaften, Historische Kommission,
*Übersicht über die Bestände des sächsischen Landeshauptarchivs und
seines Landesarchivs* (Leipzig, 1955). A worthwhile introduction to the

present contents of the Hardenberg *Nachlass* (a major source for my study) was published by Hans Haussherr, "Die Lücke in den Denkwürdigkeiten des Staatskanzlers Fürsten von Hardenberg," *Archivar und Historiker: Studien zur Archiv- und Geschichtswissenschaft. Festschrift für Heinrich O. Meisner* (Berlin, 1955). There is a recent *Guide to the Diplomatic Archives of Western Europe* (Philadelphia, 1959), edited by Daniel Thomas and Lynn M. Case, but I found the section on Germany to be of little value for my study; none of the inventories and articles published since 1945 on German archival holdings are mentioned.

Among the first group of non-German depositories listed below, in which were found a number of important isolated pieces, are archives which were German until recently and hence, strictly speaking, are not foreign. But to avoid confusion, I have entered them here on the basis of *uti possidetis*. The Archiwum Radziwiłłowie (the Radziwill family archive) is now housed at the Archiwum główne akt dawnych in Warsaw. This collection, for the most part unexploited as far as I was able to determine, could be used to great advantage on a number of topics in central European history in the early nineteenth century. There is a typescript inventory, prepared under German supervision during the Second World War. I found valuable for this study the letters of Prince Anton Radziwill from 1795 to 1811, Oddział XIII, Listy w książach 13.

At the Archiwum państwowe miasta Wrocławia i Województwa Wrocławskiego we Wrocławiu (Wrocław), papers from the former Staatsarchiv Breslau as well as from private collections in Silesia have recently been gathered. I found two useful fascicles from the collection of the Hatzfeldt family in the Archiwum Hatzfeldt'ów: No. 673 (former German Sig: I Abth., 18 Absch., Tit. IV, No. 38), "Korrespondenz des Prinzen Louis mit dem Oberpräsidenten von Sack, des Fürsten von Hatzfeldt mit dem Minister von Voss, etc., betr. Bestreitung der Kriegslasten 1808/1809"; and No. 743 (former German Sig: I Abt., 18 Absch., Tit. V, No. 30), "Dépêches officielles de Dresde pour l'année 1808." There is a note on the Hatzfeldt collection by Colmar Grünhagen, "Das fürstliche Hatzfeldsche Archiv zu Trachenberg," in the *Zeitschrift des Vereins für die Geschichte und Alterthum Schlesiens*, XIII (1876), 269–270. According to the mimeographed list of holdings provided by the Wrocław archivists the archive, formerly housed in the Schwedenturm of the castle at Trachenberg (Żmigród), is no longer completely intact.

The French diplomatic archives contain a number of items useful for understanding the internal struggle in Prussia as well as the relations between Prussia and France for this period. At the Archives des affaires étrangères in Paris, volumes 242 and 243 of the "Correspondance politique, Prusse, 1808" and supplementary volume 13, for 1806 to 1811, contain letters and Prussian diplomatic despatches captured by the French as well as Prussian correspondence directed to the French foreign office and French materials relevant to relations with Prussia. Of extraordinary usefulness to me was the "Correspondance de la grande Armée," with its reports of French commanders in the field as well as the information supplied by the corps of French spies, which is on deposit at the Archives historiques du ministère de la guerre in Vincennes. I examined the volumes numbered C 64* (the correspondence of Marshal Soult from January to October 1808) and C2 77 through C2 82, "Correspondance de la grande Armée," from June through December 1808. This is a very useful catalogue of the French military archives: M. A. Fabre, and others, eds., *Inventaire des archives conservées au service historique de l'état-major de l'armée (Château de Vincennes). Archives modernes,* 2nd ed. (Paris, 1954). A more recent inventory of the Daru collection at the National Archives (which I regrettably could not examine) has been compiled under the sponsorship of the French archival administration: Suzanne d'Huart, ed., *Les Archives Darus aux Archives nationales: Inventaire* (Paris, 1962).

The Public Record Office in London has three volumes of correspondence directly relevant to this period: FO, Prussia, 64/78 through 64/80. These contain reports from British agents in Königsberg as well as official correspondence covering negotiations between Prussia and Great Britain. There are also some interesting documents from the hands of important Prussians, chiefly from Gneisenau, which are important as a revelation of the state of mind as well as of the activities of the patriots in Königsberg.

II. BIBLIOGRAPHICAL GUIDES TO PRINTED MATERIALS

Because this study involves both domestic and diplomatic history, bibliographies for several nations could be used profitably. The standard German bibliography since 1918 has been the *Jahresberichte der deutschen Geschichte* (for 1918, Jg. I, Breslau, 1920), edited by Viktor Loewe and M. Stimmung (originally by Loewe and O. Lercha), which was published in Breslau until Jahrgang VII, for 1924 (Breslau, 1926). Then a new series was begun under the editorship of Albert Brackmann and Fritz Hartung under the title *Jahresberichte für deutsche Geschichte,* Jge. I–XVI (Leipzig, 1927–1942). Hartung continued as editor of the second new series, called "neue Folge," Jge. I–VI for 1949–1954 (Leipzig, 1952–1959). The most recent volumes of the newest series (Jg. VII/VIII, for 1955 and 1956, and Jg. IX/X, for 1957 and 1958), appeared in Berlin for 1962 and 1963 under the editorship of Die Arbeitsgruppe [!] Bibliographie des Instituts für Geschichte an der deutschen Akademie der Wissenschaften zu Berlin. Hartung is said to have resigned the editorship because ideological criteria had been superimposed by the Academy as guidelines for selection of materials (a Marxist scheme of organization having long since been employed). It may therefore be expected that this volume as well as future volumes may not be as complete as in the past, the consequence of political decisions as regrettable as they are ridiculous.

The standard shorter bibliography for German history is *Dahlmann-Waitz: Quellenkunde der deutschen Geschichte,* edited by Hermann Haering, and others, 9th ed., 2 vols. (Leipzig, 1931–1932). A new edition, unavailable to me, is in the offing. The *Dahlmann-Waitz* can be supplemented for the war years by Walther Holtzmann and Gerhard Ritter, *Die deutsche Geschichtswissenschaft im zweiten Weltkrieg: Bibliographie des historischen Schrifttums deutscher Autoren 1939–1945,* 2 vols. (Marburg/Lahn, 1951).

The lacunae in the volumes listed above can be filled by reference to provincial and local bibliographies, a number of which are quite comprehensive, as well as by bibliographies directed toward special topics. The standard provincial bibliographies, some relatively dated by now, are: Viktor Loewe, *Bibliographie der schlesischen Geschichte* (Breslau, 1927); Herbert Marzian, ed., *Ostdeutsche Bibliographie,* an annual publication, parts 1–5 (without place or date of publication), published since part 6 (for 1955) in *Jahrbuch der Albertus-Universität zu Königsberg/Preussen,* vol. VII (Würzburg, 1957); Niedersächsische Landesbibliothek, Hanover, *Katalog des Schrifttums über den deutschen Osten, I: Ost-und Westpreussen* (Hanover, 1958), and *II: Schlesien* (Hanover, 1956); and Ernst Wermke, *Bibliographie der Geschichte von Ost- und Westpreussen* (Königsberg, 1933), with supplements under the same title for 1933–1942 (Königsberg, 1944), 1939–1951 (Marburg/Lahn, 1953), and 1952–1956 (Marburg/Lahn, 1956).

Two series that began publication relatively recently are dedicated to the history of Berlin but include materials relevant for the study of Prussia in general. The Berliner Stadtbibliothek has published a quarterly bibliography, *Unser Berlin in Buch und Zeitschrift* (Jge. I-V, for 1956–1960). Joachim Lachmann and others have edited a yearly bibliography, "Bibliographie zur Geschichte Berlins," starting with 1954–55, in *Der Bär von Berlin: Jahrbuch des Vereins für die Geschichte Berlins*, vol. V (1956).

Potentially of great value for many historical topics are the publications by the Deutsche Bücherei: *Bibliographie der versteckten Bibliographien aus deutsch-sprächigen Büchern und Zeitschriften der Jahre 1930–1953* (Leipzig, 1956); and a yearly supplement, *Bibliographie der deutschen Bibliographien: Jahresverzeichnis* . . . (Jge. I–VI, for 1954–1959; Leipzig, 1957–1962).

Because of the shifting territorial borders as well as interlocking interests the Polish historical bibliographies were of some importance. The basic bibliography for Polish history is Ludwik Finkel, *Bibliografia historyi polskiej*, 3 vols. (Warsaw, 1956), a facsimile reprint of the 1891 edition with the supplement of 1914. From 1924 to 1938 an annual bibliography of Polish history, edited by Marja Marzankówna, Kazimierz Tyszkowski, and Jan Baumgart, *Bibliografja historji polskiej* (Lwów, 1925–1939), was published with some regularity. Beginning with publications originating in the year 1949, the bibliographical volumes were resumed on a yearly basis in Wrocław in 1954. The latter series in particular dedicates large sections to the German eastern provinces which have been incorporated by Poland.

French national bibliographies proved particularly useful. I used Pierre Caron and Henri Stein, *Répertoire bibliographique de l'histoire de France*, vols. I–VI, covering the years 1920–1931 (Paris, 1923–1938). For the years since 1955 the Comité français des sciences historiques has edited the *Bibliographie annuelle de l'histoire de France du cinquième siècle à 1939* (Paris, 1956—). G. Brière and others, *Répertoire méthodique de l'histoire moderne et contemporaine de la France*, 10 vols. (Paris, 1898–1914), is available for the earlier period.

Several special bibliographies are dedicated to Napoleon. Especially rewarding because it singles out by means of short bibliographical essays the areas of possible study as well as the most useful work already accomplished is Louis Villat, *Napoléon (1799–1815)*, which is volume II of his *La Révolution et l'empire* (*1789–1815*). Both volumes appeared in Paris in 1936. The standard but now obsolescent Bonaparte bibliography is Frédéric M. Kircheisen, *Bibliographie du temps de Napoléon*, 2 vols. (Geneva, 1908, 1912), which was also published in German in Berlin. Less useful is Gustave Davois, *Bibliographie napoléonienne française jusqu'en 1908*, 3 vols. (Paris, 1909–1911). Georges Lefebvre periodically reviewed recent literature on the French Revolution and Napoleon for the *Revue historique*, CLXIX (1932), 116–159; CLXXVI (1935), 65–90, 234–287; CLXXXVII (1939), 63–112, 184–256; CXCVI (1946), 185–214. A very useful analysis of the memoirs of the military figures of the early nineteenth century was compiled by Karl Linnebach, *Denkwürdigkeiten der Befreiungskriege*, Bibliographisches Reportorium, vol. VI (Berlin-Steglitz, 1912). There are some valid critical observations and a great deal of nonsense in the review by Heinz Heitzer, "Arbeiten über die Geschichte der Befreiungskriege (1806–1813)," *Historische Forschungen in der DDR* (Sonderheft of *Zeitschrift für Geschichtswissenschaft*, Jg. VIII, Berlin, 1960), 188–200. The third volume of the classic Bruno Gebhardt, *Handbuch der deutschen Geschichte*, 8th ed., edited by Herbert Grundmann and others (Stuttgart, 1962), has a short, selective bibliography which is valuable as an introduction to the study of the age of reform.

Although I found the standard international bibliographies to be of little use except in pointing out major surveys and bibliographies, one very commendable bibliographical aid now makes available important studies of article length which had been extraordinarily difficult to find before: Comité international des sciences historiques, *Bibliographie internationale des travaux historiques publiés dans les volumes de "mélanges," 1880–1939* (Paris, 1955).

III. Printed primary sources

Newspapers for the period are of limited value for a study of this nature because they were so closely censored. Most useful among newspaper sources for my study would have been the *Königsberger Zeitung*, but I was unable to find it. I had at my disposal the *Danziger Zeitung* (at the City Library in Gdańsk) as well as complete runs for the year 1808 of the two Berlin newspapers (both in Widener Library, Harvard University) *Berlinische Nachrichten von Staats- und gelehrten Sachen* (better known as the *Spenersche Zeitung*), and the *Königlich privilegirte*

Berlinische Zeitung von Staats- und gelehrten Sachen (more famous as the *Vossische Zeitung*). All of these were under French control or censorship during the time covered by this study.

I have grouped the collections of correspondence and other contemporary documents relevant for this study under two rubrics in the following paragraphs: those gathered to illustrate the history of special topics, and the letters and works of important personalities. The most important series of documents for a study in this period of the history of Prussia is that subsumed under the official series title "Publikationen aus den Preussischen Staatssarchiven" ("P.P.S.A."), of which the last volume, the ninety-fourth, was published in 1938. Five volumes are among the primary sources for this study, though three of them were part of publications which were never completed.

Documentation of Prussian foreign policy with a textual commentary was the purpose of Paul Hassel, *Geschichte der preussischen Politik, 1807–1815,* Publicationen aus den Königlichen Preussischen Staatsarchiven, vol. 6 (Leipzig, 1881). Part I, which covers 1807 and 1808, was the only one published. The documentation, though vital, is not complete, and the text, which occupies half of the volume, is by now manifestly dated. Georg Winter edited *Vom Beginn des Kampfes gegen die Kabinettsregierung bis zum Wiedereintritt des Ministers vom Stein,* Publikationen aus den Preussischen Staatsarchiven, vol. 93 (Leipzig, 1931), the first of a set of volumes having the general title *Die Reorganisation des preussischen Staates unter Stein und Hardenberg.* This collection is only of tangential value for a study like mine which deals in the main with the period after Stein's ministry had begun. The volumes on civil reform succeeding this one have never been issued. Rudolf Vaupel was the editor of *Das preussische Heer vom Tilsiter Frieden bis zur Befreiung, 1807–1814,* Publikationen aus den Preussischen Staatsarchiven, vol. 94 ([N.F., erste Abt., zweiter Teil], Leipzig, 1938), the second volume under the general title *Die Reorganisation des preussischen Staates unter Stein und Hardenberg.* As in the case of Winter's collection, the publication is pure documentation without accompanying text. Vaupel's volume extends up to the end of 1808, and thus is also valuable for the study of the civil reforms, which interlocked with the military, but no sequel was ever published. A fourth volume of the "P.P.S.A." bears directly on my study: Hermann Granier, ed., *Berichte aus der Berliner Franzosenzeit, 1807–1809,* Publikationen aus den Königlichen Preussischen Staatsarchiven, vol. 88 (Leipzig, 1913), but I discovered during my own visit to the Archives de Guerre in Vincennes, from which Granier drew much of his material, that he failed to include the greatest part of the French documentation which would have made his work significant. It is scarcely to be doubted that, had Granier done a thorough job of publishing the relevant sections of the French War Archives, as his collection purports to do, earlier scholars would have been led to undertake the sort of study I have made.

Three volumes of the four-volume study under the same general title planned and begun by Magnus Friedrich von Bassewitz, *Die Kurmark Brandenburg im Zusammenhang mit den Schicksalen des Gesamtstaats Preussen während der Zeit vom 22. Oktober 1806 bis zum Ende des Jahres 1808*, 2 vols. (Leipzig, 1851, 1852); and *Die Kurmark Brandenburg im Zusammenhange mit den Schicksalen des Gesammtstaats Preussen während der Jahre 1809 und 1810*, ed. Karl von Reinhard (Leipzig, 1860), were important for this study. Though not government publications, they are so rich in documents as to warrant inclusion among official publications. The volume covering 1809 and 1810, the last in the series, has an index covering all four. The text is not wholly reliable, but contains some first-hand observations by Bassewitz which (his staunchly conservative bias taken into account) make it a primary source, being a personal memoir of the history of the period.

Collections of diplomatic documents important for this study also appear in the following articles: Otto Karmin, "Documents relatifs à la correspondance secrète avec la cour de Berlin (1808–1809)," *Revue historique de la révolution et de l'empire*, IV (1913), 384–398, 577–598; and Karmin's later supplement, "A propos des négociations anglo-prussiennes de 1808," *ibid.*, VI (1915), 129–133. Alfred Stern published documents touching on the relations of Prussia and France at this time in "Documents sur le premier empire," *Revue historique*, XXIV (1884), 308–329.

The atmosphere at the court of Prussia as well as a part of the official correspondence of the king and queen are available. Paul Bailleu edited the *Briefwechsel König Friedrich Wilhelm's III und der Königin Luise mit Kaiser Alexander I*, Publicationen aus den Königlichen Preussischen Staatsarchiven, vol. 75 (Leipzig, 1900). An edition of the French originals of the same letters was simultaneously published by Bailleu, although not as part of the "P.P.S.A.," in Leipzig. Karl Griewank first edited the *Briefwechsel der Königin Luise mit ihrem Gemahl Friedrich Wilhelm III, 1793–1810* (Leipzig, 1929), which was followed by two editions of the queen's letters and notes: *Königin Luise: Briefe und Aufzeichnungen* (Leipzig, n.d.); and *Königin Luise: Ein Leben in Briefen* (Leipzig, 1943). The atmosphere as well as daily events at the court are reflected in the diaries of Princess Louise Radziwill: Louise de Prusse, Princess Antoine Radziwill, *Quarante-cinq années de ma vie, 1770 à 1815,* 2nd ed. (Paris, 1911); and Sophie Marie von Pannewitz, Countess von Voss, *Sixty-nine Years at the Court of Prussia,* trans. Emilie and Agnes Stephenson, 2 vols. (London, 1876). The Voss diaries are supposed to have been edited severely before publication. Court affairs are viewed from the entirely different standpoint of the royal tutor by Friedrich Delbrück, the educator of the crown prince, whose extensive diaries were edited by George Schuster under the title *Die Jugend des Königs Friedrich Wilhelm IV und des Kaisers und Königs Wilhelm I: Tagebuchblätter ihres Erziehers Friedrich Delbrück,* Monumenta Germaniae Paedagogica, vols. 36, 37, 40, 3 vols. (Berlin, 1907). Volume III covers the year 1808.

Every student of the Stein period must inevitably depend on the new edition of Stein's correspondence which is presently being published under the general editorship of Walther Hubatsch (volume I was edited by Erich Botzenhart), *Freiherr vom Stein: Briefe und amtliche Schriften.* Volume II, part 2 (Stuttgart, 1960), and volume III (Stuttgart, 1961) cover the period of this study. In view of the fact that Hubatsch and his collaborators are building their multivolume collection on the already monumental edition published in the 1930's by Erich Botzenhart, *Freiherr vom Stein: Briefwechsel, Denkschriften, Aufzeichnungen,* 7 vols. (Berlin, n.d.), it is all the more to be regretted that they did not seek out every Stein letter and correct all of the errors in the earlier edition. It will surely be some time before another edition of Stein's letters is begun, yet even this most recent effort is to be inaccurate and incomplete. I am certain of the existence of some Stein letters which did not appear in the relevant volume of the Botzenhart and Hubatsch collections—an indication to me that there are probably others equally available—and I have indicated in the footnotes at least one occasion where an important letter is obviously falsely dated, as is evident from the evidence in the text itself. Because the last volumes of the Hubatsch edition have not yet appeared, the student interested in Stein's later years still must depend on the Botzenhart edition. The same is true for the scholar in need of an index to the Stein correspondence. Fortunately Stein's autobiography, written in 1823, is presently available in a corrected third edition by Kurt von Raumer, *Die Autobiographie des Freiherrn vom Stein* (Münster, 1960).

A published edition of Hardenberg's papers which makes any claim to definitiveness is regrettably lacking. We have only Leopold von Ranke, *Denkwürdigkeiten des Staatskanzlers von Hardenberg,* 5 vols. (Leipzig, 1877), which is partial and selective. There is no printed edition of Hardenberg's letters. With the exception of materials emanating from Stägemann and Schön, there exists little published correspondence from among the ranks of Stein's civilian collaborators and foes. A few of Beyme's letters to Karl von Schroetter, very suggestive as an introduction to Beyme himself, his way of expression and cast of mind, were published as "Briefe des Grafen von Beyme aus den Jahren 1797, 1807 und 1808," in the *Allgemeine Conservative Monatsschrift,* 1886, vol. II, pp. 937–949. Two volumes of the extensive Niebuhr correspondence have been edited by Dietrich Gerhard and William Norvin, *Die Briefe Barthold Georg Niebuhrs,* 2 vols. (Berlin, 1926, 1929). A continuation has been planned for some time. One of the best printed sources for the history of Prussia in the early nineteenth century is the edition by Franz Rühl, *Briefe und Aktenstücke zur Geschichte Preussens unter Friedrich Wilhelm III. vorzugsweise aus dem Nachlass von F. A. von Stägemann,* 3 vols. (Leipzig, 1899), and a supplement, *Aus der Franzosenzeit* (Leipzig, 1904), which was most useful for my study. Perhaps more valuable yet are the several volumes of papers and correspondence which make up the printed papers and letters of Theodor von Schön. Anonymously edited, they are *Aus den Papieren des Ministers und Burggrafen von Marienburg Theodor von Schön,* 4 vols. (variously printed in Halle and Berlin, 1875–1876); *Beiträge und Nachträge zu den Papieren des Ministers und Burggrafen von Marienburg Theodor von Schön* (Berlin, 1879); and *Weitere Beiträge und Nachträge zu den Papieren des Ministers und Burggrafen von Marienburg Theodor von Schön* (Berlin, 1881). These can be supplemented by the interesting correspondence edited by Franz Rühl, *Briefwechsel des Ministers und Burggrafen von Marienburg Theodor von Schön mit G. H. Pertz und J. G. Droysen* (Leipzig, 1896); and, corroborating Schön's earlier testimony on the period here under study, there are several letters edited by Ludmilla Assing, "Karl Theodor von Schön: Aus dem Nachlass Varnhagens von Ense," *Gegenwart,* II (1872),

68–71. For a long time, Schön's acidulous comments, his gift for over-statement, and his somewhat uncharitable attitude toward some of his bygone contemporaries had put his word under suspicion among historians. More recently, that suspicion has been dispelled. For my work Schön's Nachlass, published and unpublished, was a major source, and I can recall no occasion on which Schön's account of what occurred differed significantly from the same events as they appeared from the evidence developed from other sources.

Fortunately, Stein's colleagues among Prussia's military heroes have been given more thorough treatment in terms of the reproduction of their Nachlässe than his civilian contemporaries. This is doubly fortunate, in view of the destruction in 1945 of the Heeresarchiv, when the vast majority of their letters and papers were burned. It is also an indication of where historical interest lay as well as what publishers believed would sell in Germany before 1945. In addition to volume 94 in the "P.P.S.A.," by Vaupel, I have used Karl Linnebach's *Karl und Marie von Clausewitz: Ein Lebensbild in Briefen und Tagebuchblättern* (Berlin, 1916). Carl von Clausewitz, *Nachrichten über Preussen in seiner grossen Katastrophe,* Kriegsgeschichtliche Einzelschriften, vol. 10 (Berlin, 1888), is a fine commentary on the state of Prussia and its chief figures in 1806. Hans Rothfels published "Eine Denkschrift Carls von Clausewitz aus den Jahren 1807–1808," *Preussische Jahrbücher,* CLXXVIII (1919), 223–245, which clearly shows young Clausewitz among those thinking in terms of an insurrection against the French. Karl Griewank, ed., *Gneisenau: Ein Leben in Briefen,* 2nd ed. (Leipzig, 1939), should be supplemented for this period by the documents (regrettably not complete) published by Alfred Stern, "Gneisenaus Reise nach London im Jahre 1809 und ihre Vorgeschichte," *Historische Zeitschrift,* LXXXV (1900), 1–44, from the Public Record Office in London. The plans for an uprising printed and discussed by Friedrich Thimme, "Zu den Erhebungsplänen der preussischen Patrioten im Sommer 1808: Ungedruckte Denkschriften Gneisenau's und Scharnhorst's," *Historische Zeitschrift,* LXXXVI (1901), 78–111, were reprinted by Vaupel in volume 94 of the "P.P.S.A." Karl Linnebach also edited *Scharnhorsts Briefe, I:* Privatbriefe (Munich, 1914), the only volume of a proposed set. There is also an extensive edition of the valuable memoirs of Boyen: Friedrich Nippold, ed., *Erinnerungen aus dem Leben des General-Feldmarschalls Hermann von Boyen,* 3 vols. (Leipzig, 1889–1890). I have also used the following memoirs of Prussian military figures, which are particularly important for the study of the conspiracy in which Stein became involved: Ernst Salzer, ed., *Denkwürdigkeiten des Generals Friedrich von Eisenhart, 1769–1839* (Berlin, 1910); Friedrich Carl Freiherr von Müffling (sonst Weiss genannt), *Aus meinem Leben*, 2nd ed. (Berlin, 1855), which is said to be not always reliable; *Denkwürdigkeiten aus dem Leben des Generals der Infantrie von Hüser; grösstentheils nach dessen hintergelassenen Papieren zusammengestellt und herausgegeben von M.Q., mit einem Vorwort von Professor Dr. Maurenbrecher* (Berlin, 1877).

The following memoirs provide important commentaries and information on the personalities and events of the time: Adolf Ernst, ed., *Denkwürdigkeiten von Heinrich und Amalie von Beguelin aus den Jahren 1807–1813 nebst Briefen von Gneisenau und Hardenberg* (Berlin, 1892); Hans Joachim Schoeps, ed., *Aus den Jahren Preussischer Not und Erneuerung: Tagebücher und Briefe der Gebrüder Gerlach und ihres Kreises, 1805–1820* (Berlin, 1963). This is the beginning volume of a new edition of the Nachlass of the Gerlach family which will succeed the older, partial edition of the correspondence and memoirs of Ludwig and Leopold von Gerlach. The proofs of the sections of the new volume relevant to my study were made available to me before their publication for inclusion in this study through the kindness of the editor, Professor Hans Joachim Schoeps of the University of Erlangen-Nürnberg. Bearing directly on diplomatic matters is Ludwig Freiherr von Ompteda, *Politischer Nachlass des hannoverischen Staats- und Cabinets-Ministers Ludwig von Ompteda aus den Jahren 1804 bis 1813*, Abt. 1 (1804–1809), which is volume II of Ompteda's *Zur deutschen Geschichte in dem Jahrzehnt vor den Befreiungskriegen*, 3 vols. (Jena, 1862–1869). Prince Richard Metternich, ed., *Memoirs of Prince Metternich, 1773–1815*, trans. Mrs. Alexander Napier, 3 vols. (New York, 1880) is invaluable for the comments of Metternich on the Prussians he knew and on Prussian policies. Also valuable is the bitter and perceptive evaluation of the members of the Prussian cabinet by Gentz published by Paul Wittichen under the title "Das preussische Kabinett und Friedrich von Gentz: Eine Denkschrift aus dem Jahre 1800," *Historische Zeitschrift*, LXXXIX (1902), 239–273.

Friedrich Meusel has edited documents with a commentary from the Nachlass of Marwitz: *Friedrich August Ludwig von der Marwitz: Ein märkischer Edelmann im Zeitalter der Befreiungskriege*, 3 vols. (Berlin,

1908–1913). Marwitz was later active as a violent opponent of Hardenberg's reforms, though he appears to have taken no major part in the
opposition to Stein. His Nachlass is, however, important as a direct reflection of the state of mind of the passionate foes of reform.

The contemporary influences in philosophy and literature can be
gauged by reference to J. G. Fichte, *Reden an die deutsche Nation,* ed.
Fritz Medicus, Philosophische Bibliothek, vol. 131 (Leipzig, n.d.), and
still better by the earlier, more comprehensible, *Characteristics of the
Present Age,* trans. William Smith as volume II of "The Popular Works
of Fichte" (London, 1849). The interesting lectures given by J. H.
Süvern are printed in part as "Aus Süverns Vorlesungen über Geschichte
1807–1808," *Mitteilungen aus dem Litteraturarchive in Berlin,* vol. III
(1901–1905). The student may also wish to give some attention to the
eruption of nationalism in literature. It appears in violent form in
Kleist's "Hermannsschlacht" and in the poetry written in the last few
years of his life. Kleist's works as well as those of the leading patriotic
litterateurs of the time (chiefly Arndt) are available in many editions.

For the French side three volumes of the 32-volume *Correspondance
de Napoléon Ier publiée par ordre de l'empereur Napoléon III,* XVI
(Paris, 1864), XVII (1865), and XVIII (1865), cover the events in this
study. These were supplemented several times by: *Supplément à la correspondance de Napoléon Ier* (Paris, 1887); Léon Lecestre, ed., *Lettres
inédites de Napoléon Ier,* 2nd ed., 2 vols. (Paris, 1897); Léonce de Brotonne, ed, *Dernières lettres inédites de Napoléon Ier,* 2 vols. (Paris, 1903);
Ernest Picard and Louis Tuetey, eds., *Correspondance inédite de Napoléon Ier conservée aux Archives de la guerre,* 5 vols. (Paris, 1912–1914);
and Arthur Chuquet, ed., *Ordres et apostilles de Napoléon (1799–1815),*
4 vols. (Paris, 1911–1912). Napoleon's ambassador at St. Petersburg left
an important set of memoirs which were published by Jean Hanoteau,
ed., *Mémoires du général de Caulaincourt, duc de Vicence, grand écuyer
de l'Empereur,* 3 vols. (Paris, 1933). Volume I, *L'Ambassade de Saint-
Petersburg et la campagne de Russie,* is important for the diplomacy
of this period. Caulaincourt was closer to the emperor than most of his
servants. The recollections of Jean Baptiste Champagny, *Souvenirs de
M. de Champagny, duc de Cadore* (Paris, 1846), who conducted many
of the negotiations with the Prussians in August, September, and October 1808, unfortunately do not cover affairs in the east but do reflect the
anxieties which the defeats in Spain had caused. Volume II of the edition

by Charles de Mazade of the *Correspondance du Maréchal Davout . . . 1801–1815,* 4 vols. (Paris, 1885), bears directly on the question of the relations between France and Prussia as they were conducted in 1808. Louis P. E. Bignon, *Histoire de France sous Napoléon,* 14 vols. (Paris, 1829–1850) is, for the period covered in volumes VII and VIII, which deal with the events of my study, the personal reminiscences of the author and hence correctly belongs among the primary sources.

The correspondence of the Russian ambassador in Paris, Count Tolstoy, is valuable as a major source of information on the relations between France and Russia and for the insight into the problems of Russian diplomats abroad which it provides: N. K. Schilder, ed., *Posol'stvo grafa P. A. Tolstogo v Parizhe v 1807 i 1808 gg. Ot Til'zita do Erfurta,* Sbornik russkogo istoricheskogo obshchestva, vol. 89 (St. Petersburg, 1893).

A note on missing primary sources. Many of the central European archival and library collections were destroyed during the Second World War. Some of the major holdings, such as the Heeresarchiv, were completely lost, as were large parts of the former Prussian and Reich central archives (now housed in the Deutsches Zentralarchiv, Abteilung I in Potsdam, and Abteilung II in Merseburg), the major part of the collections in the Staatsarchiv Breslau and the Staatsarchiv Stettin, and the Polish state archives in Posen. Parts of the Staatsarchiv Königsberg and the Warsaw archives were likewise lost, as were many private and family collections. Thus the Beyme papers, which had apparently been scattered by the end of the nineteenth century, are now missing completely. There are only fragments of the Voss Nachlass in the Deutsches Zentralarchiv, II, in Merseburg. I have found no trace of the Zastrow papers, which were presumably kept in private possession. The Kalckreuth (a Silesian magnate family) papers are not listed in the inventory of the Polish State Archive in Wrocław. The Dohna Archive was apparently burned with the family estate in 1945.

Since the end of the war the Polish government has established its own archives in Wrocław (Breslau), Szczecin (Stettin), Gdańsk (Danzig), and Olsztyn (Allenstein), where they have gathered the holdings of the former German archives, insofar as they are intact, in the same territorial areas, as well as the private and personal papers which could be recovered in those areas. Catalog lists of the holdings of the Polish provincial archives have been made and information is available through the Naczelna Dyrekcja Archiwów Państwowych, Warsaw, Ul. Miodowa 10.

It is to be hoped that publication of the "P.P.S.A." on a major scale will soon be resumed, but in view of the destruction of almost the whole of the Heeresarchiv in 1945 and of important pieces from other collections it is certain that Vaupel's study can never be completed on the scale on which it was begun and that the succeeding volumes to Winter's work will presumably be considerably diminished. The fact that a complete edition of the Hardenberg papers is not available would in part be remedied by the publication of his official documents with the resumption of the series of volumes entitled *Die Reorganisation des preussischen Staates unter Stein und Hardenberg.* The same work could fill some of the great gaps in the published correspondence of King Frederick William III and bring to light the official correspondence marking the remaining long careers (which lasted well into the third and fourth decades of the nineteenth century) of Beyme, Voss, and Altenstein, among others.

IV. SECONDARY SOURCES
1. Prussia

The most recent general survey of German history which introduces the background of the period under study is Kurt von Raumer, *Deutschland um 1800: Krise und Neugestaltung, 1789–1815,* Handbuch der deutschen Geschichte, edited by Leo Just, vol. III, pt. 1 (Constance, 1961). It merits inclusion in a selective bibliography from which other more famous surveys have been deliberately excluded not only because of its newness, but also because Raumer has previously written on topics in the history of Prussia directly related to the year 1808. His direct knowledge of the field is evident in the more general volume. The student's attention should also be drawn to the irreverent (hence refreshing, in spite of their age) essays "1807 bis 1812. Von Tilsit nach Taurogen," and "Stein und Schön," which are among those gathered from the writings of Franz Mehring under the title *Zur preussischen Geschichte: Von Tilsit bis zur Reichsgründung* (Berlin, 1930). Mehring was a Marxist historian at a time when it was not a disrespectable calling. His shrewdness and impiety in dealing with the secular deities of the imperial age cover to a considerable extent the defects in his research and cause him to stand out from the crowd of court historians who were his contemporaries. The same impiety is apparent in the work of the French historians who undertook the analysis of the German phenomenon after 1870 (one suspects) with a view to lecturing and thus presumably edifying their own national society. By far the most detailed previous account of the events I have described was written by Godefroy Cavaignac in volume I of *La Formation de la Prusse contemporaine*, 2 vols. (Paris, 1897, 1898). Cavaignac made use of the French war archives as well as the standard German secondary sources and printed some of the most important documents in appendices. Cavaignac's fresh interpretation was imitated by his countryman J. Vidal de la Blanche, *La Régénération de la Prusse après Iéna* (Paris, 1910). There is merit in a number of the characterizations of individual personalities in Friedrich Meinecke, *Das Zeitalter der deutschen Erhebung (1795–1815)*, 3rd ed. (Bielefeld, 1924), but it is doubtful if all of Meinecke's generalizations would bear careful scrutiny today. On the other hand Fritz Valjavec, *Die Entstehung der politischen Strömungen in Deutschland, 1770–1815* (Munich, 1951), contains a worthwhile chapter dedicated to Prussia before 1806 and a good section on Theodor von Schön. The general background of the idea of reform in Prussia was soberly treated by Otto Hintze, "Die preussische Reformbestrebungen vor 1806," *Historische Zeitschrift*, LXXVI (1896), 413–445. Standard background studies for the reform movement are Ernst von Meier, *Die Reform der Verwaltungs-Organisation unter Stein und Hardenberg*, 2nd ed. (Leipzig, 1912); and Georg Friedrich Knapp, *Die Bauernbefreiung und der Ursprung der Landarbeiter in den älteren Theilen Preussens*, 2nd ed., 2 vols. (Leipzig, 1927). More recently, attention has been fixed on the reorganization of the Prussian army. William O. Shanahan dedicated a monograph to this question: *Prussian Military Reforms, 1786–1813* (New York, 1945), but he did not go beyond his topic to discover and analyze the nature of the opposition to the reforms. It is disappointing not to find some consideration of the question of the conspiracy against Napoleon and the political involvements of the officers who figured prominently in the events I have described in the general surveys by Walter Görlitz, *The German General Staff: Its History and Structure, 1657–1945*, trans. Brian Battershaw (London, 1953); and Gordon Craig, *The Politics of the Prussian Army, 1640–1945* (Oxford, 1955). Gerhard Ritter devotes a chapter to this period in volume I of *Staatskunst und Kriegshandwerk: Das Problem des "Militarismus" in Deutschland*, 2nd ed., 2 vols. (Munich,

1959), which carries on his polemic against the mixture of politics and passions, one of Ritter's chief themes, as Andreas Dorpalen, "Historiography as History: The Work of Gerhard Ritter," *Journal of Modern History*, XXXIV (1962), 1–18, has pointed out. Walter M. Simon, "Variations in Nationalism during the Great Reform Period in Prussia," *American Historical Review*, LIX (1953–54), 305–321, deals specifically with one of the themes Friedrich Meinecke introduced in *Weltbürgertum und Nationalstaat: Studien zur Genesis des deutschen Nationalstaates*, 7th ed. (Munich, 1928). Those who were not satisfied with the approach taken in Meinecke's book will presumably be little more pleased by Simon's article. Simon has also written a very sturdy history, *The Failure of the Prussian Reform Movement, 1807–1819* (Ithaca, 1955). Although a number of my conclusions in this study are incompatible with Simon's, I do not think that the approaches to the period, Simon's more general and mine more particular, are in any way irreconcilable.

The personalities at the court of Prussia received uncritical biographies like those of Paul Bailleu, *Königin Luise: Ein Lebensbild* (Berlin, 1908); and Tessa Klatt, *Das politische Wirken der Königin Luise von Preussen* (Berlin, 1937). Friedrich Thimme, "König Friedrich Wilhelm III.: Sein Anteil an der Konvention von Tauroggen und an der Reform von 1807–1812," *Forschungen zur brandenburgischen und preussischen Geschichte*, XVIII (1905), 1–59, is a painful effort to advance the reputation of the king. But Alfred Herrmann has included a good critical summary of historical opinion on Frederick William with his meritorious short essay on the military reform movement, "Friedrich Wilhelm III. und sein Anteil an der Heeresreform bis 1813," *Historische Vierteljahrsschrift*, XI (1908), 484–516. There is also a happily forthright essay on Frederick William III in Eugene N. Anderson, *Nationalism and the Cultural Crisis in Prussia, 1806–1815* (New York, 1939). A German dissertation very much above average is that of Leonie Wuppermann, *Prinzessin Marianne von Preussen geborene Prinzessin von Hessen-Homburg in den Jahren 1804–1808* (Bonn, 1942), which made use of the family archives in Darmstadt as well as the former Hausarchiv in Berlin-Dahlem and includes important extracts from the correspondence of Prince William and Princess Marianne in 1808.

Stein has never lacked competent biographers. Georg H. Pertz, *Das Leben des Ministers Freiherrn vom Stein*, 2nd ed., 6 vols. (Berlin, 1850–1855), is based on archival research remarkably complete for its time.

Max Lehmann, *Freiherr vom Stein,* 3 vols. (Leipzig, 1902–1905), undertook the same sort of fundamental research and added materials from non-German archives to produce a fresh and still useful study. Gerhard Ritter, *Stein: Eine politische Biographie,* 3rd ed. (Stuttgart, 1958), first published in 1931, the centenary of Stein's death, was an effort at a complete re-evaluation of the life and times of Stein based on a re-examination of the archives with the addition of information from recent monographic research. It was written in part as a treatise on political behavior in opposition to Lehmann and the earlier generation of German nationalist historians. This spirit still permeates the third edition, which has not been brought completely up to date as the author would have us believe. For Max Lehmann, the biographer of Scharnhorst as well as of Stein, there is a new and valuable interpretive study (like that of Dorpalen for Gerhard Ritter): Waltraut Reichel, *Studien zur Wandlung von Max Lehmanns preussisch-deutschem Geschichtsbild.* Göttinger Bausteine zur Geschichtswissenschaft, vol. 34 (Göttingen, 1963).

There are two studies of Stein in English and one in French which bear mentioning. Sir John R. Seeley, *Life and Times of Stein: Or, Germany and Prussia in the Napoleonic Age,* 3 vols. (Boston, 1879), is not based on primary research, but is a survey of the German historical scholarship up to the time. It is useful only if Pertz is unavailable. Guy Stanton Ford, *Stein and the Era of Reform in Prussia, 1807–1815* (Princeton, 1922), is likewise derived from published materials, but as it is considerably shorter it is still of value to students who would not venture to read Seeley's three-volume resumé of obsolescent nineteenth-century German histories. Constantin de Grunwald, *Stein: L'Ennemi de Napoléon* (Paris, 1936), draws on the French archives, though it, like the most recent German biography by Walter Görlitz, *Stein: Staatsmann und Reformator* (Frankfurt/Main, 1949), is essentially a competent attempt at popular history.

The question of Stein's fall and banishment has been taken up in a number of articles: Godefroy Cavaignac, "La Saisie de la lettre de Stein en 1808," *Revue historique,* LX (1896), 69–93, drew for the first time on the important French archival materials. Alfred Stern first turned his attention to Baron Wittgenstein's curious role in "L'Origine du décret de proscription lancé par Napoléon contre Stein," *Revue historique,* LX (1896), 333–336. Gerhard Ritter superbly builds the case against the baron in "Die Aechtung Steins," *Nassauische Annalen,* LII (1931),

1–17; I have shown above how Ritter's indictment can be strengthened by the addition of evidence from the French war archives. Alfred Stern dedicated a number of solid essays to the age of reform which are contained in *Abhandlungen und Aktenstücke zur Geschichte der preussischen Reformzeit, 1807–1815* (Leipzig, 1885): "Der Sturz des Freiherrn vom Stein im Jahre 1808 und der Tugendbund" is still one of the best accounts in spite of its vintage; "Geschichte der preussischen Verfassungsfrage, 1807–1815" is a long essay touching on the Altenstein-Dohna-Beyme government as well as Hardenberg's ministries. Stern includes a number of valuable documents. Hermann Granier has discussed the question of "Der angebliche Vergiftungsbrief der Oberhofmeisterin Gräfin Voss," *Hohenzollern-Jahrbuch*, XVI (1912), 95–101. The French censorship and the background of the Schmalz episode was reported by Paul Czygan, "Über die französiche Zensur während der französischen Okkupation von Berlin und ihren Leiter, den Prediger Hauchecorne in den Jahren 1806 bis 1808," *Forschungen zur brandenburgischen und preussischen Geschichte*, XXI (1908), 99–137.

The long-term relations of Stein and Hardenberg have recently been sketched out by Hans Haussherr, "Stein und Hardenberg," *Historische Zeitschrift*, CXC (1960), 267–289. Haussherr, who was one of the most active contemporary scholars in early nineteenth-century Prussian history, had access to the Hardenberg diaries in Merseburg, but apparently did not carefully examine the correspondence from the same period which bore on the topic he examined. The most useful product from the same author is *Die Stunde Hardenbergs* (Hamburg, 1943). The rancid political ideology of Nazism penetrates this study, but it is nevertheless at bottom a serious effort to evaluate the Hardenberg ministry. Georg Siegrist, *Stein als Staatsmann und sein Gegensatz zu Hardenberg und Metternich* (Basel, 1940), develops the Stein-Hardenberg antithesis in traditional, partisan terms and also includes material from several German dissertations on the same topic which were unavailable to me. Haussherr planned a complete biography of Hardenberg but was able to complete only the first volume (1750–1800) before his death: *Hardenberg: Eine politische Biographie*, Kölner historische Abhandlungen, vol. 8 (Cologne, 1963). There is a very succinct introduction to the question and problems of a biography of Hardenberg by Walter M. Simon, "Prince Hardenberg," *Review of Politics*, XVIII (1956), 88–99. Aspects of Hardenberg's role in Prussian history surrounding the Stein ministry are detailed (for foreign affairs) by Fritz Zierke, *Die deutsche Politik Hardenbergs in der ersten Periode seines staatsmännischen Wirkens, 1770–1807* (Frankfurt am Main, 1932); Karl Griewank, "Hardenberg und die preussische Politik, 1804–1806," *Forschungen zur brandenburgischen und preussischen Geschichte,* XLVII (1935), 227–308; Ursula Seyffarth, *Zur Aussenpolitik des Staatskanzlers Freiherrn von Hardenberg von 1810–1812* (Würzburg, 1939); and (for domestic affairs) Fritz Hartung, *Hardenberg und die preussische Verwaltung in Ansbach-Bayreuth von 1792–1806* (Tübingen, 1906); and Ernst W. Zeeden, *Hardenberg und der Gedanke einer Volksvertretung in Preussen, 1807–1812,* Historische Studien, vol. 365 (Berlin, 1940). The whole question of the constitution was taken up again by Paul Haake, "König Friedrich Wilhelm III., Hardenberg und die preussische Verfassungsfrage," *Forschungen zur brandenburgischen und preussischen Geschichte,* XXVI (1913), 523–573; XXVIII (1915), 175–220; XXIX (1916), 305–369; XXX (1918), 317–365; XXXII (1920), 109–180. Bibliographers should give attention to the curious essay by Matthew Arnold, "Stein plus Hardenberg," in *Essays, Letters, and Reviews by Matthew Arnold,* ed. Fraser Neiman (Cambridge, Mass., 1960).

Biographies of the men who were contemporaries of Stein and Hardenberg are largely inadequate or incomplete. Günther Ross used the Altenstein papers for "Das Leben des Freiherrn von Altenstein bis zum Jahre 1807," unpub. diss., University of Berlin, 1925. The best existing account of the ministry of Stein's immediate successors was compiled from official archival sources and the Dohna family papers by Rudolf Lobethal, "Verwaltung und Finanzpolitik in Preussen während der Jahre 1808–1810," unpub. diss., University of Berlin, 1914 (first two chapters published, Berlin, 1914). Otto Linke edited and discussed important papers relating to the same ministry in "Der Geschäftsbericht des Ministers Grafen zu Dohna," *Jahresbericht der schlesischen Gesellschaft für vaterländische Kultur,* LXXX (1902), Abt. 3, pp. 1–62. Karl Disch made a deliberate effort to explain away the charges of weakness and vacillation often levied against Beyme in "Der Kabinettsrath Beyme und die auswärtige Politik Preussens in den Jahren 1805–1806," *Forschungen zur brandenburgischen und preussischen Geschichte,* XLI (1928), 331–366, and XLII (1929), 93–134. Ludwig Dehio, "Eine Reform-Denkschrift Beymes aus dem Sommer 1806," *Forschungen zur brandenburgischen und preussischen Geschichte,* XXXVIII (1926), 321–

338, reports favorably on a phase of the controversial adviser's earlier biography. A detailed consideration of the period up to 1806 by Hermann Hüffer, *Die Kabinettsregierung in Preussen und Johann Wilhelm Lombard: Ein Beitrag zur Geschichte des preussischen Staates, vornehmlich in den Jahren 1797 bis 1810* (Leipzig, 1891), also contains a positive judgment of Beyme. So does the short biographical sketch by Hans Saring, "Karl Friedrich von Beyme," *Jahrbuch für brandenburgische Landesgeschichte*, VII (1956), 35–46, but Saring gives no information which would clarify Beyme's attitude toward Stein during the last few months of 1808.

The civilians among Stein's party have received only partial consideration. Gustav Hasse, *Theodor von Schön und die Steinische Wirtschaftsreform* (Leipzig, 1915) estimated Schön as contributing vitally to the Stein reforms by his reconciliation of formal theory and practicality. Eduard W. Meyer, "Politische Erfahrungen und Gedanken Theodors von Schön," *Historische Zeitschrift*, CXVII (1917), 432–464, is an examination of the reformer's political thought. A favorable reassessment of Schön's memoirs is contained in chapter I of Hans Rothfels, *Theodor von Schön, Friedrich Wilhelm IV. und die Revolution von 1848*, Schriften der Königsberger Gelehrten Gesellschaft, Geisteswissenschaftliche Klasse, Jg. XIII (1936–37), Heft 2 (Königsberg, 1937). Friedrich Leopold von Schroetter's contributions to the reform movement through 1807 have been assessed on the basis of materials then in the Königsberg Staatsarchiv by Gottlieb Krause, *Der preussische Provinzialminister Freiherr von Schroetter und sein Anteil an der Steinschen Reformgesetzgebung*, I (Königsberg, 1898). No further parts seem to have been published. Kurt von Raumer considered Schroetter's earlier career in "Friedrich Leopold von Schrötter und der Aufbau von Neu-Ostpreussen," *Historische Zeitschrift*, CLXIII (1941), 282–304, and added an essay on the background of the East Prussian liberals, "Schrötter und Schön," *Altpreussische Forschungen*, XVIII (1941), 117–155. The reader must take into account the anti-Polish and anti-Semitic coloring of Raumer's writings originating in this period.

The nature and extent of the domestic conservative opposition to Stein has never been discussed as such for the period before the restoration, but Johann Gustav Droysen, *Das Leben des Feldmarschalls Grafen York von Wartenburg*, 10th ed., 2 vols. (Leipzig, 1897), makes the best possible case for York's opposition to the reforms of Stein and Scharnhorst. The family biographer, Otto von Zastrow, is concerned with showing his ancestor, General Zastrow, in the best possible light in *Die Zastrowen: Zusammengestellt in den Jahren 1862 bis 1869 aus dem ausgefundenen Materialen,* 2 vols. (Berlin, 1872, 1920). A passionately nationalistic attack on Hardenberg is contained in Walter Kayser's reevaluation of the archconservative Friedrich Ludwig von der Marwitz: *Marwitz: Ein Schicksalsbericht aus dem Zeitalter der unvollendeten preussisch-deutschen Erhebung* (Hamburg, 1936). Ernst Rudolf Huber, *Deutsche Verfassungsgeschichte seit 1789,* 3 vols. (Stuttgart, 1957–1963), includes thumbnail biographies of the leading reformers as well as of members of the "restoration party." The classification does not always appear meaningful: Beyme and Altenstein are considered under "reformers," Nagler as a "restorer." But these volumes on the whole are full of useful information drawn from secondary materials.

As in the case of primary sources, the published secondary materials on Stein's colleagues among the military are far more complete than those for all but one or two of his civilian contemporaries. Max Lehmann wrote a solid biography, *Scharnhorst,* 2 vols. (Leipzig, 1886, 1887), which is as satisfactory in its own sphere as his later Stein biography is in its. An important fragment of a major study on Scharnhorst by Rudolf Stadelmann was published as *Scharnhorst: Schicksal und geistige Welt* (Wiesbaden, 1952). One of the best informed, most balanced biographies of the imperial period of history writing is Hans Delbrück, *Das Leben des Feldmarschalls Grafen Neidhardt von Gneisenau,* 4th ed., 2 vols. (Berlin, 1920). More recent is the unpublished dissertation by Helmut Salewski, "Politisches Denken und Handeln Neidthardts von Gneisenau 1807–1831: Beiträge zu seiner politischen Beurteilung," Free University of Berlin, 1950. For the ardent reformer Grolman there is Emil von Conrady, *Leben und Wirken des Generals der Infantrie und kommandirenden Generals des V. Armeekorps Carl von Grolman,* 3 vols. (Berlin, 1894–1896), based on and including excerpts from the family papers.

There is a mass of literature dating from an earlier day on the suffering of various German provinces and cities under the French conquest and on the political effects of the temporary French administration. Aspects of the partisan reaction to the occupation are considered by Hermann Granier, "Die Franzosen in Berlin, 1806–1808," *Hohenzollern-Jahrbuch,* IX (1905), 1–43. Paul Schwartz, *Berlins Kriegsleiden in der*

Franzosenzeit: Ein zeitgemässiger Kapitel aus der Vergangenheit (Berlin, 1917), accounts for the causes of public unrest. The earlier conspiracies against the French occupation are outlined by Albert Lionnet, *Die Erhebungspläne preussischer Patrioten Ende 1806 und Frühjahr 1807* (Berlin, 1914), who deals with Prussia, and by Anton Ernstberger, *Eine deutsche Untergrundbewegung gegen Napoleon, 1806–1807* (Munich, 1955), who deals with southern Germany. The same author had earlier described a similar movement in *Die deutschen Freikorps 1809 in Böhmen* (Prague, 1942). The later activities of Count Chasot, leader of the Berlin cell of the conspiracy in 1808, were portrayed by Heinrich Ulmann, "Graf Chasot inmitten der preussischen Erhebungspartei im Jahre 1811," *Forschungen zur brandenburgischen und preussischen Geschichte,* XIV (1901), 141–150. There is no complete account of the effort to raise an insurrection against France in 1808, though Wilhelm Dilthey, "Schleiermachers politische Gesinnung und Wirksamkeit," *Preussische Jahrbücher,* X (1862), 234–277, touched on the question in connection with some letters he published from the Schleiermacher papers. My recent article, "A New Schleiermacher Letter on the Conspiracy of 1808," *Zeitschrift für Religions-und Geistesgeschichte,* XVI (1964), 209–223, contains important new evidence on the subject. There are unsatisfactory sections on the conspiracy in the standard biographies of the leading participants, Stein, Scharnhorst, and Gneisenau. Hugo von Wiese used the Götzen family archive and the former archive of the Prussian General Staff for materials supporting his histories of the opposition to the French in Silesia in *Friedrich Wilhelm Graf von Goetzen: Schlesiens Held in der Franzosenzeit 1806 bis 1807* (Berlin, 1902), which is continued in part by an earlier article, "Die patriotische Tätigkeit des Grafen Götzen in Schlesien in den Jahren 1808 und 1809," *Zeitschrift des Vereins für die Geschichte und Alterthum Schlesiens,* XXVII (1893), 28–53. The role of the Tugendbund in the planned national resurrection was debated in a number of nineteenth-century memoirs by its members, but two scholarly accounts are the best references today: August Fournier, "Zur Geschichte des Tugendbundes," *Historische Studien und Skizzen* (Prague, 1885), and Paul Stettiner, *Der Tugendbund* (Königsberg, 1904), which is based on the reports of investigations in the former Preussisches Geheimes Staatsarchiv. Gerhard Ritter's student Ulrich Meurer undertook to show that the "masses" had played little part in the wars of liberation against France in "Die Rolle nationaler

Leidenschaft der Massen in der Erhebung von 1813 gegen Napoleon," unpub. diss., University of Freiburg, 1953.

The effect of the outburst of nationalist spirit among the Prussian intellectuals on the eve of the wars of liberation was assessed in part by Friedrich Janson, *Fichtes Reden an die deutsche Nation: Eine Untersuchung ihres aktuellpolitischen Gehaltes* (Berlin, 1911), and by Rudolf Körner, "Die Wirkung der Reden Fichtes," *Forschungen zur brandenburgischen und preussischen Geschichte*, XL (1927), 65–87. The ideological background of the Prussian reform movement was examined generally by Wilhelm Wagner, *Die preussischen Reformer und die zeitgenössische Philosophie* (Cologne, 1956). The more controversial question of the relation of the reforms in Prussia to the program of the French revolutionaries was sympathetically treated by Max Lehmann, "Die preussischen Reformer von 1808 und die französische Revolution," *Preussische Jahrbücher*, CXXXII (1908), 211–229. Eduard Spranger, "Altensteins Denkschrift von 1807 und ihre Beziehungen zur Philosophie," *Forschungen zur brandenburgischen und preussischen Geschichte*, XVIII (1905), 471–517, measured the influence of contemporary philosophical trends on Altenstein. Hans Haussherr examined the ideology behind "Hardenbergs Reformdenkschrift Riga 1807," *Historische Zeitschrift*, CLVII (1938), 267–308. It was a time when the *Historische Zeitschrift* was captive to the Nazis, and Haussherr's article is strongly colored by the antiliberal, anti-Western spirit which was necessary to bring it into print. Richard Samuel, "Heinrich von Kleist und Karl Baron von Altenstein: Eine Miszelle zu Kleists Biographie," *Euphorion*, XLIX (1955), 71–76, further delineates the connection between the intellectual and political worlds. My own article, "Schleiermacher's Political Thought and Activity, 1806–1813," *Church History*, XXVIII (1959), 374–390, measures the contributions of the famous pastor-philosopher to the reform movement as well as to the patriotic cause. My unpublished dissertation, "The Course of Political Idealism in Prussia, 1806–1813," Harvard University, 1957, compares the political activities of Fichte and Schleiermacher during the period from Jena to the beginning of the wars of liberation. Edward J. Goodman, "Spanish Nationalism in the Struggle against Napoleon," *Review of Politics*, XX (1958), 330–346, was interesting to me for purposes of a comparison which Germans of the anti-Napoleonic camp had so often made.

International background

Volume seven of Albert Sorel, *L'Europe et la révolution française,* subtitled *Le Blocus continental—Le Grand Empire 1806–1812,* 5th ed. (Paris, 1904), is the best single text on the subject. I used also Louis Madelin, *Histoire du consulat et de l'empire, VII: L'Affaire d'Espagne* (Paris, 1945), and André Fugier, *La Révolution française et l'empire napoléonien,* Histoire des relations internationales, ed. Pierre Renouvin, vol. IV (Paris, 1954), for information on international relations. Edouard Driault, *Napoléon et l'Europe,* 5 vols. (Paris, 1910–1927), is no friend to the Germans, but for that reason is a useful corrective in a study like this one. Volume III, *Tilsit, France et Russie sous le premier Empire: La Question de Pologne (1806–1809),* covers the period. The subtitles that some of these general volumes bear indicate the small importance that events in Prussia had in the eyes of the French historians writing about the Napoleonic period.

Nine volumes of Friedrich M. Kircheisen, *Napoleon I: Sein Leben und seine Zeit* (Munich, 1911–1934), had been prepared by the time of the author's death. Volumes VII and VIII deal with general events of the year 1808, but there is little specific attention given to the question of Prussia. The same is less true of Georges Lefebvre's now standard biography *Napoléon,* 4th ed., Peuples et civilisations, vol. 14 (Paris, 1953), which has a chapter on affairs in Germany. Robert B. Mowat's interestingly written *The Diplomacy of Napoleon* (London, 1924) is regrettably superficial. R. P. Dunn-Pattison, *Napoleon's Marshals* (London, 1909), heroicizes Davout, but is the only volume on the topic which gives attention to Davout's role in military government as well as to his position as field commander. H. A. L. Fisher, *Studies in Napoleonic Statesmanship: Germany* (Oxford, 1903), is short on facts to buttress its general remarks. More scholarly is Erwin Hölzle, "Das Napoleonische Staatssystem in Deutschland," *Historische Zeitschrift,* CXLVIII (1933), 277–293. Some aspects of Napoleon's diplomacy which bear on the background of diplomatic affairs in central Europe in 1808 are considered by Edouard Driault, *La Politique orientale de Napoléon: Sebastiani et Gardane (1806–1808)* (Paris, 1904).

The late nineteenth-century reconciliation between France and Russia brought forth a spate of publications on the important question of French relations with Alexander I. Albert Vandal, *Napoléon et Alex-*

andre Ier: L'Alliance russe sous le premier empire, 3 vols. (Paris, 1896–1897), is also pro-French, but not uncritical. Also useful are Serge Tatischeff, *Alexandre Ier et Napoléon d'après leur correspondance inédite, 1801–1812* (Paris, 1891); and Nicolas Mikhailowitsch Romanoff, Grand Duke of Russia, *Les Relations diplomatiques de la Russie et de la France d'après les rapports des ambassadeurs d'Alexandre et de Napoléon (1808–1812)*, 6 vols. (St. Petersburg, 1905–1908). From the same period is the general survey by A. K. Dzivelegov, *Aleksandr I i Napoleon: Istoricheskie ocherki* (Moscow, 1915). There is a short but good re-evaluation of the relations between Russia and France by Charles de Larivière, "Le Tsar Alexandre Ier dans ses relations avec Napoléon," *Revue des études napoléoniennes*, XXX (1930), 151–170, 202–216. Larivière is certain that all is not yet known about the enigmatic Alexander and his role in Napoleonic Europe. A largely unknown aspect of the conflict between the two great empires at the time of the romance of Alexander and Bonaparte in Europe (from Tilsit to Erfurt) is revealed by A. R. Ioannisian, "Iz istorii franko-russkikh otnoshenii na vostoke v 1807–1808 gg.," *Izvestiia akademii nauk armianskoi SSR* (Erivan), Obshchestvennye nauki, 1957, No. 5, pp. 27–51. For Alexander himself, I referred to the biography by Kazimierz Waliszewski, *La Russie il y a cent ans: Le Règne d'Alexandre Ier*, 3 vols. (Paris, 1923–1925). Volume I covers the period from 1801 to 1812. The classic Russian biography is N. K. Schilder's beautifully appointed *Imperator Aleksandr pervyi: Ego zhizn' i tsarstvovanie*, 2nd ed., 4 vols. (St. Petersburg, 1904–1905). Andrei A. Lobanov-Rostovsky, *Russia and Europe, 1789–1825* (Durham, N.C., 1947), is a very helpful introduction to the complications of diplomatic events.

Prussia's place in Napoleonic Europe is discussed dispassionately by Max Lenz, "Napoleon I. und Preussen," *Cosmopolis: Internationale Revue*, IX (1898), 580–595, 859–874. Lenz's short survey, like the publication in which it appeared, must have been conceived as part of an effort to overcome national and linguistic borders between the feuding peoples of Europe at the turn of this century. One of the best revelations of the weaknesses of the Prussian system before Jena is Reinhold Koser, "Die preussische Politik, 1796–1806," in his essays collected under the title *Zur preussischen und deutschen Geschichte* (Stuttgart, 1921). Paul Bailleu published a Prussian view of "Die Verhandlungen in Tilsit," *Deutsche Rundschau*, CX (1902), 29–45, 199–221, which also includes the correspondence between Queen Louise and Frederick William. René Bittard des Portes, "Les Préliminaires de l'entrevue d'Erfurt (1808),"

Revue d'histoire diplomatique, IV (1890), 94–144, is derived from papers in the Archives des affaires étrangères and the correspondence of Napoleon. The negotiations with France leading to the Convention of September 1808 and the evacuation of Prussia are the subject of Hans Haussherr, *Erfüllung und Befreiung: Der Kampf um die Durchführung des Tilsiter Friedens 1807/1808* (Hamburg, 1935), which is based in part upon the records in the former Preussisches Geheimes Staatsarchiv. Just the opposite feeling from Haussherr's nationalistic resentment at French oppression permeates Charles Lesage, *Napoléon I, créancier de la Prusse (1807–1814)* (Paris, 1924), which shows how the rascally Prussians wriggled out of paying a debt. There was undoubtedly meant to be a contemporary reference for Lesage's lesson in history.

The question of Prussia's entrance into war against France after the fall of the Stein government has been argued in detail by Maximilian W. Duncker in two articles: "Preussen während der französischen Okkupation," *Aus der Zeit Friedrichs des Grossen und Friedrich Wilhelms III: Abhandlungen zur preussischen Geschichte* (Leipzig, 1876), and "Friedrich Wilhelm im Jahre 1809," *Abhandlungen aus der neueren Geschichte* (Leipzig, 1887). Both were conceived in defense of Frederick William, as was the Berlin dissertation by Udo Gaede, *Preussens Stellung zur Kriegsfrage im Jahre 1809* (Hanover, 1897), which is based on substantial archival research. Less dedicated to the exoneration of the king from the charge of vacillation is Paul Bailleu, "Zur Geschichte des Jahres 1809," *Historische Zeitschrift*, LXXXIV (1900), 451–459. Two documented articles by Alfred Stern, "Aktenstücke zur Geschichte des Jahres 1809," and "Die Mission des Obersten von Stegentisch nach Königsberg im Jahre 1809," printed in *Abhandlungen und Aktenstücke zur Geschichte der preussischen Reformzeit, 1807–1815* (Leipzig, 1885), add to the general portrait of the meandering course of Prussian foreign policy in the spring of 1809.

The question of Prussia's relations with Russia is considered in part by O. P. Backus, "Stein and Russia's Prussian Policy from Tilsit to Vienna," unpub. diss., Yale University, 1949. Prussia's conduct of secret negotiations for military aid with England in 1808 is revealed in Otto Karmin, *Sir Francis d'Ivernois, 1757–1842: Sa vie, son oeuvre, et son temps* (Geneva, 1920), which is soundly grounded on the D'Ivernois family papers and on British sources in the Public Record Office in London.

Austria's role in the diplomatic and military coalitions against Bonaparte is the subject of Adolf Beer, *Zehn Jahre österreichischer Politik, 1801–1810* (Leipzig, 1877). Beer's book, based on research in the Vienna Staatsarchiv, is a contribution to the squabble between nineteenth-century Austrian and Prussian historians of German nationalist persuasion about which of the two nations filled the most honorable role in the final exclusion of the French from Germany. Alfred Ritter von Arneth, *Johann Freiherr von Wessenberg*, 2 vols. (Vienna, 1898), is a biography of the agent who was charged with enlisting the Prussians in the war of 1809 against the French. Helmut Rössler, *Oesterreichs Kampf um Deutschlands Befreiung: Die deutsche Politik der nationalen Führer Oesterreichs, 1805–1815*, 2 vols. (Hamburg, 1940), is a more recent taking of sides in the Austro-Prussian argument which is further enlightened by National Socialist ideology. This brings the author to denigrate liberals, Jacobins and Smithians (that is, Prussians), and English influences on the one hand and, on the other, term the Austrians like Stadion (and Hitler?—note the use of "nationale Führer" in the title) leaders of a conservative nationalist revolution (Stein miraculously fits this bill too). Only the date of publication of Rössler's study can account for the obvious testimonials to Russian friendship. Yet the whole book is based upon the most extensive archival research and thus, if carefully sifted, is a fund of information. There are two political biographies of Gentz, neither of which contributes much to clarifying Gentz's role in the negotiations of 1808: Paul R. Sweet, *Friedrich von Gentz: Defender of the Old Order* (Madison, 1941); and Golo Mann, *Friedrich von Gentz: Geschichte eines europäischen Staatsmannes* (Zurich, 1947), which has a somewhat different subtitle in the English edition: *Secretary of Europe*. Gentz's role as an English agent is the subject of Paul Wittichen, "Friedrich von Gentz und die englische Politik, 1800–1814," *Preussische Jahrbücher*, CX (1902), 463–501. Minna R. Falk has recently summarized Stadion's political activities for the years just before the Austro-French War of 1809: "Stein, adversaire de Napoléon (1806–1809)," *Annales historiques de la révolution française*, XXIV (1962), 288–305.

There is no adequate account of the role of the Grand Duchy of Warsaw in the diplomacy of Napoleonic Europe, nor of its domestic history. The most recent history is that of Stefan Kieniewicz and Witold Kula, eds., *Historia polski*, vol. II (Warsaw, 1958). Part 2 covers the period from 1795 to 1831. But the whole series of volumes has been fitted into the procrustean bed of the Marxist organization of history. Since it is now necessary for Polish historians to deal with the eastern German territories which fell to Poland in 1945 as if they had always been Polish (and to ignore the eastern Polish territories seized by the Soviet Union in 1945), there is a stab at including the Prussias and other areas which were never part of the Grand Duchy, but without really saying what is being done or included. The question is left vague and indefinite by historians who are seemingly caught between ideology and conscience. The relations of Prussia and the Grand Duchy in 1808 are discussed with animus by Juliusz Willaume in several articles. "Rozgraniczenie Ks. Warszawskiego z Prusami," *Przegląd zachodni*, VII (1951), no. 1, 474–492, deals with the problems of defining the border between the two states. Financial negotiations between Prussia and Warsaw are the subject of "Polsko-pruskie stosunki finansowo-gospodarcze (1807–1813)," *Roczniki historyczne*, XIX (1952), 99–132. Diplomatic relations as such are the topic of two articles: "Stosunki sąsiedzkie Księstwa Warszawskiego z Prusami," *Przegląd zachodni*, VII (1951), no. 3, 396–427; and "Prusy a sprawa polska za Księstwa Warszawskiego," *Roczniki historyczne*, XVII (1948), 378–398. Willaume based his articles on the Warsaw archives (Akta rady stanu Xięstwa Warszawskiego), but I have read the same volumes of correspondence, which in no way sustain the one-sided interpretation he gives them.

I was surprised to find no complete accounts of the conduct of British foreign policy in the Napoleonic period and, especially, of London's attitude toward Continental movements of resistance. Volume I of A. W. Ward and G. P. Gooch, eds., *The Cambridge History of British Foreign Policy*, 3 vols. (Cambridge, 1922–1923), deals with the period of Napoleon but is wholly unedifying on what would appear to me to be an important subject. Godfrey Davies, "English Foreign Policy," *Huntington Library Quarterly*, V (1942), 419–478, is suitable for the general background only, as is H. W. C. Temperley, *Life of Canning* (London, 1905). There is not much of substance behind J. Holland Rose, "Canning and the Spanish Patriots in 1808," *American Historical Review*, XII (1906–07), 39–52. More recently, present-day notions of research have inspired several articles dealing with the period, though not with the specific topic of British-Prussian relations and the question of military aid during the ministry of Stein and his immediate successors. Richard Glover, "Arms and the British Diplomat in the French Revolutionary Era," *Journal of Modern History,* XXIX (1957), 199–212; and Raymond Carr, "Gustavus IV and the British Government, 1804–9," *English Historical Review,* LX (1945), 36–66, do not deal with Prussia itself, but the evidence they adduce for Spain and Scandinavia may by analogy apply to Germany. Friedrich Thimme dealt with the problem of English aid for the German patriots in "Die hannoverschen Aufstandspläne im Jahre 1809 und England," *Zeitschrift des historischen Vereins für Niedersachsen,* 1897, pp. 270–364, but he is anti-English to the extent that one must suspect his use of evidence and hence his conclusions.

Addendum. A helpful review article, "Neues Schrifttum über den Freiherrn vom Stein: Ein Beitrag zum Stein-Jubiläumsjahr," by W. Klötzer, in *Nassauische Annalen,* LXIX (1957–1958), 292–298, covers the dozens of contributions to the Stein bibliography that appeared in 1956 and 1957 alone.

INDEX

Culture, Prussian, 7, 166

Danzig, 12, 15, 32, 131
Danziger Zeitung, 12
Daru, Pierre, Intendant-General, 31;
negotiations with Stein, 2–3; negotiations with Prussia, 23–24, 55–56, 96–
97, 102–105
D'Aubier, Chamberlain, 135–136
Davout, Marshal Louis Nicholas, 83n,
105–107, 122, 129–130, 139, 159–160;
suppression of Prussian insurrection
plans, 48, 81, 103–104, 130–132, 159–
160; and Poles, 48n; and French
agents, 97n, 150n; alarmism, 103–104,
129–136, 142, 157, 159–161, 172;
opposition to Stein, 104, 127–133, 136,
156–157, 159–162; suppression of
Prussian domestic reform, 130–131;
and Frederick William III, 136
Denmark: insurrection of Spanish troops
in, 16; aided by Great Britain, 22
Deutschtum, 8
Diplomacy: Prussia–France, 2, 32, 50–56,
64, 94–97; Süvern's attitude, 8; Prussia–Austria, 14–15; Prussia–Great Britain, 17–19; Prussia–Russia, 17–20, 53–
54
Dohna, Count Alexander von, 123; selection as minister, 122–124, 141, 146–
147; and Hardenberg, 122–124, 143,
171, 174; role in domestic reform, 123;
and Stein, 123, 141, 154; and Altenstein, 142–143, 174; and Nagler, 142–
143, 146–147, 174; ministry, 140n,
149, 153, 158, 163, 168, 171, 174

Education, 43, 166
Enghien, Duke of, 78, 109
Erfurt, conference of, 46, 50n, 54, 64–69,
80, 89–90, 94–97, 102–104, 113, 115,
136
Europe: dissolution of Third Coalition, 1;
French domination, 2, 4, 7, 11, 46–47,
95–96, 159; revolutionary atmosphere,
7, 16; national awakening, 9. *See also*
Balance of power

Faudel, Privy Counselor, 135n
Ferdinand, Prince of Prussia, 82
Feudal organization, 28
Fichte, J. G.: significance for Prussia,
8, 43; influence on Beyme, 35, 92, 166;
influence on Altenstein, 108, 166
Finance, Ministry of, 121, 141–142
Finances, Prussian, 40, 52, 95, 98, 109–
110, 122, 142–143. *See also* Reparations
Finland, 21
Fouché, Joseph, 169
France: Napoleonic Wars, 1–2; occupation of Prussia, 1–2, 12, 16, 51–52, 64–
65, 96–97, 103–105, 112, 121–128,
136, 158–159, 163–164; Stein's role
in negotiations with, 1–3, 17, 29, 31,
37, 52, 55–56, 73, 93n, 110, 125;
confiscation of Prussian taxes, 3; and
Prussia, 3, 32, 35, 47–52, 62, 81–82,
88, 93–96, 101–104, 137n, 173; Austrian policy, 4, 22, 164; army, 12,
15, 46, 57, 70n, 103, 173; Silesian
policy, 14; treaty with Prussia, 23–24,
50–54, 62–67, 69–73, 113, 115, 123,
125, 136, 168–169; blockade, 46; suspicion of Austro-Prussian alliance, 47–
49; opposition to Stein, 49–50; censorship, 77, 130–131, 133; bureaucracy,
78–79; military character, 81; suppression of Prussian insurrection plans,
81, 103–104, 130–133, 136, 142, 159–
163; opposition to Prussian domestic
reform, 84, 130–131, 133; shipping,
131; and Prussian church, 160. *See
also* Bonaparte, Napoleon; Davout;
Reparations; Revolution, French
Frederick the Great, 1, 27, 131, 174
Frederick William III, 13, 58–61, 70,
107, 167–169; powers, 11, 13, 59–60,
105, 169; and Stein, 11, 37, 39–40,
42–43, 52–72, 78, 100, 105–107, 112,
127–128, 137–138, 141–142, 163, 167,
169, 172; attitude toward Prussian insurrection plans, 13, 16–17, 20, 24–25,
152, 163; French policy, 13–15, 17,
30, 52–55, 136, 157, 160, 164; Silesian

WITHDRAWN